Global Sport Business

Global Sport Business: Community Impacts of Commercial Sport involves a range of pressing issues that come with the arrival of sport as a commodity in the world economy. It can be argued that, throughout the past two centuries, sport has always been recognised as both a frivolous pursuit of spending leisure time with friends and family, and as an activity that has substantial commercial value to be mined by entrepreneurs. However, only during the most recent wave of globalisation, spurred by technological advancements that have led to achieving global reach in regard to potential customers, has sport entered a global marketplace that offers tremendous financial rewards for those who manage to control international sport organisations and events.

In this book, global sport business is viewed from a number of different perspectives including a value chain approach to describing the sport industry; the ever increasing impact of the international media on sport business; how globalisation influences the style of (sport) management; how social capital can be generated through sport business; and the emergence of social sport business. Overall, the different contributors to the book reflect on how sport's global (and as such commercial) attractiveness can, and often will impact locally, on communities of people and individuals.

This book was previously published as a special issue of *Sport in Society*.

Hans Westerbeek is the Director of the Institute of Sport, Exercise and Active Living (ISEAL) and Professor of Sport Business in the School of International Business at Victoria University (VU) in Melbourne, Australia. He also holds an appointment as Professor in Sport Management at the Free University of Brussels in Belgium.

Global Sport Business
Community Impacts of Commercial Sport

Edited by
Hans Westerbeek

Routledge
Taylor & Francis Group

LONDON AND NEW YORK

First published 2011
by Routledge
2 Park Square, Milton Park, Abingdon, Oxon, OX14 4RN

Simultaneously published in the USA and Canada
by Routledge
711 Third Avenue, New York, NY 10017

Routledge is an imprint of the Taylor & Francis Group, an informa business

First issued in paperback 2012

British Library Cataloguing in Publication Data
A catalogue record for this book is available from the British Library

ISBN13: 978-0-415-45763-7 (hbk)
ISBN13: 978-0-415-82823-9 (pbk)

Typeset in Times New Roman
by Taylor & Francis Books

Disclaimer
The publisher would like to make readers aware that the chapters in this book are referred to as articles as they had been in the special issue. The publisher accepts responsibility for any inconsistencies that may have arisen in the course of preparing this volume for print.

Contents

SPORT IN THE GLOBAL SOCIETY – CONTEMPORARY PERSPECTIVES

Series Editor: Boria Majumdar

GLOBAL SPORT BUSINESS

Community Impacts of Commercial Sport

Sport in the Global Society – Contemporary Perspectives
Series Editor: Boria Majumdar

The social, cultural (including media) and political study of sport is an expanding area of scholarship and related research. While this area has been well served by the Sport in the Global Society Series, the surge in quality scholarship over the last few years has necessitated the creation of *Sport in the Global Society: Contemporary Perspectives*. The series will publish the work of leading scholars in fields as diverse as sociology, cultural studies, media studies, gender studies, cultural geography and history, political science and political economy. If the social and cultural study of sport is to receive the scholarly attention and readership it warrants, a cross-disciplinary series dedicated to taking sport beyond the narrow confines of physical education and sport science academic domains is necessary. Sport in the Global Society: Contemporary Perspectives will answer this need.

Titles in the Series

Sport management and sport business: two sides of the same coin?[1]

Hans Westerbeek

Institute of Sport, Exercise and Active Living, Victoria University, Melbourne, Australia and Free University of Brussels, Brussels, Belgium

The ambitious title that this special issue carries raises expectations about its contents. Sport business in a global context, and within that context the impact of commercial sport on communities ... a whole range of potentially complex issues packaged into one title.

A special issue offers the opportunity to thematically focus, and to raise issues outside the mainstream of research in the discipline area. In this case, sport business implies commerce and trade in the sport industry, and how commerce and trade impact on communities – the latter ranging from groupings of sport participants and sport spectators to the array of stakeholders that have close or remote relations with sport and sport organizations. The net is purposely cast widely in this special issue with both global and local examples of (different types of) impact on a variety of 'communities'. Rather than specifying types of communities – an intellectual effort that is required in future work but for which the collection of articles in this issue remains too diverse – 'community' in this special issue refers to 'the people living in one particular area or people who are considered as a unit because of their common interests, social group or nationality'.[1] Contributing author Raymond Boyle focuses on 'hybrid communities of mediated sport fans' and the impact new media is having on their congregation and consumption behaviour, whereas Shakya Mitra looks at a new community of (middle class Indian) sportfans and what has been the impact of the rapid rise to sport business success of the Indian Premier League cricket competition. Koji Kobayashi, John M. Amis, Richard Unwin and Richard Southall debate the impact of globalizing forces on the management behaviour of the senior corporate communities of two Japanese sporting-goods manufacturers. Corporate decision makers are not an end-user community, but an instrumental stakeholder in the value chain of sport nevertheless (see also Figure 1 later in this article). Ramon Spaaij and Hans Westerbeek propose a different approach to determining 'impact' through a typology of markets for social capital in the sport business environment. Although their discussion is limited to identifying marketplaces for 'social capital', their typology provides a starting point for describing different types of 'end-user communities', in this case communities that may benefit from different types of social capital. In a way, Fred Coalter precedes this line of thinking by questioning what may be the impact of sport-for-development programmes on local communities of socially and economically deprived citizens, how impact is measured, and what can and cannot be expected of such programmes. Marc Theeboom, Reinhard Haudenhuyse and Paul De

Knop query how community sport programmes benefit socially deprived groups. Their focus is on questioning the positive impact that traditional (sport and government) organizations have, if they possess the best organizational purpose and structure for the effective delivery of these programmes. The authors also provide a potential alternative group of organizations for the delivery of community sport s in order to improve positive impact.

Reflecting on the work that has been submitted for this special issue, it made me more aware of the exponential journey that sport has travelled regarding academic programmes that have been established and research that has been conducted in the name of revealing the many unknowns in the sport industry. In order to talk about sport business we may briefly need to reflect on sport management, and how the professionalization of an industry has been fast-tracked by the onset of globalization, delivering an increasingly complex, dynamic and competitive arena of business. Sport management in that regard is about how to run sport, how to develop its management, how to improve its offering and output – a clear focus on the production of sport. Sport business on the other hand is about the wider perspective of industry, its marketplaces and the congregation of producers and consumers. It focuses on the commodification of sport, how to best commercialize potential products and how to sell them to a growing and progressively more segmented marketplace. This introductory article is about setting the scene for this special issue, in the process debating some conceptual and definitional confusion that may exist.

It all started with sport management?

Although universities in North America have delivered academic programmes in sport management and sport administration since the 1960s, the applied discipline of the management of sport organizations has only recently been embraced by (some) universities as a serious field of academic inquiry and teaching. A valid proxy for sport management's academic ascendance may well be the establishment of regional associations of sport-management academies, the oldest being the North American Society for Sport Management (NASSM)[2] founded in 1985. The establishment of NASSM was followed by the European Association for Sport Management (EASM, founded in 1993)[3], the Sport Management Association of Australia and New Zealand (SMAANZ, founded in 1995)[4] and the Asian Association for Sport Management (AASM, founded in 2002).[5] Interestingly, the majority of early, established sport-management programmes did not emerge in faculties, schools or departments of management but, rather, were mostly created in academic environments of applied sport science such as kinesiology, exercise science, physical education and human movement sciences. It seems that disciplines closest to the organizational practice of what was predominantly volunteer-driven sport activity were also the first to detect (or even feel) the need for more professional sport management.

Fast-forward to 2010 when business schools seem to have discovered the inherent attractiveness of sport as a means to (cross) promote their programmes, coinciding with a significant demand for sport-industry-specific degree programmes. As a result they have incorporated professional and research sport-industry programmes into their offerings. Not only are universities competing with each other in regard to offering degrees in sport management, but internally there seems to be an arm-wrestle looming between the applied-sport disciplines and the business schools delivering management and marketing degrees, about who is best suited to deliver sport-management programmes. The applied sport scientists argue that they best know *sport,* which is countered by the business professors who argue that it is about *management and marketing* applied to sport organizations.

This friendly clash of mother disciplines of sport management – applied sport science and management/marketing – reflects the increasing complexity of the sport industry. Only a few decades ago the majority of organizational activity in sport was delivered through non-commercial, volunteer and community-based initiative. Today the sport-industry landscape is dramatically different. The majority of financial resources in sport are generated and spent by highly skilled and experienced professionals who are in the sport industry to make a living. The organizations that they run vehemently compete for limited resources and even when they are not-for-profit by nature, they still require a no-nonsense rational business approach to their management in order to survive and ultimately thrive. Not only has the increasing importance of this business approach to sport led to a partial shift of sport management educational programmes to be housed in business schools, it has also led to (re)defining the scope of the sport industry. As such it may extend the discipline domain of sport management as well. As foreshadowed in the title of this article, where sport management may have been focused on the production of sport, sport business extends this focus on exchange between producers and consumers in the sport industry as a whole. In the next section this wider industry perspective is visualized using a value-chain[6] approach.

A value-chain approach to describing the sport industry

In a consulting report to the Australian Government's Department of Culture, Information Technology and the Arts (DCITA), Westerbeek and Smith adapted Porter's value-chain approach to describe the sport industry. An 'industry' can be defined as 'the people and activities involved in producing a particular thing, or in providing a particular service'.[7] A more elaborate definition states that industry is 'a department or branch of a craft, art, business or manufacture: a division of productive or profit-making labour; especially one that employs a large personnel and capital; a group of productive or profit-making enterprises or organizations that have a similar technological structure of production and that produce or supply technically substitutable goods, services, or sources of income'. The last part of this definition is critical, in that the categorization of businesses under the banner of a single industry is largely dependent on the types of goods or services that they produce. More to the point, these goods and services need to satisfy similar needs and wants of consumers, and production of those goods and services take place along similar technological lines. Therefore, when attempting to define the 'sport industry', one describes and categorizes all suppliers of goods and services that satisfy (or indirectly contribute to satisfying) sport needs. The point in the context of this paper is that it dramatically increases the range of organizations that have an involvement in producing, delivering and selling sport, and as such require (at least some form of) sport management. Westerbeek and Smith[8] propose the following sport-industry definition:

> The sport industry encompasses all upstream and downstream value adding activities emanating from the delivery of sport products and services. A sport product or service occurs when a human-controlled, goal-directed, competitive activity requiring physical prowess (irrespective of competency) is delivered or facilitated.
>
> Upstream value adding activities include sectors or organizations which provide supplies, infrastructure or support products or services to allow or facilitate the delivery of a sport product or service. Downstream value adding activities include sectors or organizations which provide distribution, marketing or customer relationship (after sales) products or services to a sport product or service.

Government Federal, State Ministries of Sport Local Government Authorities Legislation Physical Infrastructure					
Supplies and inbound logistics	Production, infrastructure and support services	Sport organization and operations	Sport delivery and activity	Media and Broadcasting	Marketing and after-sales
				facilities and venues	

Construction	Fitness Centres	National sport organizations	Private and membership clubs	Print	Consulting
Manufacturing	Heath and Medical	State sport organizations	Athletes	Television	Advertising and public relations
Equipment	Recreation Agencies	Non-government sport agencies and organizations	Sport development programmes	Pay television	Event support services
Apparel	Trainers and coaches	Events	Community sport programmes	Internet	Athlete management
Food, drinks and Supplements	Sponsors	Leagues and competitions	Development through sport programs	Gaming and gambling	Sport law
Consulting services	Education services	Sport festivals		Private and public facilities	Hospitality
	Research services	Education institutions		Public centres	
	Sport development institutes			Parks and gardens	
	Intellectual property				
	Information technology				

Figure 1. A value-chain-based model of the sport industry including some product examples (adapted from Westerbeek and Smith, 2004).

They go on by developing a visual model of how a value-chain-based model may apply to the describing the sport industry. The simplified model that is presented in Figure 1 needs to be 'read' from left to right (from upstream 'raw materials' to downstream 'end products', and from 'input' to 'throughput' to 'output'). The top layer of the model represents organizations and processes that impact all stages of value adding, either by providing financial or physical resources or how they influence the value-adding process through policy or legislation.

It is beyond the scope of this article to further elaborate on the specific contents of the sport-industry typology. As briefly outlined in the introductory paragraph of this article – because an intellectual effort is required to further specify types of communities in future work – Figure 1 may well serve as a starting point to describe all relevant stakeholder communities in the sport value chain, and also specify what the differential impact of their value-adding activities is. However, for this article it is sufficient to observe that the value-chain approach offers interesting opportunities to visualize the expanding scope of the sport industry and, as such, the extension of the domain of sport management. With the scope of the industry being about derived sport value, management of organizations in the industry can be referred to as sport management. In other words, where a few decades ago the focus of academic education and research would have been on the professionalization of sport organizations and its delivery management (the middle two columns in Figure 1), today this only represents a small part of creating and mining sport's value. The expansion of the industry has led to a range of value-adding activities becoming sub-industries in their own right. It can indeed be argued that sport as an industry has grown up – that organizations[9] and professions[10] have matured and that volunteer-driven management has largely been replaced with managers educated to operate in the executive office.[11] Beyond the process of professionalization and returning to the theme of this special issue, it can be observed that sport-management knowledge is required in unexpected market environments such as Third World countries, urban ghettos, multimedia company boardrooms and a range of government ministries that are not responsible for sport policy, but require sport's value in their production process nevertheless.

Ergo, although the applied discipline of sport management possibly best describes the range of academic programmes that are offered it does not unite international perspectives on the diversifying nature and scope of sport products. It is a(n) (value-chain) industry perspective that better allows for a discussion about sport business in a global context.

So what is sport business?

We are forced to consider the answer to the above question in the context of globalization as it can be argued that driving forces of globalization, such as economic liberalization and technological progress, have been critical in sport becoming an arena of big business.[12] The breakdown in the economic frontiers between nations has allowed sport to become more widespread, to gather more fans, and to present the opportunity for greater business development. Globalization has also brought with it the availability of large amounts of venture capital. Not only are emerging market nations benefiting from greater interest from venture capitalists, businessmen and entrepreneurs, but the opportunity to expand domestic leagues, clubs and events as well as exporting local sporting products are being capitalized on around the world.[13] Rapid development of information technology allows users access to all types of information, including high-quality footage of live sporting events, and has led to an expansion of market size for sport, not seen before in the history of the industry. Training programmes and training techniques can now also be accessed without travelling overseas to those who could monopolize the knowledge that was available. Overall, some of the driving forces that have facilitated a move towards globalization have particularly favoured the propensity for doing business in the sport industry. It is also important to note that globalization is often equated with capitalism and, as such, with ruthless commercialism that favours the rich and marginalizes those who already are poor. Muhammad Yunus argues that 'globalization, as a general business principle, can bring more benefits to the poor than any alternative. But without proper oversight and guidelines, globalization has the potential to be highly destructive'.[14] This also applies to sport and to sport consumers. The have-nots are in danger of being marginalized in favour of those who already own the majority of the pie. The opportunity to develop sport business comes with the potential that commercialized sport negatively (but also positively!) impacts communities (of consumers and stakeholders).

For the purpose of this special issue it can be argued that sport business is the profit-seeking or surplus-seeking production of sporting goods or services. In other words, the argument is that all sport business is commercialized, but the driving objective can be achieving a profit or a surplus (that is returned into the sport business). Sport business takes place in the sport industry (as described earlier in this article) and is about the exchange of value inherent in sport. Exchange takes place in (the) sport market(s) – gathering places where suppliers (not necessarily producers) and buyers (this can be individuals or groups/communities) meet to negotiate and conduct the exchange of sport's (derived) value.

Myth or fact: global sport as ruthless business?

Let us cut to the chase, sport can be as much an arena of ruthless and unforgiving combat as any other area of business. Irrespective of past (and current!) perceptions about sport being constrained to frivolously playing or spectating physically competitive games, sport is now deconstructed as a 'product' that in many different guises, and to many different consumers, can be offered for sale. This implies value and this inherent value of sport leads to competition off the field of play for resources that are required to keep the producers of sport 'in business'. It does not matter if the mode of business is 'for profit' or 'for surplus', it remains an ongoing struggle for limited resources that will see the fittest survive. However, we may be deceived into believing that modern sport business, or commercialized sport is all about making money for those who have amassed substantial wealth already. Indeed numerous examples prove this insight to have merit . . . but there is also increasing evidence that a commercial approach to delivering sport (products) to so called lower-chance communities – those who are offered limited opportunity in life – can bring excellent outcomes for both producers and consumers of such products. As always the crucial question remains how one generates good ideas and how one produces quality products at affordable and self-sustaining prices. In this special issue these dilemmas are looked at from a number of perspectives; such as the power and influence of new media and mediated sport; in regard to the capacity of sport (where and how) to create social capital; what is the influence of national culture on the management of sport organizations; how cultural identity is formed based on mediated sport; and how (commercial) sport intervention programmes (can) impact community repair and/or development. If anything, this special issue further exemplifies the increasing complexities and intricacies of an industry continuing its rapid growth and diversification. It will also foreshadow the latent potential of sport as a source of social business ventures, an exciting prospect that also may solve problems regarding self sustainability. I will briefly return to this point in the concluding article.

Notes

[1] *Cambridge Advanced Learner's Dictionary*, http://dictionary.cambridge.org/define.asp?key=15490&dict=CALD (accessed 5 May 2009).
[2] See also http://www.nassm.com/.
[3] See also http://www.easm.net/.
[4] See also http://smaanz.cadability.com.au/.
[5] See also http://aasm.tw/welcome/.
[6] See Porter, *Competitive Advantage*.
[7] See Westerbeek and Smith, 'Sport and Leisure Exports'.
[8] See Westerbeek and Smith, 'Sport and Leisure Exports'.
[9] See Slack and Hinings, 'Understanding Change in National Sport Organizations'.
[10] See Shilbury, Deane and Kellett, *Sport Management in Australia*.
[11] See Slack, *Understanding Sport Organizations*.
[12] See Westerbeek and Smith, *Sport Business*; and Smith and Westerbeek, *The Sport Business Future*.
[13] See Westerbeek and Smith, *Sport Business*.
[14] See Yunus, *Creating a World Without Poverty*.

References

Porter, M. *Competitive Advantage*. New York: The Free Press, 1984.

Shilbury, D., J. Deane, and P. Kellett. *Sport Management in Australia: An Organizational Overview*. 3rd ed. Melbourne: Strategic Sport Management, 2006.

Slack, T. *Understanding Sport Organizations: The Application of Organization Theory*. Champaign, IL: Human Kinetics, 1997.

Slack, T., and C.R. Hinings. 'Understanding Change in National Sport Organizations: An Integration of Theoretical Perspectives'. *Journal of Sport Management* 6 (1992): 114–32.

Smith, A., and H. Westerbeek. *The Sport Business Future*. London: Palgrave Macmillan, 2004.

Webster's Third New International Unabridged Dictionary. Springfield, MA: Merriam-Webster, 2000.

Westerbeek, H., and A. Smith. 'Sport and Leisure Exports: Industry Definition and Statistical Modelling'. Confidential report prepared for the Department of Culture, Information Technology and the Arts, Canberra, Australia 2004.

Westerbeek, H., and A. Smith. *Sport Business in the Global Marketplace*. London: Palgrave Macmillan, 2003.

Yunus, M. *Creating a World Without Poverty: Social Business and the Future of Capitalism*. New York: Public Affairs, 2007.

Sport and the media in the UK: the long revolution?

Raymond Boyle

Centre for Cultural Policy Research, University of Glasgow, Glasgow, UK

'It seems to me that we are living through a long revolution, which our best descriptions only in part interpret. It is a genuine revolution, transforming men and institutions; continually extended and deepened by the actions of millions, continually and variously opposed by explicit reaction and by the pressure of habitual forms and ideas. Yet it is a difficult revolution to define, and its uneven action is taking place over so long a period that it is almost impossible not to get lost in its exceptionally complicated process.'[1]

The dialectics of the relations between globalization, national identity and xenophobia are dramatically illustrated in the public activity that combines all three: football. For, thanks to global television, this universally popular sport has been transformed into a worldwide capitalist industrial complex (though, by comparison with other global business activities, of relatively modest size).[2]

Introduction

While, in the opening quote, Williams was talking about the relationship between communications and culture over 40 years ago, it seems appropriate to use his argument – from, incidentally, a cultural critic who thought that sport was one of the very best things on television – as an apt starting point in reflecting on the relationship between sport, the media and its stakeholders in contemporary society. This article aims to look at how the media have increasingly become the financial underwriter of global elite sport and examine the impact that sports content continues to play across the broadcast, print and online media industries, both at a national and international level. It also reflects on the ways in which both sports and their governing bodies have been shaped by the growing influence that the media play in the broader sports culture and focuses on some of the issues around trust and integrity that are emerging in both the media and sports industries. This paper also aims to address to what extent this relationship has been beneficial to all the various stakeholders in the sports–media nexus and examines the degree to which sporting communities themselves have shaped the wider media-sport landscape. It also highlights some of the particular challenges that may lie ahead for the UK sports industry as it continues to set the agenda for the broader European sports market.

Continuity and change in the media landscape

At the core of this article is a broader argument about the nature of continuity and change in contemporary culture. From a media-industries perspective, the dominant paradigms that have shaped the media landscape for decades are being challenged and restructured as we move from an analogue environment to a digital age characterized by the increasing convergence of technologies.[3] This is having a profound impact on how media content is produced, distributed and consumed. However, this process is one characterized by strong elements of continuity in patterns of media usage and consumption as well as dramatic change.

For example, television remains a central element of popular culture and sports content a key component in its mix, as it has been for over 50 years, but its place in media consumption is also changing. Over the coming years the key shift regarding sports content will be to think about the relationship between screens (big, small, portable, flexible, in the home, in the office, in the car, at the airport) and the types of content that appears on these screens (sport, news, drama, information), the process by which content gets onto the these screens (pulled down, scheduled, time shifted) and how – and if – we pay for this content (license fee, pay-as-you-go, subscription, advertising). Driving this process is a mixture of factors from technological change, through to explicitly political and economic impulses. In any case, technological development always takes place within particular political and economic frames of reference. Without the marketization of the broadcasting industry instigated by the Thatcher government in the 1980s in the UK – by which we mean the extent to which the principles of the free market were increasingly extended into all areas of public life – the conditions allowing the growth of a pay-TV platform such as BSkyB would not have evolved. Indeed it could be argued within a UK context that the driving through of market values into sectors of the communications industry, over the last 30 years or so, has been absolutely crucial in creating a climate that has allowed the specific growth and development of the sports economy in that country. It is the liberalizing of media markets that has allowed pay-TV operators such as BSkyB to channel billions of pounds into elite sports, and in the process become the financial underwriters for English Premier League football, rugby and cricket amongst others. In so doing, they have helped to restructure a range of relations that communities have with these differing sports. From dismantling some parts of the relationship (including name changes and the creation of new teams in rugby) through to the construction of new communities of identification as a younger generation has grown up with BSkyB's saturation coverage of sport.

Why sports matter in the digital age

There is now an established literature that traces and examines some of the key issues and debates around the relationship between the media and sport.[4] There has also been a growing interest in the particular relationship between journalism and sport and how this long historical relationship has evolved and developed as both journalism and the sports industry has changed in the digital age.[5] However given the pace of change across the media and creative industries in the last decade, as existing media structures have evolved in response to regulatory, technological and economic change, the current state of the relationship between sport and the media remains dynamic and intense.

At the core of the relationship between the media and sport are three key factors that are shaping its development. These are: the marketization of the media (and sport); the evolution of a digital landscape; and the globalization of labour, economy and aspects of cultural practice and identity. The marketization of media and sport, and indeed the internationalization of sports and media cultures are in themselves not new. You could also substitute the term technology for digitalization and again argue that this has always been a central component of the historical relationship between the media and sport. However it is the scale, scope and pace with which these differing forces are impacting on the sports and media industries which has become increasingly significant.

A few examples from the UK media sports market serve to illustrate the point. Between 1998 and 2008 the size of the audience for mainstream television programmes has significantly declined. In 1998, the most watched programmes on British television regularly attracted audiences of 15 million viewers, 10 years later there has been a fall-off in audiences to the extent that the figure is now in the region of 11 million.[6] However, and emphasizing the theme that the media environment is characterized by both continuity as well as significant change, the overall numbers of people watching television has remained broadly static. People in the UK still watch television in significant numbers, but in a mature multi-channel, multi-platform digital landscape they are not collectively watching the same programmes.[7]

In an age when the advent of on-demand services across the commercial and public service broadcasting terrain means that viewers increasingly can watch when they wish through the BBC iPlayer, or Sky + or Channel 4's VOD service, the collective 'appointments to view' in the schedule have become less obvious. There are clearly impacts on patterns of family life and the collective viewing of television. The process started when television sets began to multiply in the home, with people watching differing programmes in different rooms and has been extended through a culture of narrow or niche broadcasting, aimed at particular segments of the family or audience.

In part this changing pattern of media consumption, which looks set to intensify over the coming decade as the ability to pull-down content directly onto your television becomes a mass-market phenomenon, has seen a return of 'event television'. These are programmes such as the *X Factor* (ITV) or *Strictly Come Dancing* (BBC) that play on their 'liveness' and are less easy to time-shift. To this end sport, and particularly live sports such as football, have found that in such a media environment, not only have they retained their value, but their commercial value has actually increased. For example, when England played Sweden in the 2006 FIFA World Cup, ITV attracted its largest audience of the year, 18.8 million viewers. The 2007 Rugby World Cup saw 14 million tune into the England versus South Africa final in October of that year, and as F1 motor racing enjoyed a ratings surge with Lewis Hamilton's attempt to secure the world title in his inaugural season, almost eight million tuned into ITV's coverage of the Brazilian Grand Prix that same weekend.[8]

The combination of Rugby World Cup and FI motor racing gave a struggling ITV network an 'event' weekend television schedule that provided it with its biggest-grossing advertising revenue weekend of that year. ITV sold over £16 million's worth of advertising around these two events. Such is the integral nature of major international sports content (when it has a British dimension, of course) to commercial television in the UK, that when England failed to qualify for the 2008 European Championships, it was not simply football fans who lost out. ITV's advertising revenue projects for the summer were dramatically scaled back and while viewing figures held up well, they never scaled the heights that ITV would have expected had there been British interest at the tournament. The case of ITV is a good example of the systematic structural turbulence in the media markets that is directly impacting on sports content. However, as media analyst Emily Bell argues:

> The sums paid for TV sports rights have often been criticized in the past twenty years as unrealistically over-inflated, yet sports events have proved the most reliable part of the schedule; and their singular importance to money machines such as BSkyB is so overwhelming that there is no point in the foreseeable future when the price of rights will not suffer from hyper-inflation.[9]

Sports content in a changing broadcasting market

In the UK there now is a three-tier system of television. In one tier you have the BBC as a public service broadcaster (PSB), funded by the license fee for at least the next few years; you then have ITV, ostensibly a public service commercial broadcaster funded via advertising, who in the light of advertising spend migrating online and declining audiences in the multi-channel age, are keen to dispense with many of their PSB obligations, and finally there is a subscription pay-TV market dominated by BSkyB, with limited competition from Setanta. In addition Channel 4 has PSB obligations, carries advertising and is facing a significant revenue shortfall if it is to continue to offer the BBC competition in the PSB market.

Thus, within a decade the UK television sports marketplace has changed out of all recognition. Sky Sports, once the 'new kid on the block' created the pay-TV sports market in the UK in the 1990s, but has now become part of the media establishment and finds a rival company Setanta, who muscled into the market in the wake of EU regulation which broke Sky's monopoly of live Premiership football, nibbling at its ankles.

Lest we forget the scale of the change in British television sport, it is worth reminding ourselves that in the late 1980s television paid £3 million a season for top-flight English football. Fast-forward 20 years and the current combined BSkyB and Setanta deal with English football's elite division is worth £567 million a season. It is the TV executives who are now the financial underwriters of this sport and many others in the UK and elsewhere in Europe. Tennis, golf and rugby all feed off television money and exposure as part of – in the UK alone – a staggering 36,000 hours of sports broadcast in 2007.

For ITV, locked into an advertising revenue model, only sports that deliver within this environment are of interest. Twenty years ago, ITV Sport, although second fiddle to the vast BBC, had a significant portfolio of sport. In 2008, the channel was forced for strategic reasons to pull out of its F1 motor racing contract early, which returned to the BBC after a gap of 12 years, in order to be given a free run at securing the highly lucrative UK rights to the UEFA Champions League live free-to-air package of 18 games a season, thus extending ITV's coverage of the tournament to 2012. The BBC, on securing F1 from its old rivals dropped their interest in the sponsor-driven UEFA event allowing ITV to secure a competition that has become the backbone of its sports coverage and delivers a lucrative, male, midweek audience to ITV's advertisers. The 2008 Champions League final between Manchester United and Chelsea saw ITV's audience peak at 14.6 million making it the most watched television programme for the network in 2008. ITV also secured £10 million's worth of advertising revenue during its coverage of the final.

Thus, very specific sports content, in an increasingly commercial UK media system, remains very important for traditional broadcasters, such as ITV who are trying to find a workable post-PSB business model. In contrast, the BBC, who had seen its sporting portfolio diminish as the governing bodies of sport followed the money on offer from BSkyB, has been re-entering the market and using its digital and cross-platform presence to reassert its credentials as the *national* broadcaster. Sports content matters to the organization as it seeks to define PSB for a digital age and also for overtly political reasons to help with its future funding. As argued elsewhere:

> The 2008 Beijing Olympics, one of an increasingly small number of sporting events that cannot be exclusively captured by pay-TV, will see the BBC make 2,400 hours of extra sports coverage available through the interactive 'red button' digital service. By London 2012, the Corporation aims to make BBC1 the premium Olympic channel, and show every event live via the interactive service. This kind of commitment is only sustainable through a large well-funded broadcaster such as the BBC. At a time of funding uncertainty this will continue to be

sold by the Corporation as part of its distinctive public service remit. Given the massive public expenditure by Government on the London Games, it can be predicted that it will support the BBC as the only broadcaster capable of promoting and making Games coverage available free-to-air and across media platforms. The BBC will make the London Games part of its political argument to keep up levels of public funding. The reality is that by 2012 the way the BBC is funded is likely to change, as the license fee finally becomes an outdated mechanism through which to fund public service content in a multi-platform digital environment.[10]

A key issue for both sports and broadcasters will be the *cultural* argument about sport. This perspective views sport as making a distinctive contribution to the national and cultural life of any European country, and thus subject to special regulatory measures making it available for all. As discussed in the next section, the organizing institution of football in Europe, UEFA, has, under its president Michel Platini, increasingly been articulating this particular discourse as he attempts to rein in the power of the market-driven elite clubs of Europe. Platini's analysis is that the future of the sport requires intervention to regulate the European football marketplace on the grounds of a growing competitive imbalance within the sport. The need to regulate for the 'public good' is also echoed within the related field of the communications marketplace, where arguments about 'market failure' and 'public service content provision' have moved back onto the political agenda.[11] Thus while history suggests that the marketization of the broadcasting world will continue apace, so too will the accompanying debate – which is finding an echo in the sporting world – about when it is both necessary and useful to regulate a market for the public good. In this instance 'the public good' relates to a good or service that enhances public or collective national cultural life and well being. It also relates to the more narrow economic definition which views such goods (such as free-to-air television sport) as non-excludable (open to all regardless of their ability to pay) and non-rivalled (one fan watching does not prevent others enjoying the same experience).

So towards the end of the first decennium of the 2000s we are at another staging post in the long relationship between sport and media, there is continuity, but the times are also changing and the pace of that change appears to be quickening.

A step too far? The English Premiership, the market and national identity

You already have
NO English coach, you have
NO English players and
maybe now you will have
NO clubs playing in England. It's a joke.
EXCLUSIVE: *Uefa chief Michel Platini slams the Premier League's global mission.*[12]

When Richard Scudamore, the chief executive of the English Premier League, announced in early 2008 that a working group was being set up to examine the possibility of an 'international round' of Premiership matches, some reactions, to what quickly became dubbed the '39th step' (this phrase was a play on words as there is a well known British film called *The 39 Steps* and this would increase the games from 38 to 39 and be seen as a 'step too far' by the Premier League), suggested that the world had indeed been turned upside-down. The plan would see a round of English domestic matches being played around the globe, supposedly as a way of bringing the league to its ever growing international fan base. Scudamore also argued that this plan, estimated to generate an additional £5 million of revenue per club, would also head off a proposed world league that would tear the top teams away from their domestic competition. So – the official version explained – the plan was not about extracting even more revenue from the Premier League brand and its supporters, but rather about consolidating the 'inclusive' nature of the league.

What this proposal really signified was the synergizing of marketization, globalization and digitization trends that have been shaping the relationship between sport and the media. For while the proposed round of international matches has a certain economic logic, and in many ways was simply another stage in a model of sports development which prioritizes extracting revenue from every possible avenue of cultural production (and with digitization the possibility of doing this now exists; for example, a match that previously would never have been broadcast can generate revenue for clubs because a digital station will buy and carry it), its cultural logic was non-existent. Scudamore made plain that in the age of stakeholder democracy, the fans would be consulted about the proposal as the discussion progressed. However, which fans exactly was the chief executive actually talking about?

Fan communities in the digital age

The defining of the fan communities which sustain and nurture sports culture has become increasingly complex in the digital age of mediated sport.[13] Was it the fans that pay through season tickets and turn up to follow the team week-in week-out? The fans that help fund the game through their Sky Sports subscriptions? The fans of clubs such as Manchester United and Liverpool who are located around the globe and follow the fortunes of their team through communication networks such as the Web? Of course, some fans fall into all three categories, and others, the casual fan, may not be in any of them. Yet the proposal raised fundamental questions about the nature of the relationship between identity, location and the modern sports fan, as well as the extent to which commercial logic can simply eradicate traditionally important notions such as competition symmetry and sporting integrity. It demonstrates just how detached the game of football in England has become from its roots and its traditional communities that have sustained the sport. It also illustrates how fixated the commercial side of the game has become with securing the loyalty of potentially transient global communities of consumers.

The reaction in the UK print media and online from fans and commentators was overwhelmingly hostile to an idea that appeared to have no sporting or cultural logic, but was viewed as another revenue-generating activity using a game already awash with money from television and the supporters paying to watch live in the stadium or at home on pay-TV. However, given the wider shifts in the sport over the last few years, the proposal to change the nature of the competition was entirely predictable.

Since 2005, for example, almost half of the football teams in the Premiership have seen a change of control at boardroom level. Of these nine clubs, seven have been taken over by foreign owners, while an additional club, Chelsea, is famously being bankrolled by the Russian billionaire Roman Abramovich. At the same time, research by BBC Sport in May 2008 noted how the number of players eligible to play for the England national team starting matches in the Premier League dropped to an all-time low in 2007.[14] In that season only 34.1% of players who started games in the English Premier League were eligible to be picked for the national team, hence the president of UEFA Michel Platini's acerbic response to the 39th step proposal. The football industry in England has become a microcosm of the extent that wider economic orthodoxies have entered mainstream British political and social life. Here is a game that has modernized since the dark hooligan days of the 1980s, and that Britain exports abroad as an example of the 'soft power' that the sporting and creative industries can confer on economies that, rather than make things, sell services and images.

Sport as a business

At its core the English game is driven by a short-term, market logic, which is about maximizing revenue and is aided and abetted by a lack of rigorous governance and regulatory framework that recognizes that while football *is a business*, it is one deeply *imbued with cultural values* and subject to considerable emotional investment from an increasingly disaggregated and disenfranchised base of stakeholders; the supporters. As Westerbeek and Smith have argued in their discussion about governance and sport in a global context:

> Increasingly, the future of sport is in the hands of the private sector, where economic opportunity will provide the driving focus of investors and broadcasters, and government involvement, intervention and funding will move further to the periphery. Thus, the original owners of sports and clubs – the fans – will become further marginalized[15]

While the issue of governance in media sport and its attendant concerns of trust in the integrity of the sports culture is discussed in the following section it is worth noting that within the domain of television and the media industries more generally, the issue of trust and the relationship between the media and its audiences has begun to move centre stage in the last few years.[16]

There are parallel arguments being mobilized around the extent that a rise in consumer power enables the regulation of social and cultural activity, be it sports or television. This is a powerful political discourse centred around the notion of 'consumer sovereignty' and has run through much of the UK's political and public discourse over the last few decades. This discourse suggests that in a market-driven economy it is the consumer, through their ability to switch their purchasing power to another supplier, that enjoys a powerful position within the market, often to such an extent that external regulation of that market is not necessary. Yet the reality appears that, certainly in the UK, the marketization of broadcasting has been accompanied by a growing disregard for the audience – perhaps even contempt in some instances – as a long list of abuses of trust involving the major broadcasters and their audiences has been exposed in recent times. From simply misleading the audience, in the case of the BBC, to ITV actually financially ripping-off the viewer through rigged phone-ins, to the failure of match tickets to get to genuine fans for big football games, it appears that there are severe limits to the regulatory impact that 'consumer sovereignty' has on powerful institutions, be they media or sporting. In broadcasting it has been the statutory regulator Ofcom who has eventually intervened, fining ITV, for example, £5.67 million in May 2008 for 'misconduct in viewer competitions and voting'[17]. Channel 5, Channel 4, GMTV and the BBC have all been fined in 2008 for misleading the public in some capacity.

In a sporting market, large sections of the fan base of, say British football teams, remain impervious to the notion of the 'rational consumer', where if you don't like what is on offer you buy something else or simply switch loyalties to another team. So despite changes in fan communities, fans do not all act rationally, in an economic sense.

In the sporting universe, the Premier League's 39th-step idea has not gone away despite concerted opposition from FIFA, UEFA, the popular press and supporters groups. In late 2008 it remains on the agenda as the drive to maximize overseas revenues and consolidate the brand position of the league in Asian and North American markets takes precedence over any potential concerns around impact on domestic fans, the integrity of the competition and indeed on the indigenous leagues of other, potential host countries.

In an era of global franchises, it raises the question of who – in the twenty-first-century digital age – are the stakeholders of sport? It is also worth saying that in raising these issues one is not harking back to the mythical 'good old days of sport', but rather to note that sport has always been a business, but not just any business. When sports such as football simply become a rational business entity and break the link with their traditional fan base that relationship or bond can change significantly.[18] Of course 'fans' do not themselves remain still, as Brecht argued 'What was popular yesterday is not today, for the people today, are not what they were yesterday'.[19] So fans develop and change also, but they do so within particular sporting and cultural narratives and histories that sustain and make sense of this change, and central to this process is the issue of trust.

Sport, the media and trust

Until we stand back and take a longer view of what Raymond Williams famously called the 'long revolution' of communications, culture and democracy it is hard to accurately make sense of some of the underlying changes that are evident in the sports-media relationship of the last few decades. In doing so however we find something quite profound and less commented upon appears to have happened. Sports have lost their veneer of innocence, with regard to the impact that the world of business and capital has on their practices and culture. For media and sports scholars, of course, have long argued that the discourse of sporting innocence has been largely mythological in its nature.[20]

Since the Victorian age of sport, as a cultural form it has always been imbued by the wider values and ideological assumptions that shape the society that gives birth to that sport and nurtures it. As society changes, elements of the codified games remain, but the fundamental values and attitudes of that society are given expression through sport and shape the cultural hinterland that surrounds sports such as football, rugby, cricket, baseball and such like. It is this process that allows international games such as football to become carriers of wider cultural and national identities. This is a process through which mediated sports can reflect – and at times construct – distinctive collective identities that can also emphasize difference and distinctiveness.

The call of 'keep politics out of sport' has always been a mistaken aspiration, given that sports cultures have always been steeped in the politics of gender, class and power. However, what has been crucial in this process has been the complicit nature of the media in this view of a 'world of sport' divorced from the economic and political structures that shape our working lives. Television traditionally has always downplayed its role in the mediation process of sport. The dominant discourse was one of simply bringing the sport into your home, giving you the best seats in the house at centre court at Wimbledon for example, or opening up symbolic national events to the whole country such as football cup finals or the Grand National steeplechase.

The role television played in shaping these events, either though its payment for rights or in what Whannel called its 'transformation' of a sports event into a media event went by-and-large uncommented upon either by television itself or by the media more generally.[21] In truth television got sport for so many years on the 'cheap' that the money it put into events had a marginal impact on structures. However, the governing bodies of sport have always viewed television as important, not least for the potential leverage it gives them with sponsors, that often they were only too happy to alter rules, change times and schedule themselves for television.

However all this changed in the 1990s in the UK with the marketization of broadcasting and the twin accompanying forces of technological change and the internationalizing of economies. Again neither of these forces was new, and the history of sports media is one characterized by technological innovation and the international nature of certain sporting forms and governing bodies such as the International Olympic Committee (IOC) and FIFA.

What was significant was that the 1990s saw the market being positioned as the central driver within a range of areas of the economy, such as health and education, that previously had remained largely immune to its influence.

The deregulation of the financial sector of the City of London in the 1980s blew away many of the old regulated structures and globalized the money networks in such a profound manner that 20 years later we are still working through its impact on British economic life. The massive re-calibrating of the private and public sector economies in the UK and the introduction of market mechanisms across the public sector from health to education have all had a significant impact in reshaping the public and private lives of British people. We have moved from a supply-led media environment to an increasingly demand-led culture, from restricted citizens, to supposedly liberated consumers. Sports and the various sports cultures in the UK have been dramatically shaped, either directly or indirectly, by this major socio-economic and political changeof the last two decades and the rise of new orthodoxies regarding the centrality of the market in our public and private lives.

The growth of public relations and marketing agencies concerned with what Schlesinger and Tumber[22] called the 'promotional age' is one such example of how the newly expanded media became an increasingly important element in shaping public opinion and attitudes. Davies,[23] for example, notes that public relations (PR) does not simply play a role in articulating the position of certain organizations, but has increasingly come to usurp what we understand to be the nature of journalism and journalistic enquiry, noting how people who work in public relations now outnumber journalists in the UK. Elsewhere I have argued that sports journalism has been significantly altered by the rise of PR and marketing agencies that now operate in and around the sports economy. As a result, clubs, associations or individual stars are concerned about protecting their image and tightly controlling access to information.[24]

What these broader changes have done is complex, but significant for sports. At an obvious level, the marketization of the media has massively increased what is offered and, in a demand-led media culture, sports (or more accurately certain sports such as football) have finally been given the media profile their popularity merits. For example, 20 years ago the coverage of sports in the broadsheet press in the UK was limited, now the coverage is extensive and recognizes the very public popularity of sports among sections of the population. In this sense the marketization of the media has brought certain benefits for the sports fans and consumer. For example, access to information for fans about, say, European football and the top leagues throughout the continent is much greater than existed even a decade ago.

In this broader process sports have become industries in the UK, as the level of revenue from television has grown in a manner nobody envisaged. Governing bodies of sport, and the broader governance of sport more generally, were singularly ill equipped to deal with this change; and the shifting of power relations between players, clubs and associations has been one of the defining components of the sporting landscape over the last two decades. The inability of organizations to deal openly and honestly with a range of accusations regarding the abuse of power and privilege in either national organizations such as the Premier League[25] or global bodies such as FIFA and the IOC[26] suggest that these bodies appear to think that the normal standards of governance for institutions in public life are not applicable to them. Money and the expanded media have created stars, and shifted the balance of power to elite stars and elite clubs. The PR and marketing industries mentioned earlier have moved into sport to shift the lexicon of the 'promotional age' centre stage into sporting discourse, from discussions about global sports 'franchises' to the 'branding' of football clubs.

Sports fans, certainly those willing and able to pay the vastly inflated prices to either watch sport live or mediated through pay-TV have never had it so good. But something else has also happened. Television and the expanded digital and online media environment are no longer able to sustain some of the myths about sport it so deeply cherished for many years. Despite attempts by organizations such as the BBC to sell the sporting image of events such as the Olympics, other parts of the corporation, in this demand-led media culture, will be castigating the IOC for its poor governance of the Games or highlighting the contradictions between a Beijing Games based on peace and goodwill and China's poor human-rights record in Tibet. The BBC will provide extensive radio coverage of sports such as cricket while running television documentaries exposing the gambling corruption that appears to lie at the heart of the modern game.

It is simply no longer sustainable to argue that sport is divorced from the broader economic culture that shapes our lives. We are continually told that sport is now a *business* and most sports fans are aware of this. As noted above, in an age where trust in institutions and indeed in the media and journalism more generally is falling, sport is also caught in this wider cultural shift. This may be a particularly culturally rooted phenomenon but, in the UK, events such as the Olympics do not occupy the same position that they once did in terms of the affections of the public. There are a range of factors explaining this, of course. The relative lack of high-profile British athletes that transcend their sport in the manner of previous Olympians has been important, but so to is a deeper loss of innocence about the nature of elite sport. As the ever-increasing number of drug cheats has been exposed, so, using the language of twenty-first-century sport, the Olympic brand has been damaged. How many medals are now won by clean athletes? Who can you trust? Even while the coverage of the role of drugs in sport has increased, the media is still reluctant to acknowledge the implicit role they play in the process. As the amounts of money in sports escalate so the risks associated with cheating become worth taking given the financial rewards that are on offer in an age where celebrity media status awaits those at the top of their sport.

This is not simply a concern among media sports scholars. Jon Holmes, a former football agent, has written about what he views as the looming crisis for football in England, fuelled by the massive amounts of money that are being poured into the sport. For Holmes the issue that is being ignored by the sport is simple: it is corruption and the inability of the game to address its corrosive impact on trust. He argues:

> Self-regulation has not worked in the financial services industry and will not work in football. If the game is not to lose its integrity over financial malfeasance – as athletics has to some extent, and cycling over drugs, and cricket, to a lesser degree, over gambling – then those at the top need to seek help from the government. Independent authorities, free from the influence of the self-interested, need to be created so that the game can really face up to the challenges that success in the modern world brings. Once the public lose trust, it's a rocky path for sport.[27]

Just as Barnett has argued that if we distrust journalism then we will eventually destroy it,[28] so is trust also vital for the long-term health of sports. There may never have been an age of complete innocence for sports and its supporters, but greater openness and accountability in sports media culture is required as never before. Changes are taking place. The 2008 Wimbledon tennis grand-slam event began with a UK Sunday newspaper leading with a front page splash of 'Anyone for backhanders?'[29] and a story about the setting up by the tennis authorities of a new anti-corruption squad, staffed by former Scotland Yard detectives to investigate growing concerns about betting corruption and match-fixing in the sport. The leader comment in the newspaper, under the headline, 'Advantage Tennis', praised the authorities for meeting the challenges posed by the fact that, after football and racing, tennis attracts the greatest amount of money in betting than any other sport. However the current configuration of sports journalism with its entertainment and PR focus also suggests that journalism has been less than rigorous in acting as the watchdog of the public in calling institutions and individuals to account.[30]

Conclusion: into tomorrow

> The globalization of football has created a culture in which the leading players are now absolutely separated from the people who pay to watch them – us, the fans – and, indeed, also from those who write about the game ... Football has ceased to be the people's game, in any meaningful sense. It has become a game defined by rapacity and greed, and by a grotesque, mercantile, neo-liberal winner takes-all ethos.[31]

The above quote comes from the editor of the *New Statesman* magazine and former editor of the *Observer Sports Monthly* (OSM) reflecting on how sport changed during his time (between 2003 and 2007) at the helm of OSM. It also encapsulates what an increasing number of fans and commentators feel about the changes that have restructured a sport such as football, both domestically and internationally.[32] Money always both drives and distorts markets over a long period of time, and the football industry is no different. In 2008 we have a combination of vast domestic payouts to clubs fuelled by exclusive pay-TV money, allied with European Champions League revenues. The money and talent follows an elite number of European clubs clustered in the cities of Barcelona, London, Madrid and Milan who hoover up the top stars and shape the footballing talent market for all the other clubs as well as alter the balance of players available for international teams.

In reflecting on the contemporary structure of elite sport and its deeply embedded links with the media, one has to ask does any of this matter? Sport appeals to the media because it evokes passion among its followers and has been sustained by communities who have invested financially and emotionally in teams, clubs, players and managers.

Well it does matter, because without attention to, and recognition of, the complex mutual relationships that exist between sporting communities and the sports they sustain traditional aspects of that relationship may become lost. If a football club like Celtic choose to ignore the narratives of community and identity that have sustained it over the years, then it would over time simply become one other leisure option among many for supporters. The best sports writing and journalism understands this potent chemistry and use sports culture to illuminate wider social trends and deepen our understanding of particular societies such as England and Italy,[33] or Ireland and its continuing love affair with indigenous Gaelic games.[34]

The business side of sport has never stood still, always had one eye on the main deal, often taken their fan base for granted even, and indeed especially, in the so called 'good old days'. However the challenge is to strike a balance between short-term goals and long-term sustainability; playing this long game is something at which the governing bodies of sport have rarely been good.

Media technology will continue to develop apace. We are moving to an age where debates about old and new media are becoming outdated and the new paradigm is one that places the relationship between content and screens at its core. By this we mean an age where technology allows screens to be held in your hand, be on your work desk, be in any room of your home and increasingly occupy public spaces from shopping malls to airports. The debate will be about how we pull content down onto these screens and how money is made from this transaction. If this emerging media ecology is driven solely by marketization this will impact on sports, keen to take the money and run. European media regulators struggle to strike a balance between the commercial and cultural role of broadcasting and media in society and ask, what should be the continued role of public service broadcasting? Where do notions of the public good fit into media and political discourse? How do we combat 'market failure' in media content provision? In the same context, sports should also reflect on their relationship with the range of diverse stakeholders who sustain the industries, both financially and also culturally.

Lest one thinks that this author despairs about the future of sport, a couple of examples illustrate the sustaining power of communities that have been nurtured in and through sporting culture.

The death in 2008 at the age of 51 from cancer of Celtic Football Club's first team coach Tommy Burns provoked a widespread public and media outpouring of grief. Burns had played for Celtic from an early age and also managed the club for a period in the 1990s. He was also an assistant manager to the Scotland national team serving under both Berti Vogts and Walter Smith. Burns was a man defined by his love of family, his Catholic faith and his passion for Celtic and football. The scenes as his funeral cortege passed by Celtic Park, with the streets lined with thousands of supporters, offered a poignant reminder of the role that heroes such as Burns played and continue to play in the lives of ordinary supporters. It was not simply empty rhetoric that saw both the Celtic chairman, John Reid, and chief executive Peter Lawwell speak about the importance of Burns to the 'Celtic family' and how his early death meant that that family, around the globe, was in mourning for a much loved son. The open emotion with which Celtic manager Gordon Strachan spoke intimately about the last hours he spent with his friend, and the very public grief of his friend and Rangers assistant boss Ally McCoist, demonstrated in a very public manner how at key moments sport has the power to transcend the rivalries that are deeply embedded in its culture and speak to the dignity and the honour that still resides in aspects of the culture that sustains the sport.

The other example has been the enjoyment provided by the Euro 2008 football tournament that has been a free-to-air television success in the UK despite no home nation teams being present. Across BBC television, radio and online the engagement of the public has vindicated the argument that such events, when free-to-air, capture the imagination not only of the sports fan, but of the wider public pulled into the drama, colour and intrigue which has been associated with this event. For football fans, the pleasure of watching a tournament characterized by positive football and exciting games reminds one that, stripped of the hinterland that has grown up around the football industry over the last few decades, it is the game and how it is played that remains the most important ingredient in helping to sustain its popularity.

To borrow from Williams,[35] the media sports relationship is part of a long revolution, and we are entering another staging post in that journey. What is becoming clear is that we have tensions between older notions of sporting communities and the new hybrid communities of mediated sports fans. The challenge is for the governing bodies of sport to respect and seriously engage with, rather than pay lip-service to, notions of stakeholder democracy within this emerging, complex new landscape. The sports media relationship has always been one of change, shot through with strong patterns of continuity. It is the cultural component of this process of connection, through shared collective memory, identity, tradition and history that makes sport such a compelling, competitive and potentially powerful cultural form, informed by the local, but connected to the global. The long-term health of sporting culture will depend on the ability of sports to meaningfully engage with all the differing communities that move within its orbit. As these communities evolve and change, often in line with developing patterns of media consumption, this presents a considerable challenge. A continual re-evaluation about who sport is for and its role in society must be part of that debate.

Notes

[1] Williams, *The Long Revolution*, 10.
[2] Hobsbawn, *Globalisation, Democracy and Terrorism*, 90.
[3] Jenkins, *Convergence Culture*.
[4] Boyle and Haynes, *Power Play*; Brookes, *Representing Sport*; Rowe, *Sport, Culture and the Media*; Blain and Boyle, 'Sport as Real Life'.
[5] Boyle, *Sports Journalism*; Steen, *Sports Journalism*.
[6] Broadcasting Audiences Research Board (BARB) figures.
[7] Ofcom, *The Communications Market 2007*.
[8] BARB, 20 October 2007.
[9] Bell, 'A Toehold in Football'.
[10] Blain and Boyle, 'Sport as Real Life'.
[11] Richards, Foster and Kiedrowski, *Communications*.
[12] *The Daily Telegraph*, 9 February 2008, Sport section.
[13] King, *The European Ritual*; Williams, '"Protect Me From What I Want"', Williams, 'Rethinking Sports Fandom'.
[14] BBC Sport, 'England Player Numbers at New Low', 27 May 2008, http://www.bbc.co.uk/sport.
[15] Westerbeek and Smith, *Sport Business in the Global Marketplace*, 36.
[16] Beckett, *Supermedia*; Davies, *Flat Earth News*; Monck, *Can You Trust the Media?*
[17] Ofcom, *Annual Report 2007/2008*, 20.
[18] Goldblatt, *The Ball is Round*.
[19] Brecht, 'Against Georg Lukacs', 51.
[20] Boyle and Haynes, *Power Play*; Brookes, *Representing Sport*; Rowe, *Sport, Culture and the Media*; Blain and Boyle, 'Sport as Real Life'.
[21] Whannel, *Fields in Vision*.
[22] Schlesinger and Tumber, *Reporting Crime*.
[23] Davies, *Flat Earth News*, 85.
[24] Boyle, *Sports Journalism*.
[25] Bower, *Broken Dreams*; Conn, *The Beautiful Game?*
[26] Jennings, *The Great Olympic Swindle*; Jennings, *Foul!*; Sugden and Tomlinson, *Great Balls of Fire*.
[27] Jon Holmes, 'A Whole New Ball Game', *GQ Magazine*, January 2008.
[28] Barnett, 'On the Road to Self-destruction'.
[29] The *Independent on Sunday*, 22 June 2008.
[30] Boyle, *Sports Journalism*.
[31] Jason Cowley, 'A New Era', *Observer Sports Monthly*, no. 100, June 2008.
[32] Bazell, *Theatre of Silence*; Samuels, *The Beautiful Game is Over*.
[33] Vialli and Marcotti, *The Italian Job*.
[34] Humphries, *Dublin v Kerry*.
[35] Williams, *The Long Revolution*.

References

Barnett, Steven. 'On the Road to Self-destruction'. *British Journalism Review* 19, no. 2 (2008): 5–13.

Bazell, Matthew. *Theatre of Silence: The Lost Soul of Football*. London: Elliot Mackenzie Publishers, 2008.

Beckett, Charlie. *Supermedia: Saving Journalism So It Can Save the World*. London: Wiley-Blackwell, 2008.

Bell, Emily. 'A Toehold in Football is Worth All the Ferraris in Cheshire'. *The Guardian*, 24 March 2008, Media Guardian.

Blain, Neil, and Raymond Boyle. 'Sport as Real Life'. In *The Media: An Introduction* 3rd ed., edited by Paul Cobley and Daniele Albertazzi, 519–533. London: Longman, 2009.

Bower, Tom. *Broken Dreams: Vanity, Greed and the Souring of British Football*. London: Pocket Books, 2007.

Boyle, Raymond. *Sports Journalism: Context and Issues*. London: Sage, 2006.

Boyle, Raymond, and Richard Haynes. *Power Play: Sport, the Media and Popular Culture*. London: Pearson, 2000.

Brecht, Bertolt. 'Against Georg Lukacs'. *New Left Review* 84 (1974): 39–53.

Brookes, Rod. *Representing Sport*. London: Arnold, 2002.

Conn, David. *The Beautiful Game? Searching for the Soul of Football*. London: Yellow Jersey Press, 2005.

Davies, Nick. *Flat Earth News*. London: Chatto & Windus, 2008.

Goldblatt, David. *The Ball is Round: A Global History of Football*. London: Penguin, 2007.

Hobsbawn, Eric. *Globalisation, Democracy and Terrorism*. London: Little Brown, 2007.

Humphries, Tom. *Dublin v Kerry: The Story of the Epic Rivalry that Changed Irish Sport*. Dublin: Penguin, 2007.

Jenkins, Henry. *Convergence Culture: Where Old and New Media Collide*. New York: NYU Press, 2006.

Jennings, Andrew. *Foul! The Secret World of FIFA: Bribes, Vote Rigging and Ticket Scandals*. London: HarperCollins, 2007.

Jennings, Andrew. *The Great Olympic Swindle*. London: Simon and Schuster, 2000.

King, Anthony. *The European Ritual: Football in the New Europe*. Aldershot: Ashgate, 2003.

Monck, Adrian. *Can You Trust the Media?* London: Icon Books, 2008.

Ofcom. *The Communications Market 2007*. London: Ofcom, 2007.

Ofcom. *Annual Report 2007/2008*. London: Ofcom, 2008.

Richards, Ed, Foster, Robin, and Kiedrowski, Tom, eds. *Communications: The Next Decade*. London: Ofcom, 2006.

Rowe, David. *Sport, Culture and the Media*. Maidenhead: Open University Press, 2004.

Samuels, John. *The Beautiful Game is Over: The Globalisation of Football*. London: Book Guild Publishing, 2008.

Schlesinger, Philip, and Howard Tumber. *Reporting Crime: The Media Politics of Criminal Justice*. Oxford: Clarendon, 1994.

Steen, Rob. *Sports Journalism: A Multi-media Primer*. London: Routledge, 2008.

Sugden, John, and Alan Tomlinson. *Great Balls of Fire: How Money is Hijacking World Football*. Edinburgh: Mainstream, 1999.

Vialli, Gianluca, and Gabriele Marcotti. *The Italian Job: A Journey to the Heart of Two Great Footballing Cultures*. London: Bantam, 2007.

Westerbeek, Hans, and Aaron Smith. *Sport Business in the Global Marketplace*. Houndmills: Palgrave Macmillan, 2003.

Whannel, Garry. *Fields in Vision: Sport, Television and Cultural Transformation*. London: Routledge, 1992.

Williams, John. '"Protect Me From What I Want": Football Fandom, Celebrity Cultures and "New" Football in England'. *Soccer and Society* 7, no. 1 (2006): 96–144.

Williams, John. 'Rethinking Sports Fandom: The Case of European Soccer'. *Leisure Studies* 26, no. 2 (2007): 127–46.

Williams, Raymond. *The Long Revolution*. London: Chatto & Windus, 1961.

The IPL: India's foray into world sports business

Shakya Mitra

Department of Sports Studies, University of Stirling, Stirling, UK

In the three years since its inception, the Indian Premier League (IPL), a Twenty20 cricket tournament based in India, has become one of world sports' foremost properties. The IPL as of 2010 has a valuation of $4.13 billion and is the second highest paying league in the world. This article seeks to identify the factors that could be accounted for in the phenomenal growth of the IPL brand. While the IPL, in its short lifespan, has shown tremendous growth, the shortness of life span should be taken into account when passing a judgment on its 'success'. Thus any conclusions drawn on the IPL's relative success will be gained in an interim rather than a definite sense. Cricket is immensely popular in India to the extent that other sports often receive only passing mention in the country. However, the popularity of cricket alone could not have made the IPL run. The success of any league, and not just the IPL, is dependent on the presence of a solid foundation. The article thus attempts to identify the extent to which the IPL is based on such a solid foundation.

Introduction

It is not a case about putting the Indian Premier League before my county. Yes, I am excited about coaching and captaining the Rajasthan Royals and I believe that the IPL will give a huge boost to cricket worldwide.'[1]

(Shane Warne)

The Indian Premier League (IPL), a franchise-based Twenty20 cricket competition initiated by the Board of Cricket Control of India (BCCI), has in a span of just three years grown into one of world sports' foremost properties.[2] Where other sports across the world had ventured into franchise-based ownership, this was a first for cricket.[3] Franchise-owned sport was clearly a new avenue for cricket, but as its soaring valuation of $4.13 billion after three years would indicate, it has clearly been successful for the IPL.[4]

If professional sports across the world have a rival from the game of cricket, then that is the IPL. This can be represented by the fact that the players' average annual salary is the second highest in the world, only after the National Basketball Association (NBA).[5] Despite its rapid growth which has made it Twenty20 cricket's most marketable property, the IPL was not the format's first venture. Twenty20 cricket was first introduced in 2003 by the England and Wales Cricket Board (ECB). The ECB, noticing dipping attendances and reduced revenues in longer forms of cricket, such as first-class Test cricket and 50-overs a side one-day cricket, decided to come up with the formula of Twenty20 cricket, a game involving two teams, each with a single innings, batting for a maximum of 20 overs.[6] The first official Twenty20 tournament, the Twenty20 Cup, was marketed with the slogan 'I don't like cricket, I love it'.[7] The results were immediate, with packed stadiums and increased revenues in the very first season of the tournament. The first Twenty20 game held at Lords, on 15 July 2004, between Middlesex and Surrey attracted a crowd of 26,500, breaking all previous attendance records in one-day cricket.[8] The results and outcomes of that tournament turned out to be spectacular. The Twenty20 Cup became a benchmark for other cricket-playing countries and domestic Twenty20 competitions were soon introduced in Australia, South Africa, West Indies and other major cricketing nations.[9] What makes the IPL different from the Twenty20 cricket organized in all these countries is its franchise-based nature.[10]

Despite the difference in the way the IPL is organized compared to the Twenty20 cup, it still maintains many similarities with the elements introduced during that tournament. These include making the game's time-span shorter and closer to that of other popular team sports, the use of cheerleaders and scheduling of games during the evening hours when most people are free to come to the stadium. These features have helped to create a lively form of the game which would be attractive to spectators at the ground and viewers on television.[11] This paper will make an evaluation of the IPL on the basis of academic literature available on the way leagues are organized in both Europe and North America, keeping in mind the differences in the organization of sports in both parts of the world. In the process, it uses concepts of sports finance and sports economics such as uncertainty of outcome, competitive balance, ownership of teams, revenue-sharing pattern, player valuations and salary caps.

The former Chairman of the IPL Lalit Modi has been the central figure of the IPL over its first three seasons, with the league credited as being his brainchild.[12] However it must be added that it was not Modi alone who helped develop the IPL concept. Prior to launching the IPL in September 2007, Modi hired the services of International Management Group (IMG), one of the best-known sports management companies in the world. More significantly he also consulted two leading sports academics Stefan Szymanski and Stephen Ross to help them in fine tuning the league structure. Szymanski and Ross are experts in the area of sports league, so their involvement would clearly have been beneficial to the IPL.[13] This paper, while using the academic work or any other viewpoint raised by either Szymanski or Ross, keeps aside their consultancy role with the IPL.

The objective of the paper is to establish the 'success' of the IPL on the basis of the manner in which the league is run. A conclusion on its 'success' in an interim sense will be made on the basis of the IPL's league structure and policies that have been adopted. Though the league structure and policies will be the primary criteria through which the IPL's success will be evaluated, there is some other contextual information that can be taken into account. In 2009, the second season of the IPL was shifted out of India to South Africa. This was because of the clash of dates with the Indian general elections and the inability of the Indian government to assure the IPL of adequate security cover.[14] The *Guardian* newspaper hailed Lalit Modi in the wake of this decision to move the IPL out of India, describing him as one of the most effective sports administrators in history. It also added that Modi's foresight, decisiveness and 'staggering self-belief' rescued the tournament from collapsing.[15] Despite the IPL's rapid growth, its brand image was hurt severely in the wake of the corruption scandal and allegations of financial irregularities against Lalit Modi, which eventually led to him being sacked as the Chairman of the IPL. While the allegations are indeed severe, they in no way influence this paper in making a judgment on the success of the IPL since the facts on these allegations are unclear as investigations are not yet complete.[16]

Ownership of franchises

The auction process that decided the eight participating teams in the inaugural edition of the Indian Premier League (IPL-1) and their owners took place on 24 January 2008.[17]

The floor price of a team was set at $50 million. It was also stipulated that interested bidders would be able to bid for just one team.[18] The eight cities that received the highest bid would be considered for franchise; the remaining four cities would miss out.[19]

As Table 1 suggests, these are fairly high prices for a league that is at its inception phase. Rodney Fort suggests that these high prices are usually an outcome of demand for the product that is cricket.[20] To put the spending that took place during the 2008 franchise auction into perspective, one must consider the example of English Premier League club Aston Villa. In 2006, Randy Lerner, who owned the National Football League (NFL) club Cleveland Browns, bought Aston Villa for $115 million. This was just over $3 million more than what Reliance Industries paid to buy the Mumbai franchise. Here the differences come in, whereas Aston Villa was a club that had been in existence since 1874, and was the fourth most successful club in English football history, comparatively Mumbai was a new team in a new league.[21] Mumbai topped the spending at the franchise auction which reached the level of $723.5 million or an average franchise spending of over $90 million per team. This was a figure that satisfied the then IPL chairman Lalit Modi. Modi's publicly stated ambition was to make the IPL as big as the English Premier League. He felt that over a period of time the league was going to get bigger considering India's one billion plus population as well as the increasing following of cricket across the world.[22]

Rising ticket sales is one of the major reasons why location plays such a crucial role in the auction process.[23] Not surprisingly the two cities that had the highest demand prior to the franchise auction were Mumbai and Delhi, the two most commercially viable cities in the country. There were 15 bidders interested in bidding for the Mumbai franchise compared to 9 bidders interested in Delhi.[24] Mumbai, India's commercial capital, fetched the highest price at the auction–$111.9 million.[25] Delhi, despite being India's political capital and possessing a strong cosmopolitan population, went for a lower figure $84 million, the fifth highest at the auction.[26]

One of the new elements brought in with franchise ownership in cricket which is similar to professional sports in North America and Europe is the business of the owners.[27] The money paid by Vijay Mallya and T.V. Reddy, to buy the Bangalore and Hyderabad franchises respectively, may seem inflated in cricketing terms. Professor Stefan Szymanski though feels the expenditure is justified because a lot of the money will be recouped through the primary businesses of the franchises which are based in these cities. In other words, the popularity of these cricket teams, it was felt, would help boost the sale of spirits and wines produced by Mallya or the sale of newspapers brought out by Reddy.[28]

Table 1.   Selected franchises

City franchise	Value	Owners	Principal industry
Mumbai (Mumbai Indians)	$111.9 million	Reliance Industries	Petrochemicals
Bangalore (Royal Challengers Bangalore)	$111.6 million	UB Group	Breweries
Hyderabad (Deccan Chargers)	$107 million	Deccan Chronicle	News media
Chennai (Chennai Super Kings)	$91 million	India Cements	Cement
Delhi (Delhi Daredevils)	$84 million	GMR	Construction
Punjab (Kings XI Punjab)	$76 million	Preity Zinta, Ness Wadia and others	Textile
Kolkata (Kolkata Knightriders)	$75 million	Red Chillies Entertainment	Film production
Jaipur (Rajasthan Royals)	$67 million	Emerging Media	Media property

Source: Srinivas and Vivek, 2009.

Compared to the prices that were paid during the 2010 franchise auction, the purchase of the Mumbai, Bangalore and Hyderabad franchises seemed like bargains. Sandy, Sloane and Rosentraub's theory is that more teams invest in a league when it (the league) becomes more successful.[29] The fact that the above mentioned franchises were bought at bargain prices was accentuated by the astonishing prices at which the Pune and Kochi franchises were sold for during the 2010 auction, over $300 million, more than three times the price paid for Mumbai.[30] With a base price of $225 million each for the two new franchises – double of what the Mumbai franchise went for – there were fears of bidders being put off. At the auction, though, the winning bids comfortably exceeded the base price. The Pune franchise was bought for $370 million by Sahara Sports, while the Kochi franchise was bought by Rendezvous Sports World for $333 million.[31] The huge prices paid to acquire the Pune and Kochi only justify Sandy, Sloane and Rosentraub's theory that the success of a league will encourage new franchises to enter. The $300 million plus purchases of both franchises affirm the IPL's growing brand value. To put these purchases into perspective, the price paid to buy Liverpool in 2007, the most successful English football club, was £219 million ($326.3 million). This was less than the price paid to buy both the Pune and Kochi franchises. Even Manchester City, regarded as the world's richest club, was bought for less, £200 million ($298 million) when it was purchased in 2008.[32]

League structure

The IPL comes under the category of league structure that is described as 'closed'.[33] Scholars such as Stephen Ross, Stefan Szymanski and Roger Noll have been critical of 'closed' leagues. They see a perceived lack of excitement in 'closed' leagues as well as an encouragement of mediocrity through the permanent league status which they provide to their teams. From the first three seasons of the IPL, there seems to be little evidence of either of these factors. What Ross and Szymanski, through the example of Major League Baseball (MLB), seem to suggest about 'closed' leagues is that once teams fall out of contention to reach post-season play, they begin to lose motivation and incentive to perform.[34] The IPL also has post-season play just as in the MLB with the four best teams qualifying for the semi-finals.[35] It must be mentioned that the MLB is a much older and larger league than the IPL, thus making a comparison between the two difficult. However, the three IPL seasons have been extremely competitive so far, the allure of reaching the semi-finals is very strong, with three out of the four semi-finalists qualifying to play in the lucrative Champions League (the two finalists and the winner of the game between the two losing semi-finalists).[36]

Ross and Szymanski also mention that one of the reasons 'open' leagues are better is because there are more exciting matches, with teams having to fight to keep their place in the division.[37] The financial consequences of relegation to a lower division in football can be massive.[38] In a similar manner, the race to reach the IPL semi-finals is equally intense because of the large amounts of prize money that qualifying for the Champions League brings.[39] The Champions League is a global tournament in which the 10 best teams of various Twenty20 cricket tournaments worldwide (there were 12 in 2009) participate.[40]

The intensity factor which manifests itself in the race to the semi-finals is visible through the television ratings. In season one, the encounter between Delhi Daredevils and Mumbai Indians that was played on 24 May 2008 garnered a television rating of 6.41.[41] A win for Mumbai would ensure a place in the semi-finals, while a win for Delhi would give their hopes of reaching the semi-finals a huge boost.[42] These sub-plots definitely boost the ratings of games that are crucial for the progress of teams to the semi-finals.

In fact, all games played between 13 and 24 May, that is, the latter phase of the tournament, that involved Delhi, Kolkata Knightriders or Mumbai delivered a television viewership rating of over 6.[43] These were the three teams in contention for the last semi-final slot. Direct confrontations between the teams were even more popular – the Delhi-Kolkata encounter of 13 May delivered a TV rating of 6.98, the third highest in the tournament.[44]

Noll argues that a poor performing team in a higher division is usually a better financial alternative than a better performing team in a lower division.[45] Taking into account Noll's earlier point on how closed leagues encourage mediocrity by providing permanent league status to poor performing teams, we could assert that in Noll's view 'closed' leagues are good from a financial viewpoint but bad from a playing one. Noll does make a point when he asserts that permanent league status for poor performing teams does make a league more mediocre. However, in the case of the IPL there seems to be little suggestion of this happening. In season 1, Deccan Chargers finished last with a record of two wins in 14 games, one position ahead of them were Royal Challengers Bangalore with a record of four wins in 14 games.[46] Had the IPL been an 'open' league, there may have been a case for both franchises to be relegated. In season two, these were the two best performing franchises with the final being contested between the two teams.[47] This might be taken to prove Noll's assertion that lower ranked teams in a higher division are not necessarily poorer alternatives to high ranking teams in a lower division. Even if Noll's assertion is in a financial context, the example of IPL 2 proves that his theory can have sporting relevance as well.

Salary caps, competitive balance and uncertainty of outcome

The salary cap was a mechanism introduced in the 1970s in North America to prevent the payment of salaries from going out of control in the new era of free agency.[48] The more common reason for the implementation of the salary cap is that it enables a level playing field. This is a point which Lalit Modi took into account whilst implementing the salary cap, arguing that he did not want a situation akin to that in the English Premier League where a few rich clubs like Manchester United and Chelsea dominate.[49] Modi later added that the salary cap was necessary to provide an element of unpredictability.[50] With a salary cap in place, all the teams would get an opportunity to buy the best players, rather than them being concentrated amongst the strong teams.[51] While Modi's reasoning for introducing a salary cap is that it ensures a more level playing field amongst participating teams, he also acknowledges that it has regulated players' salaries from going out of control. In fact Modi added that if a salary cap did not exist, IPL cricketers could have been the world's most well-paid sportsmen.[52]

Even though the salary cap was introduced so as to create a sense of equality in the spending of teams, this did not quite become the case in the IPL 2008 auction. In fact, many teams did not observe the $5 million salary cap, with certain teams taking their spending to over $1 million over the cap. At the same time, there was the case of Rajasthan Royals who spent a much lower $3.3 million.[53] Rajasthan's spending patterns might affirm Roger Noll's theory that the salary cap is not a mechanism which helps weaker teams to compete with the strong ones but a mechanism whereby the strong teams compete for one another's players.[54] However, Rajasthan's decision to spend less at the auction had nothing to do with them being a weak team, but rather it was a strategy which saw them go for younger but talented players. Unlike their rivals, Rajasthan put a premium on efficiency over flamboyance which could explain why their spending was lower. It might be pointed out that they were also involved heavily during the bidding for Ishant Sharma – the fourth most expensive player in the 2008 auction. The bidding war to acquire Ishant, which took place between Rajasthan and Kolkata Knightriders, went right to the very end, where at a price of $950,000 Rajasthan gave up. Had they won the bid, they would have had an expensive and flamboyant cricketer in their squad.[55] Rajasthan's most expensive player was former India batsman Mohammad Kaif bought for $675,000. This value was much less compared to what the other franchises spent on their most expensive players.[56]

Quirk and Fort argue that in order to maintain interest in any league, it is a necessity to maintain competitive balance.[57] If there are too many strong teams, it will take away interest from the weak teams, and over a period of time this domination by the strong teams will take away interest from their fans as well. The salary cap is one such mechanism that helps maintain this competitive balance. An evenly balanced league provides more scope for exciting contests than an unevenly balanced one.[58] This brings us to the uncertainty of outcome hypothesis. One could argue that over the first three seasons of the IPL there has been an even balance of results. There have been three different winners and out of the eight participating teams, seven have reached the semi-finals at least once.

The disparities as showcased in Table 2 are not massive, four teams have a winning percentage in the range of 53% and 58% while three teams have winning percentages less than 46%. However, three seasons might be too short a lifespan to draw such conclusions.

The winning percentage theory was postulated by Sandy, Sloane and Rosentraub (2004) who argued that provided all teams spend an equal sum of money they should record roughly equal winning percentages.[59] However, the IPL may not be the right place to apply their theory. The winning percentages do not tell the true picture of the franchises over the three seasons, in these circumstances it would be better to observe how they performed over different seasons. The case of Rajasthan Royals and Deccan Chargers might provide an appropriate example in the above context. Rajasthan's winning percentage over three seasons of 58.13% is far superior to Deccan Chargers' 41.3%. However, over three seasons it could be said that the Chargers have been, in relative terms, a better side, measured by the fact that alongside their title in 2009 they also reached the semi-final in 2010 (see Table 2). Rajasthan's high winning percentage is on account of their excellent season in 2008 when they won 13 out of their 16 games.[60] That very same season the Chargers recorded a poor two wins in 14 games.[61] So despite winning the IPL in 2009 and reaching the semi-finals the following year (Table 2), the Chargers possess a poor winning percentage on account of their 2008 season. On the other hand, despite possessing the best winning percentage amongst all teams over the three seasons, Rajasthan have failed to qualify for the semi-finals in both 2009 and 2010 (Table 2).

Table 2. Team records 2008–2010

Team	2008 rank	2009 rank	2010 rank	Total wins	Total losses	Win percentage
Chennai	2	T3*	1	26	20	56.52%
Delhi	T3*	T3*	5	24	19	55.81%
Bangalore	7	2	3	21	25	45.65%
Deccan	8	1	4	19	27	41.30%
Rajasthan	1	6	7	25	18	58.13%
Mumbai	5	7	2	23	20	53.48%
Punjab	T3*	5	8	21	22	48.83%
Kolkata	6	8	6	16	24	40%

Source: *cricinfo.com*
Note: * T3 is tied for third which is for both losing semi-finalists during 2008 and 2009 when there was no playoff match to determine third and fourth place.

A true measure of the salary cap providing competitive balance comes across through the Chargers responding to their 8th placed finish in 2008 to win the IPL the following season.[62] Sandy, Sloane and Rosentraub's theory of winning percentage does not take such intricacies into account. At the same time, by no means would it be right to call Rajasthan the most dominant IPL team considering that they followed up their win in 2008 with a 6th placed finish in 2009 and 7th placed finish in 2010 (Table 2). Sports leagues look to have two evenly matched teams as often as possible in order to prevent the uncertainty of outcome in those contests. Szymanski though argues that the contest between two unevenly matched teams can have an uncertainty of outcome as well.[63] According to him, the possibility of the unexpected – that is the weaker team beating the stronger team – is what keeps the viewers interested. We will take the example of the 2008 IPL to demonstrate this.

Prior to the start of the 2008 IPL Rajasthan Royals were described as the tournament's weakest team. This was on account of their low spending as well as reliance on fewer superstars compared to their rivals.[64] This underdog status may well have been a factor with the audiences because their first three games against stronger opponents Delhi, Punjab and Deccan Chargers garnered good viewership rates.[65] However, after recording back-to-back wins over Punjab and Deccan, it was noticed that their viewership in succeeding games began to decline.[66] This could have been a case of the audience realising that Rajasthan was a stronger team than their wage bill suggested. Rajasthan may have the least fancied team in IPL 2008, but it was the Deccan Chargers who were the worst in terms of on-field performance.[67] The viewership rates for the Chargers games in the 2008 IPL were reasonably good.[68] In fact, the only game in which their viewership was poor was their encounter against Bangalore on 3 May 2008. That particular game recorded a poor rating of 3.11 [69] despite being a clash of two evenly matched teams who were battling to avoid dropping to the bottom of the league.[70] While this evenly matched contest delivered a poor rating, Deccan's next two games against stronger opposition Chennai Super Kings and Rajasthan delivered better ratings of 4.92 and 5.29 respectively.[71] This proves that in order to deliver exciting games in a league, it is not necessary that teams are evenly matched. Uncertainty of outcome is not necessarily created by a competitive balance of teams.

Revenue sharing arrangements

The franchises' main source of income is through the revenue-sharing formula of the IPL's sale of television rights. Prior to the first season, the league cut a 10-year deal worth $1.026 billion with Sony Entertainment, a division of Sony Corporation and World Sports Group.[72] It was determined that 20% of the annual television revenue would be kept by the league, while the remaining 80% would be distributed equally amongst the franchises.[73] In comparison, teams in the English Premier League get 50% of the broadcast money equally, with 25% decided by the respective team's position in the league and 25% by television exposure.[74] There was an unexpected financial bonus for the franchises prior to the second season when the IPL renegotiated the television deal with Sony (now known as Multi Screen Media (MSM)) for a much higher amount of $1.63 billion for nine years. This meant the franchises' share of broadcast income would increase substantially.[75]

An equal sharing of television revenue has its advantages, especially for franchises playing in smaller market areas or in areas where there is less interest in the game. However, there could be negative aspects to this kind of revenue-sharing as well. As Kesenne (2004) suggested, equal revenue-sharing makes rich teams poorer and poor teams richer.[76] The owners who have paid a higher amount to acquire a franchise for a larger market area may feel it is unfair for them to get the same amount as those who have paid less for small market areas. This also amounts to a team that is performing well being penalised and one that is performing poorly being rewarded. The renegotiated broadcasting deal with MSM was crucial to helping franchises recoup their losses from the second edition of the IPL that was held in South Africa. It was estimated that the shift to South Africa led to a 75% drop in revenue earned through gate receipts.[77] The Indian Cricket Board compensated the franchises for loss of earnings through gate receipts and sponsorship.[78] This was a huge bonus for franchises located in relatively weaker markets. However, those franchises located in larger market areas, who were successful in drawing crowds during season one, would feel cause to be aggrieved at losing out on major sources of revenue such as gate receipts and sponsorships with the event being held in South Africa.

While revenue-sharing is clearly beneficial for creating competitive balance among the teams, in the context of the IPL it has also prevented teams from getting either too rich or too poor. However, from the point of view of franchises that have been successful in earning revenue from other sources or have contributed more in creating a buzz about the tournament, the system of receiving an equal share of television revenue is probably unfair.

Financial results

In the first season of the IPL, only two franchises, Rajasthan Royals and Kolkata Knight Riders, made profits.[79] Surprisingly in the second season, every franchise made a profit despite the dramatic fall in gate receipt revenues.[80] As mentioned in last section, shifting the tournament to South Africa saw a drop in revenue of 75% in gate receipts for the eight franchises. That the franchises still made a profit is because of the renegotiated broadcasting deal with MSM. As just three seasons of the IPL have been completed, it is difficult to draw definitive conclusions on the financial success of the league and adequately benchmark it against North American or European soccer leagues. In its second issue of August 2009, *Forbes* magazine lists Mumbai Indians as the most valuable IPL franchise at $80 million. In terms of revenue earned during season two, Chennai was listed as the most profitable franchise with revenue of $24.7 million. The average franchise value was listed at $67 million with Mumbai being one of three franchises with a valuation exceeding $70 million.[81]

Forbes magazine's July 2010 list of the 50 most valuable sports teams has English Premier League club Manchester United at number one with a valuation of $1.83 billion. In second place is the National Football League (NFL) franchise Dallas Cowboys at $1.65 billion. The NFL clearly is the world's most valuable league – of the 25 teams with a valuation of $1 billion and above, 19 come from the NFL. Spanish football club Real Madrid earns the highest revenue with $563 million.[82] In terms of valuation, clearly there is a huge difference between franchises in the NFL and the IPL. However, the NFL has been in existence since 1920, nearly 90 years longer than the IPL.[83] In this regard, the fact that three IPL teams have achieved valuations of over $70 million after just two seasons can be seen as a significant achievement.

The example of Major League Baseball's New York Yankees should encourage the IPL franchises. In 1973, when they were bought, the Yankees had a value of just $10 million. Now, 37 years on, they are the world's third most valuable sports team worth $1.6 billion[84]. Through the example of the Yankees, and on the basis of their earnings in the first two seasons, the IPL franchises could feel optimistic about their prospect of emulating their counterparts from North America and Europe.

Valuation of players

The formation of the IPL must be put into context with the parallel Indian Cricket League (ICL) which was launched in April of 2007.[85] However, the ICL failed to get recognition from the International Cricket Council (ICC) and was regarded as a rebel tournament. Players joining the ICL were threatened with a ban from their national team or from other forms of official cricket.[86] Since the ICL was branded as a rebel league, the IPL, which had official status, became the natural choice among cricketers. In consonance with Hausman and Leonard's theory on star quality[87], the fact that the IPL was able to attract the world's top international cricketers was bound to make the tournament attractive.[88]

The IPL had a unique method of buying players through an open auction process. While there have been auctions in each of the three seasons, none topped the scale of the first auction held on 20 February 2008 in Mumbai. Lalit Modi described the auction as being special because of the sense of history involved, this being the first ever player auction in cricket history.[89] With 77 cricketers involved, many with well-established reputations, interest increased even further[90]. The player auction fits in well with some underlying principles in the IPL such as uncertainty of outcome and competitive balance. There is however a case that in order to fulfil these requirements, some economically irrational salaries have been paid to certain players. Modi believes this is nothing but a simple case of market economics, and players will get paid with respect to the demand for their services and value.[91] Claudio Lucifora and Rob Simmons argue that a player's salary is not simply determined by how good a player he/she is, but their overall reputation as well.[92] They point to an example in the mid-1990s where in the Italian Serie A Roberto Baggio was one of the world's highest paid footballers. In fact, he was paid a much higher salary compared to other footballers in Serie A who were only slightly less talented than him. Lucifora and Simmons argue that this is due to Baggio's reputation at the time of being one of the world's most famous footballers. Lucifora and Simmons espouse a theory about player wages in European soccer where the method of pay structure is completely different to that of the IPL. In European soccer, a player's wage is determined after private negotiations between the player and the club(s).[93] This makes it possible for a superstar like Baggio to be paid a higher salary compared to a slightly less talented player. Modi's earlier comment on the demand factor is not quite in consonance with Lucifora and Simmons' theory about superstars getting paid much more than ordinary players. This is to do with the peculiarities of the auction process in the IPL which has led to many cricketers earning more than they ever expected.[94]

An example of this peculiarity will be taken from the third IPL Auction that was held in 2010. Here, Kemar Roach, an inexperienced 21 year-old West Indies fast bowler,[95] was bought for a startlingly high $720,000 by Deccan Chargers. Bidding for Roach began at his base price of $100,000 and there was aggressive competition for his services from Chennai Super Kings. Prior to Roach's name coming up for bidding, two other fast bowlers Shane Bond and Wayne Parnell were sold for $750,000 and $610,000 respectively. The Chargers had bid aggressively for both players, they lost out on Parnell to a more aggressive Delhi Daredevils, whilst Bond was sold to Kolkata Knightriders, after a silent one-bid tie-breaker when Kolkata bid the maximum permissible amount, over the salary cap of $750,000 for the 2010 IPL.[96] The close parity in the wages that Bond and Roach are going to be earning is at variance with Lucifora and Simmons theory of superstars earning more than ordinary players. Under normal circumstances, a player like Bond with a strong reputation and an excellent cricketing record would be earning much more than a novice like Roach.[97] This is where the peculiarities of the auction come into play. With 66 players put up on the third auction list, out of which only 12 players could be picked by eight franchises, competition was bound to be fierce. The relative scarcity of fast bowlers in this list of players available for auction contributed to the high demand for Roach. It was accentuated by the fact that his eventual team, Deccan Chargers, had earlier missed out on acquiring the other highly-rated fast bowlers, Parnell and Bond, making them desperate to buy Roach. This helped raise his salary.[98]

With a much smaller pool of players available during the auction for not just the 2010 season but also the 2009 season, cases such as that of Roach are not uncommon. In fact, even during the 2009 auction, two unheralded cricketers - Tyron Henderson for $650,000[99] and Mashrafe Mortaza for $600,000 - were bought for values that far outstripped their track record and reputation.[100] However, one could find consonance with Lucifora and Simmons' theory in the 2008 Auction. Here Australian all-rounder Andrew Symonds became the second most expensive player and most expensive foreigner when Deccan Chargers (still Hyderabad at the time) paid $1.35 million to buy him.[101] Comparatively, Symonds' fellow Australian all-rounder Shane Watson was bought for just $125,000 by Rajasthan Royals, over $1 million less than Symonds. As pointed out by Lucifora and Simmons in their study of Baggio's earning, the difference in talent between Symonds and Watson does not justify such a large gap in their wages. The difference could have been the relative reputation of the two players at the time of the auction(s). Symonds was rated as one of the world's best limited-overs (One Day International and Twenty20) cricketers at the time, and a valuable member of the Australian team that won both the 2003 and 2007 One-Day International World Cup.[102] The increased demand for Symonds could also have been prompted by the intrigue and interest in him in the aftermath of a racism controversy that erupted on the eve of the auction involving him and the Indian spinner Harbhajan Singh. It was alleged that Harbhajan had racially abused Symonds during a Test match in Sydney a month and a half prior to the auction, allegations which subsequently could not be proved.[103] In contrast, Watson was a low-profile cricketer, talented but failing to cement his place in the Australian team in the period leading up to the auction because of injuries. This may have been the reason for his reduced market value.[104] The price paid to acquire a player is not just an outcome of his performance and reputation but also the peculiarities of the market, that is the auction pool. Thus Symonds will fetch a much higher price than Watson in a large auction pool. However, in a smaller auction pool like that in 2010 where choices are limited, the disparity in wages between a Roach and a Bond will not be so high.

Though the occasional irrationality exists in the pay structure of players, the salary structure is highly regarded in the IPL. In fact *The Annual Review of Global Sports Salaries* has found that the average annual salary of the IPL is the second highest amongst professional sports. The IPL, with an average annual salary of £2.5 million ($3.72 million), is just behind the highest ranked National Basketball Association (NBA), which has an average annual salary of £2.62 million ($3.9 million).[105] Three IPL teams are amongst the 30 highest paying teams in the world. These are Royal Challengers Bangalore, Chennai Super Kings and Kolkata Knight Riders.[106] Bangalore is the highest paying IPL team with an average salary of £57,833 ($86,171) a week, and it is the 12th highest paying team in the world. Interestingly, Bangalore's average weekly salary exceeds that of the English Premier League's most successful team, Manchester United, who are in 14th place with an average weekly salary of £55,818 ($83,168.8). The highest paying sports team is Major

League Baseball's New York Yankees with an average weekly salary of £89,897 or $133,946.5.[107]

Though the IPL seems to be performing well in the above aspects, it still has some way to go before its individual player wages match up to other professional sports. In fact the highest paid player in the IPL, Kevin Pietersen's annual salary of $1.55 million (£1.04 million), is much lower than that of the highest paid player in the English Premier League, John Terry. Terry has an annual salary of £7.8 million ($11.62 million), on the other hand the highest paid athlete across all team sports is New York Yankees' Alex Rodriguez who earns £20 million ($29.8 million).[108] It is interesting to note that with the IPL being a six-week tournament, Pietersen's weekly salary of $258,000 (approximately £173,000) is higher than Terry's weekly salary of £151,000 (or approximately $225,000).[109] The 'superstar' effect could explain why the weekly wages of a Pietersen exceed those of Terry. Terry is one amongst many stars in an established product such as the English Premier League. In contrast, Pietersen is amongst a few world-class players who play in the IPL which is a new league.

At one level the scarcity of superstars may have contributed to the likes of Pietersen and Symonds fetching high prices. At another level, India's triumph in theTwenty20 World Cup in 2007 also played a role in inflating the demand for players.[110] The likes of Rohit Sharma, bought by Hyderabad for $750,000, and Robin Uthappa, bought by Mumbai for $800,000[111], had been on the international circuit for just around one year. However, their presence in the 2007 Twenty20 World Cup team gave them instant stardom which was reflected in their inflated value. In comparison legends of the game such as Ricky Ponting ($400,000) and Glenn McGrath ($350,000) went for much lower values.[112]

Performance related to valuation

There are two ways of looking at a player's performance related to his valuation, first how it affects the performance of the team and second if a superstar phenomena exists in the IPL. In consonance with Adler's theory,[113] teams sign on players not only because of their playing record but also because of their popularity and reputation. Three seasons is too short to assess whether team revenues have been bolstered through signing superstars in the IPL, although there are examples in other sports. At the end of the 2007–08 season, the revenues of German Bundesliga club Bayern Munich increased by €72 million.[114] They had a good season winning their domestic league as well as the domestic cup competition.[115] They had a similar performance in 2005-06 where they also completed the league and domestic cup double.[116] However, Bayern's revenue went up by just €15 million in 2005-06,[117] compared to the €72 million in 2007-08. This higher revenue in 2007-08 could be ascribed to them signing up two world-class footballers, Franck Ribery and Luca Toni, amongst other factors.[118]

While there is no evidence as yet of the superstar effect boosting revenues in the IPL, it is clear that a superstar effect does exist. This could explain why franchises like Deccan Chargers and Bangalore are ready to pay over a million dollars to acquire the likes of Symonds and Pietersen respectively. The second way of judging performance related to valuation is to evaluate their on-field performance in relation to their salary. In 2008 Rajasthan was much derided for spending the least amount of money at the player auction. Therefore it came as a massive surprise to everyone when they went on to win the tournament.[119] At the heart of their success were Shane Watson ($125,000) and Sohail Tanvir ($100,000)[120] whose performances far outweighed their demand which was reflected in their salaries. Watson with 472 runs and 17 wickets was declared the Player of the Tournament,[121] while Tanvir with 22 wickets was the tournament's leading wicket-taker.[122] An even bigger value for money purchase, compared to both Watson and Tanvir, was Shaun Marsh who was bought for a meagre $30,000 by Kings XI Punjab. The then uncapped Australian opener was the 2008 IPL's leading run-scorer with 616 runs.[123]

If Watson, Tanvir and Marsh were clear bargain purchases then Ishant Sharma was a very expensive failure. In fact he failed to do any justice to his $950,000 price tag by taking just seven wickets in 13 games in the 2008 IPL.[124] Montanaria, Silvestrib and Bfoc suggest a player's value should reflect his track record.[125] Ishant was just 19 at the time and despite a good showing in Australia prior to the auction, one could argue he was signed more on potential rather than sustained performance.[126] Unfortunately, Ishant has been mediocre through his entire three-year stint with Kolkata, taking just 25 wickets in 31 games with his side, a poor record for a frontline fast bowler.[127]

Ishant's case, however, is not necessarily a trend. Chennai's Suresh Raina is perhaps the best example of a young player who has excelled in the IPL. Raina, who cost $650,000,[128] is the leading run-getter in IPL history with 1,375 runs.[129] He is also a useful part-time bowler with 14 wickets in the IPL and an excellent fielder having taken 27 catches, the most by a player over three seasons.[130] Deccan Chargers' Rohit Sharma, who fetched a price of $750,000,[131] is another youngster who has performed well. He is the fourth highest run-getter in the IPL with 1,170 runs. Like Raina, he has useful all-round capabilities, having taken 14 wickets in three IPL seasons and 21 catches.[132]

As mentioned in the last section, younger players, particularly those who excelled at the Twenty20 World Cup in 2007, fetched higher prices compared to senior players. However, some of these senior players put in a much better performance than their auction value would reflect. The best example is that of Shane Warne, the second-highest wicket-taker in Test cricket history, bought for just $450,000, his exact base price, by Rajasthan Royals.[133] Warne, who was named captain by his franchise, went on to have a superb tournament in 2008 as he led his team to win the IPL with some innovative captaincy. He was also one of the best bowlers in the tournament taking 19 wickets.[134] While Warne's performance in the second season was less spectacular, there were other veterans who excelled. Chennai's Matthew Hayden, one of the finest batsmen in the 2000s who recently retired from international cricket, had an excellent tournament finishing as the highest run-getter in IPL-2 with 572 runs.[135] The 37 year-old Hayden was bought for just $375,000, half what Rohit Sharma, 16 years his junior, was bought for.[136] Another player who excelled in 2009 was 37 year-old Adam Gilchrist. Gilchrist, like Hayden and Warne, had also recently retired from international cricket. Gilchrist, however, fetched a higher salary than his two compatriots at $700,000 (Times of India, 2008a)[137]. Gilchrist is acknowledged as one of the most destructive wicket-keeper batsmen in cricket history.[138] His case appears to bear out Montanaria, Silvestrib and Bfoc's theory about a player's track record determining his wage. However, Gilchrist's salary is more than half that of Chennai wicket-keeper, M. S. Dhoni at $1.5 million.[139] Not only did he lead his franchise, Deccan Chargers, to win the title, he also scored the second highest amount of runs, 495 runs,[140] to be named the Player of the Tournament.[141]

Lucifora and Simmons (2003) maintain that as a player gets older, he gets less fit and more prone to injury. While the demand for Warne, Gilchrist and Hayden may have declined because of their age, the fact that they were no longer required to play for their national side, allowed them to remain focused and fit for the IPL.[142] This is in sharp contrast to a much younger cricketer like Ishant Sharma, whose poor performance in the IPL could be attributed on his over-exertion while playing for India on the international circuit.[143] The point being made is that older players are just as likely to succeed in the IPL as younger players. This is due to the fact that many of them no longer play international cricket, and this reduces their excessive exposure to bruising and tiring games, which in turn keeps them fitter and less prone to injury.

Conclusions

It could be concluded on the basis of the above discussion that the IPL over its first three seasons has been a relative success. The popularity of cricket in India as well as the presence of superstars in this billion dollar sporting extravaganza has certainly helped the IPL's cause. However, cricket's popularity as a game and superstar presence alone cannot guarantee the success of a league if it is not based on strong foundations. As this paper has tried to show, the IPL's structure and policies were sound which enabled it to succeed over and above the general basic requirements such as cricket's popularity and superstar influence. In light of the IPL's strong performance over its first three seasons, the most crucial element has been its introduction of a salary cap. This has enabled a competitively balanced league, and one where there is a strong excitement factor because of the unpredictability that such an evenly balanced league presents. The salary cap has not only ensured an even balance amongst teams but also resulted in an equitable distribution of superstars. This is a very strong development in helping maintain fan interest amongst all the franchises. It could have been a negative situation for the IPL had the allotment of superstars gone to just one or two teams. Here one must take Quirk and Fort's theory into account that if franchises become too strong, they will lead to reduced interest amongst weaker franchises and subsequently amongst stronger franchises as well.[144]

While the salary cap has clearly been one of the IPL's biggest plus points in enabling them to succeed, one should also take into account that the IPL is a 'closed' league and over its three seasons it has managed to disprove a lot of notions about the demerits of 'closed' leagues. Scholars in the past have been critical of 'closed' leagues because they are felt to be encouraging mediocrity by allowing poor performing teams permanent league status. It took the IPL just two seasons to prove this notion wrong when the 2009 final was contested between Deccan Chargers and Royal Challengers Bangalore, those very two teams who finished at the bottom of the table in IPL 2008. Had the IPL been an open league, both these franchises may not even have participated in the 2009 IPL, denying the tournament the thrill of their triumphant run that season.

When a league is evenly balanced and assures its members of permanent league status, it only enhances its financial prospects. Szymanski's theory on leagues is that when the prospect of relegation exists in leagues, it puts off team owners from financially investing in these leagues. In 2010, the Pune and Kochi franchises entered the IPL at values well over $300 million, triple the maximum price paid in 2008. One could only assume as to whether the respective team owners of either franchise would have paid such amounts if the prospect of relegation existed.

One could therefore conclude that the IPL is extremely well-structured and almost all their policies have been implemented to perfection so far. However, there are some aspects where scope for improvement exists. One of the IPL's weak links appears to be its revenue-sharing formula. Currently the money from television revenue is distributed equally amongst the franchises. While such a revenue-sharing model does help ensure competitive balance, it can be unfair to teams that are located in large market areas and have paid more money to acquire franchises in those areas. A more graded revenue sharing model as exists in the English Premier League would make more sense to be implemented.

A proportion of the revenue, say 25%, should be allocated to performance. This would encourage teams who are not earning sufficient money in small-market areas to improve their on-field performances as well as other endeavours to improve their brand value. The aspect of player salaries, though it has had mixed results over its first three seasons, is not really a problem of the IPL as it is about the individual franchises. Still, when mediocre players like Tyron Henderson, Mashrafe Mortaza and Kemar Roach are bought for inflated salaries, and then play only a minute proportion of their team's games, it sends wrong signals about the league. On the other hand, some of the game's legends such as Shane Warne and Matthew Hayden have been bought for much lower salaries and have turned out to be massive successes.

Thus a more careful selection of players is recommended to the franchises, one in which players who are bought for high salaries do not spend the season warming the benches like Henderson, Mortaza and Roach did during their stints in the IPL. At the same time, the performances of Warne, Hayden and Adam Gilchrist disprove the notion that Twenty20 cricket is a young man's game. In fact, these veteran cricketers who are formally retired turned out to be good bargains for their teams.

Finally, while the scandal that engulfed Lalit Modi has certainly hurt the IPL's brand image, it should in no way cloud any judgment on how successful it has been as a league. As long as the IPL is able to function on the basis of their strong league foundation, it should continue being successful as a league. This is a point which Professor Stefan Szymanski reaffirms as well stating that the suspension of Modi will not affect the IPL brand. He adds that the IPL is a successful product which fans want to watch and will continue to do so regardless of this scandal.[145] On the whole, the paper considers the IPL to be a positive contribution to cricket and a 'success'. We may conclude with the empowering words of Australian cricketing legend, Glenn McGrath: 'IPL has brought different cultures from different countries together. The interaction of the players help to develop friendship among the players and as a whole, it contributes to the spirit of cricket.'[146]

Notes

[1] Warne, 'It Was a Tough Decision to Leave Hampshire'.
[2] Schwartz, 'The World's Hottest Sports League'.
[3] Hughes, 'Indian Premier League on the Horizon'.
[4] Burke, 'Lalit Modi on Brink of Axe as IPL Controversy Gathers Momentum'.
[5] 'IPL 2nd Highest Paid League, Edges out EPL'.
[6] Kitchin, 'Twenty20 and English Domestic Cricket'.
[7] Smith, 'Sport on TV: Cricket Makes a Heroic Pitch to be King of the Bouncy Castle'.
[8] Kitchin, 'Twenty20 and English Domestic Cricket'.
[9] Randall, 'Twenty20 Bandwagon Ready to Roll'.
[10] Booth, 'Stars Come Out as the Eyes of the Cricket World Switch to Bangalore'.
[11] Tomlinson and Singh, 'India's Twenty20 Cricket Imports Cheerleaders, Grabs UK Stars'.
[12] 'Indian Cricket Suspends IPL Chief Modi for "Corruption"'.
[13] Narayanan, 'Economy and Law of a Cricket League'.
[14] Srinivas and Vivek, *IPL: Cricket and Commerce*.
[15] Hopps, 'Hats Off to Modi After his 48-hour Mission to Find IPL's New Home'.
[16] Rao and Basu, 'Modi All but Hanged Without Trial'.
[17] Srinivas and Vivek, *IPL: Cricket and Commerce*.
[18] Assisi and Surendar, 'Anil Ambani, Mallya in Race to Own T20 teams'.
[19] Srinivas and Vivek, *IPL: Cricket and Commerce*.
[20] Fort, *Sports Economics*.
[21] Srinivas and Vivek, *IPL: Cricket and Commerce*.

[22] Jackson, 'The Week that Changed Cricket Forever'.
[23] Fort, *Sports Economics*.
[24] Assisi and Surendar, 'Anil Ambani, Mallya in Race to Own T20 Teams'.
[25] Chang and Bellman, 'Collision Blocks Lanes at Indian Ports'.
[26] Mantri, 'Chief Mentor: Reinventing the wheel for India'.
[27] *IPL Franchise Prospectus*.
[28] Mehra, 'The IPL is an Unscripted Soap Opera'.
[29] Sandy, Sloane and Rosentraub, *The Economics of Sport*.
[30] 'New IPL Cricket Franchises Handed to Kochi and Pune After Huge Bids'.
[31] Ibid.
[32] Saxena and Hardy, 'In the Big League'.
[33] Datta, 'IPL Needs Fit and Proper Persons Tests'.
[34] Ross and Szymanski, *Fans of the World Unite*.
[35] Nair-Ghaswalla, 'Corporates Queue Up for Next IPL season'.
[36] Nayadu, 'All Not Lost Yet'.
[37] Ross and Szymanski, *Fans of the World Unite*.
[38] James, 'Why Clubs May Risk Millions for Riches at the End of the Rainbow'.
[39] Nayadu, 'All Not Lost Yet'.
[40] 'Ten Teams for 2010 Champions League'.
[41] *DLF IPL T/20 Ratings Scoreboard*.
[42] Bhaduri, 'Devils Under Mumbai Cloud'.
[43] *DLF IPL T/20 Ratings Scoreboard*.
[44] Ibid.
[45] Noll, 'The Economics of Promotion and Relegation in Sports Leagues'.
[46] *Indian Premier League 2007/08/ Points Table*.
[47] 'Back to Front'.
[48] Kesenne, *The Economic Theory of Professional Team Sports*.
[49] Briggs, 'IPL Cricketers Will Earn as Much as Lampard'.
[50] McRae, 'Test Cricket Must go Day-night to Survive'.
[51] Briggs, 'IPL Cricketers Will Earn as Much as Lampard'.
[52] Ibid.
[53] *Times of India*, February 21, 2008; 'Bangalore get Misbah, Kohli in 2nd IPL Auction'. The Total Excludes the Signings of Australians Shaun Marsh, Luke Ronchi and Dominic Thornely that were Made After the Two Auctions Held in 2008. See 'Shaun Marsh Joins Mohali'.
[54] Noll, 'Professional Basketball: Economic and Business Perspectives'.
[55] Srinivas and Vivek, *IPL: Cricket and Commerce*.
[56] *Times of India*, February 21, 2008; 'Bangalore get Misbah, Kohli in 2nd IPL Auction'.
[57] Quirk and Fort, *Pay Dirt*.
[58] Cairns, Jennett and Sloane, 'The Economics of Professional Team Sports'.
[59] Sandy, Sloane and Rosentraub, *The Economics of Sport*.
[60] *Indian Premier League 2007/08 Results, Indian Premier League 2007/08/ Points Table*.
[61] *Indian Premier League 2007/08/ Points Table*.
[62] Rao, 'CSK Do Not Want Fresh Auction in IPL'.
[63] Szymanski, 'Uncertainty of Outcome, Competitive Balance and the Theory of Team Sports'.
[64] *Times of India*, February 21, 2008; 'Bangalore Get Misbah, Kohli in 2nd IPL Auction'.
[65] *DLF IPL T/20 Ratings Scoreboard*.
[66] Ibid.
[67] *Indian Premier League 2007/08/ Points Table*.
[68] *DLF IPL T/20 Ratings Scoreboard*.
[69] Ibid.
[70] Rajesh, 'Bangalore Fight Back to Clinch Thriller'.
[71] *DLF IPL T/20 Ratings Scoreboard*.
[72] 'Sony Bags IPL Media Rights for $1 Billion'.
[73] *IPL Franchise Prospectus*.
[74] Szymanski, 'Revenue Sharing'.
[75] 'IPL Set to Bowl Over South Africa'.
[76] Kesenne, 'Competitive Balance and Revenue Sharing'.
[77] Schwartz, 'The World's Hottest Sports League'.

78 Shankar, 'BCCI to Compensate Franchises'.
79 'Revenue and Profits: IPL Season 1'.
80 'IPL Franchise Earnings for 2009'.
81 Schwartz, 'The World's Hottest Sports League'.
82 Ozanian and Badenhausen, 'The World's Most Valuable Sports Teams and Athletes'.
83 'N.F.L.'94'.
84 Goldstein, 'George Steinbrenner Who Built Yankees into Powerhouse, Dies at 80'.
85 'Zee Boss Does a Packer on BCCI'.
86 Vice, 'South African Players Warned Over Rebel League'.
87 Hausman and Leonard, 'Superstars in the National Basketball Association'.
88 Naik, 'IPL's Million Dollar Auction Today'.
89 Basu, 'Each Team Had Come With a Pre-determined Bid Strategy'.
90 Naik, 'IPL's Million Dollar Auction Today'.
91 Basu, 'Each Team Had Come With a Pre-determined Bid Strategy'.
92 Lucifora and Simmons, 'Superstar Effects in Sports'.
93 Hughes, 'Shopaholic Clubs Covet Gerrard'.
94 Richards, 'Cricket: The Latest Indian Export'.
95 'Kemar's Coming Back to Pursue Ponting'.
96 'Pollard, Bond, Roach Hottest Picks'.
97 Alderson, 'Bond Set to Cash in at IPL Auction'.
98 'Pollard, Bond, Roach Hottest Picks'.
99 Hoult, 'South African Tyron Henderson Stunned by His $650,000 IPL Sale'.
100 Premachandran, 'Pietersen and Flintoff Claim Record IPL Prices After Bidding War'.
101 David, 'Cricket's Best Sold for Millions in India'.
102 'Players/Australia/Andrew Symonds'.
103 Basu, 'Judge'.
104 'Watson Won't Give up Bowling'.
105 'IPL 2nd Highest Paid League, Edges out EPL'.
106 Ibid.
107 Harris, 'Premier League Footballers Not the Richest on the Planet-Revealed'.
108 Sawer, 'Premiership Stars are Poor Men of Sport'. John Terry was the highest paid player in the English Premier League at the time the paper was written. This is no longer the case.
109 'John Terry to Join Chelsea's Top Earners with £151k–a-week deal'.
110 Kesavan, 'India "Secures Future of Twenty 20"'.
111 *Times of India*, February 21, 2008.
112 'Players/Australia/Rickey Ponting'; *Times of India*, February 21, 2008.
113 Adler, 'Stardom and Talent'.
114 Panja, 'Real Madrid Leads Soccer Rich List for Fourth Straight Year'.
115 'Bayern Munich Win Bundesliga and Cup double'.
116 'Bayern Munich Completes its Second Straight Double'.
117 Deloitte and Touche, 'Football Money League'.
118 Kirschbaum, 'Bayern Aim for Clean Sweep After Last Season's Failure'.
119 Richards, 'The Old Men Triumph in Game Build for Youth'.
120 'IPL 2nd Highest Paid League, Edges out EPL'.
121 Premachandran, 'Young Guns Humble Greats to Catch Selectors' Eyes'.
122 Kidd, 'Rajasthan Owe IPL Litle to Unsung Squad Players'.
123 Ibid.
124 Ibid.
125 Montanaria, Silvestrib and Bfoc, 'Performance and Individual Characteristics as Predictors of Pay Levels'.
126 Agencies, 'IPL Auction Changes Ishant's Life For Ever'; Berry, 'IPL Heralds Dawn of Cricket's Fourth Epoch'.
127 www.cricinfo.com
128 *Times of India*, February 21, 2008.
129 www.cricinfo.com
130 www.cricinfo.com
131 *Times of India*, February 21, 2008.
132 www.cricinfo.com

[133] Srinivas and Vivek, *IPL: Cricket and Commerce*.
[134] Richards, 'In the Big-ticket Indian Premier League, Frugal Rajasthan Wins All'.
[135] Burnes, 'Deccan Steal IPL Show Amid the Glitz'.
[136] 'How Retirement Made Reborn Hayden King of the IPL'.
[137] Ibid.
[138] Langer, 'Playing with Gilly was a Privilege'.
[139] *Times of India*, February 21, 2008.
[140] Hopkins, 'Amazing Gilchrist Transforms Chargers'.
[141] Rao, 'IPL's New Nizams'.
[142] Richards, 'The Old Men Triumph in Game Build for Youth'.
[143] 'Should be a Hard-fought Series'.
[144] Quirk and Fort, *Pay Dirt*.
[145] Glendenning, 'In the Line of Fire'.
[146] 'McGrath talks about IPL and Warne'.

References

Adler, M. 'Stardom and Talent'. *American Economic Review* 75, no. 1 (1985): 208–12.
Agencies, 'IPL Auction Changes Ishant's Life For Ever'. *Indian Express*, February 21, 2008.
Alderson, A. 'Bond Set to Cash in at IPL Auction'. *NZ Herald*, January 17, 2010.
Assisi, C., and T. Surendar. 'Anil Ambani, Mallya in Race to Own T20 teams'. *Times of India*, November 13, 2007.
'Back to Front'. *Times of India*, May 24, 2009: 23.
'Bangalore get Misbah, Kohli in 2nd IPL Auction'. *Times of India*, March 12, 2007.
Basu, I. 'Each Team Had Come With a Pre-determined Bid Strategy'. *Times of India*, February 23, 2008: 30.
Basu, I. 'Judge: Symonds More to Blame Than Bhajji'. *Times of India*, January 31, 2008: 1.
'Bayern Munich Completes its Second Straight Double'. *New York Times*, May 7, 2006.
'Bayern Munich Win Bundesliga and Cup Double'. *Daily Telegraph*, May 5, 2008.
Berry, S. 'IPL Heralds Dawn of Cricket's Fourth Epoch'. *Daily Telegraph*, April 13, 2008.
Bhaduri, P. 'Devils Under Mumbai Cloud'. *Times of India*, May 24, 2008: 28.
Booth, L. 'Stars Come Out as the Eyes of the Cricket World Switch to Bangalore'. *Guardian*, April 18, 2008.
Briggs, S. 'IPL Cricketers Will Earn as Much as Lampard'. *Daily Telegraph*, March 1, 2008.
Burke, J. 'Lalit Modi on Brink of Axe as IPL Controversy Gathers Momentum'. *Guardian*, April 21, 2010.
Burnes, C. 'Deccan Steal IPL Show Amid the Glitz'. *Sydney Morning Herald*, May 25, 2009.
Cairns, J., N. Jennett, and P. Sloane. 'The Economics of Professional Team Sports: A Survey of Theory and Evidence'. *Journal of Economic Studies* 13, no. 1 (1993): 3–80.
Chang, A., and E. Bellman. 'Collision Blocks Lanes at Indian Ports'. *Wall Street Journal*, April 26, 2010.
Datta, K. 'IPL Needs Fit and Proper Persons Tests'. *Business standard*, April 29, 2010.
David, R. 'Cricket's Best Sold for Millions in India'. *Forbes Magazine*, February 21, 2008.
Deloitte and Touche, 'Football Money League'. *Sports Business Group*, annual report, 2007.
DLF IPL T/20 Ratings Scoreboard. Mumbai: TAM Media Research, 2008.
Fort, R. *Sports Economics*. Upper Saddle River, NJ: Prentice Hall, 1998.
Glendenning, M. 'In the Line of Fire'. *Sport Business International*, no. 157 (June 2010).
Goldstein, R. 'George Steinbrenner Who Built Yankees into Powerhouse, Dies at 80'. *New York Times*, July 13, 2010.
Harris, N. 'Premier League Footballers Not the Richest on the Planet-Revealed'. *Daily Telegraph*, March 27, 2010.
Hausman, J.A., and G.K. Leonard. 'Superstars in the National Basketball Association: Economic Value and Policy'. *Journal of Labour Economics* 15, no. 4 (1997): 586–624.
Hopkins, T. 'Amazing Gilchrist Transforms Chargers'. *Sydney Morning Herald*, May 26, 2009.
Hopps, D. 'Hats off to Modi After His 48-hour Mission to Find IPL's New Home'. *Guardian*, March 25, 2009.
Hoult, N. 'South African Tyron Henderson Stunned by His $650,000 IPL Sale'. *Daily Telegraph*, February 6, 2009.

'How Retirement made reborn Hayden King of the IPL'. *Australian*, May 14, 2009. Available at: http://www.forbes.com/2009/08/27/cricket-india-ipl-business-sports-ipl.html.

Hughes, R. 'Shopaholic Clubs Covet Gerrard'. *New York Times*, July 6, 2005.

Hughes, S. 'Indian Premier League on the Horizon'. *Daily Telegraph*, March 25, 2008.

'Indian Cricket Suspends IPL Chief Modi for "Corruption"'. *BBC*, April 26, 2010. Available at: http://news.bbc.co.uk/1/hi/8643302.stm

Indian Premier League 2007/08 Results, *Cricinfo* 2008. Available at: http://www.cricinfo.com/ipl/engine/series/313494.html

Indian Premier League 2007/08/ Points Table. *Cricinfo* 2008. Available at: http://www.cricinfo.com/ipl/engine/series/313494.html?view=pointstable

Indian Premier League 2009/Points Table. *Cricinfo* 2009. Available at: http://www.cricinfo.com/ipl2009/engine/series/374163.html?view=pointstable

Indian Premier League 2009/Results. *Cricinfo* 2009. Available at: http://www.cricinfo.com/ipl2009/engine/series/374163.html

'IPL 2nd Highest Paid League, Edges Out EPL'. *Times of India*, March 29, 2010: 1.

'IPL Franchise Earnings for 2009'. April 2010. Available at: http://en.wikipedia.org/wiki/IPL_Franchise_earnings_for_2009.

IPL Franchise Prospectus. IMG Report, 2007.

'IPL Set to Bowl Over South Africa'. *Hindu Business Line*, April 17, 2009.

Jackson, J. 'The Week That Changed Cricket Forever'. *Guardian*, February 24, 2008.

James, S. 'Why Clubs May Risk Millions for Riches at the End of the Rainbow'. *Guardian*, August 5, 2006.

'John Terry to Join Chelsea's Top Earners With £151k-a-week Deal'. *Daily Telegraph*, August 6, 2009.

'Kemar's Coming Back to Pursue Ponting'. *Sydney Morning Herald*, January 30, 2010.

Kesavan, M. 'India "Secures Future of Twenty20"'. *BBC*, September 25, 2007. http://news.bbc.co.uk/1/hi/world/south_asia/7011937.stm.

Kesenne, S. 'Competitive Balance and Revenue Sharing: When Rich Clubs Have Poor Teams'. *Journal of Sports Economics* 5, no. 2 (2004): 206–12.

Kesenne, S. *The Economic Theory of Professional Team Sports: An Analytical Treatment*. Cheltenham, UK: Edward Elgar, 2007.

Kidd, P. 'Rajasthan Owe IPL Title to Unsung Squad Players'. *Sunday Times*, June 2, 2008.

Kirschbaum, E. 'Bayern Aim for Clean Sweep After Last Season's Failure'. *Reuters UK*, August 2, 2007. Available at: http://uk.reuters.com/article/idUKL3080372220070802\

Kitchin, P. 'Twenty20 and English Domestic Cricket'. In *International Cases in the Business of Sport*, edited by S. Chadwick and D. Arthur. London: Elsevier, 2008.

Langer, J. 'Playing With Gilly Was a Privilege'. *BBC*, January 31, 2008. Available at: http://news.bbc.co.uk/sport1/hi/cricket/7221343.stm.

Lucifora, C., and R. Simmons. 'Superstar Effects in Sports: Evidence From Italian Soccer'. *Journal of Sports Economics* 4, no. 1 (2003): 35–55.

Mantri, R. 'Chief Mentor: Reinventing the Wheel for India'. *Wall Street Journal*, August 26, 2010.

'McGrath talks about IPL and Warne'. *IPL cricket live 2010*. Available at: http://www.iplcricketlive.com/ipl/indian-premier-league-quotes/

McRae, D. 'Test Cricket Must go Day-night to Survive'. *Guardian*, March 2, 2010.

Mehra, C. 'The IPL is an Unscripted Soap Opera'. *Business World*, May 5, 2008.

Montanaria, F., G. Silvestrib, and F. Bfoc. 'Performance and Individual Characteristics as Predictors of Pay Levels: The Case of the Italian "Serie A"'. *European Sport Management Quarterly* 8, no. 1 (2008): 27–44.

'N.F.L.'94'. *New York Times*, September 4, 1994.

Naik, N. 'IPL's Million Dollar Auction Today'. *Times of India Delhi*, February 20, 2008: 3.

Nair-Ghaswalla, A. 'Corporates Queue up for Next IPL season'. *Economic Times*, June 11, 2008.

Narayanan, C. 'Economy and Law of a Cricket League'. *Times of India*, September 14, 2007: 29.

Nayadu, V. 'All Not Lost Yet'. *Times of India*, April 24, 2010: 25.

'New IPL Cricket Franchises Handed to Kochi and Pune After Huge Bids'. *Guardian*, March 21, 2010.

Noll, R.G. 'Professional Basketball: Economic and Business Perspectives'. In *The Business of Professional Sports*, edited by P. Staudohar and J Mangan, 18–47. Champaign, IL: University of Illinois Press, 1991.

Noll, R.G. 'The Economics of Promotion and Relegation in Sports Leagues: The Case of English Football'. *Journal of Sports Economics* 3, no. 2 (2002): 169–203.

Ozanian, M, and K. Badenhausen. 'The World's Most Valuable Sports Teams and Athletes'. *Forbes Magazine*, July 21, 2010. Available at: http://www.forbes.com/2010/07/20/most-valuable-athletes-and-teams-business-sports-sportsmoney-fifty-fifty.html

Panja, T. 'Real Madrid Leads Soccer Rich List for Fourth Straight Year'. *Bloomberg*, February 11, 2009. Available at: http://www.bloomberg.com/apps/news?pid=newsarchive&sid=auDSZBUtcFn4&refer=uk

'Players/Australia/Andrew Symonds'. *Cricinfo*, August 2010. Available at: http://www.cricinfo.com/ci/content/player/7702.html

'Players/Australia/Ricky Ponting'. *Cricinfo*, Available at: http://www.cricinfo.com/ci/content/player/7133.html

'Pollard, Bond, Roach Hottest Picks'. *Cricinfo*, January 19, 2010. Available at: http://www.cricinfo.com/ipl2010/content/story/444986.html

Premachandran, D. 'Young Guns Humble Greats to Catch Selectors' Eyes'. *Guardian*, June 4, 2008.

Premachandran, D. 'Pietersen and Flintoff Claim Record IPL Prices after Bidding War'. *Guardian*, February 6, 2009.

Quirk, J., and R. Fort. *Pay Dirt: The Business of Professional Team Sports*. Princeton, NJ: Princeton University Press, 1992.

Rajesh, S. 'Bangalore Fight Back to Clinch Thriller'. *Cricinfo*, May 3, 2008. Available at: http://www.cricinfo.com/ipl/content/story/349874.html

Randall, C. 'Twenty20 Bandwagon Ready to roll'. *Daily Telegraph*, January 27, 2006.

Rao, K.S. 'IPL's New Nizams'. *Times of India*, May 25, 2009: 1.

Randall, C. 'CSK Do Not Want Fresh Auction in IPL'. *Times of India*, November 17, 2009: 29.

Rao, K.S., and I. Basu. 'Modi All But Hanged Without Trial'. *Times of India*, April 26, 2010.

'Revenue and Profits: IPL Season 1'. *India Broadband Forum*. Available at: http://www.indiabroadband.net/sports-forum/17631-revenue-profits-ipl-season-1-a.html

Richards, H. 'In The Big-ticket Indian Premier League, Frugal Rajasthan Wins All'. *New York Times*, June 2, 2008.

Richards, H. 'Cricket: The Latest Indian Export'. *New York Times*, March 26, 2009.

Richards, H. 'The Old Men Triumph in Game Build for Youth'. *New York Times*, May 25, 2009.

Ross, S., and S. Szymanski. *Fans of the World Unite*. Palo Alto, CA: Stanford University Press, 2008.

Sandy, R., P.J. Sloane, and M. Rosentraub. *The Economics of Sport: An International Perspective*. London: Palgrave MacMillan, 2004.

Sawer, P. 'Premiership Stars Are Poor Men of Sport'. *Daily Telegraph*, March 28, 2010.

Saxena, S., and J. Hardy. 'In the Big League: Indian Franchises Top Several EPL Heavyweights'. *Times of India*, March 22, 2010: 1.

Schwartz, P. 'The World's Hottest Sports League'. *Forbes Magazine*, August 27, 2009.

Shankar, A. 'BCCI to Compensate Franchises'. *Cricinfo*, March 25, 2009. Available at: http://www.cricinfo.com/ipl2009/content/story/396732.html

'Shaun Marsh Joins Mohali'. *Cricinfo*. April 9, 2008. Available at: http://www.cricinfo.com/australia/content/story/345650.html

'Should be a Hard-fought Series'. *The Hindu*, October 24, 2009.

Smith, G. 'Sport on TV: Cricket Makes a Heroic Pitch to be King of the Bouncy Castle'. *Daily Telegraph*, June 16, 2003.

'Sony Bags IPL Media Rights for $1 Billion'. *Financial Express*, January 15, 2008.

Srinivas, A, and T.R. Vivek. *IPL: Cricket and Commerce*. New Delhi: Roli Books, 2009.

Szymanski, S. 'Revenue Sharing'. In *Handbook on the Economics of Sport*, edited by W. Andreff and S. Szymanski, 616–618. Cheltenham, UK: Edward Elgar, 2006.

Szymanski, S. 'The Promotion and Relegation System'. In *Handbook on the Economics of Sport*, edited by W. Andreff and S. Szymanski, 685–688. Cheltenham, UK: Edward Elgar, 2006.

Szymanski, S. 'Uncertainty of Outcome, Competitive Balance and the Theory of Team Sports'. In *Handbook on the Economics of Sport*, edited by W. Andreff and S. Szymanski, 597–600. Cheltenham, UK: Edward Elgar, 2006.

'Ten Teams for 2010 Champions League'. *Cricinfo*, May 24, 2010. Available at: http://www.cricinfo.com/t20champions2010/content/story/460726.html

Tomlinson, R., and A. Singh. 'India's Twenty20 Cricket Imports Cheerleaders, Grabs UK Stars'. *Bloomberg*, September 25, 2008. Available at: http://www.bloomberg.com/apps/news?pid=newsarchive&sid=agXm3oIJqEUA

Vice, T. 'South African Players Warned Over Rebel League'. *Reuters UK*, October 1, 2007. Available at: http://uk.reuters.com/article/idUKB54037120071001

Warne, S. 'It Was a Tough Decision to Leave Hampshire'. *The Sunday Times*, March 2009. Available at: http://www.timesonline.co.uk/tol/sport/columnists/shane_warne/article3642034.ece

'Watson Won't Give Up Bowling'. *Cricinfo*. September 26, 2007. Available at: http://www.cricinfo.com/australia/content/story/312571.html

'Zee Boss Does a Packer on BCCI'. *Times of India*, e-paper. April 4, 2007.

Japanese post-industrial management: the cases of Asics and Mizuno

Koji Kobayashi[a], John M. Amis[b], Richard Unwin[c] and Richard Southall[d]

[a]School of Physical Education, University of Otago, Dunedin, New Zealand; [b]Department of Management, Fogelman College of Business and Economics, University of Memphis, Memphis, USA; [c]Department of Health and Sport Sciences, University of Memphis, Memphis, USA; [d]Department of Exercise and Sport Science, University of North Carolina, Chapel Hill, USA

This study provides an examination of two Japanese sporting goods corporations, Asics and Mizuno, to uncover the ways in which the traditional forms of Japanese management have been modified to fit within a post-industrial, global context. Our findings reveal a strong link between the cultural context of the firms and their managerial approach. However, the impact of traditional Japanese values is tempered by the existence of both firms in a global industry that have led to western values and practices becoming increasingly influential. This hybrid approach is contrasted with the explicitly marketing-oriented stance of western firms in the industry, most notably exemplified by industry leader Nike.

Although the notion of a post-industrial society has been with us for sometime,[1] it has become a more common topic of discussion as the economies of, in particular, western societies become increasingly oriented away from traditional manufacturing and extracting industries and towards those that are knowledge-based. This post-industrial shift has been accompanied by an intense scouring of the globe by corporate leaders anxious to secure preferential access to resources and markets. In particular, technological advances have compressed time and space around the globe and radically altered the ways in which corporations operate.[2]

This changed global context has, of course, transformed managerial practices. However, while the impact of globalization on western firms has been a topic of much debate and scholarly investigation, much less has been produced in western outlets about how eastern firms have modified their practices to fit with a global context. This is somewhat ironic as our fascination with Japanese firms in particular can be traced back to the 1970s and 1980s when the rapid growth of the Japanese economy and high quality of Japanese products surprised western executives and scholars. The questions of how firms located in a country lacking capital, natural resources and political power following World War II were able to compete so effectively with western corporations proved compelling and generated much discussion.[3]

While such studies have undoubtedly informed western management practices, the predominant view of globalization has been one of spreading westernization, American-ization, or more rarely 'cultural hegemony'.[4] Further, most of the research that has been carried out on Japanese firms has been focused upon the traditionally prominent automotive and electronics industries.[5] Despite some recent and notable exceptions,[6] few studies have offered considerations of the ways in which Japanese firms have responded to the global shifts that have resulted in, for example, much greater connectivity among geographically dispersed groups, outsourcing of manufacturing, increased marketing segmentation, and enhanced consumer access to information. Such work has been particularly sparse with respect to how Japanese firms in non-manufacturing industries operate, and the ways in which traditional forms of Japanese management have evolved to accommodate a changed competitive context. Consequently, our purpose was to examine how the managerial practices of two well established Japanese sporting goods firms, Asics and Mizuno, responded to changes in the social, economic, cultural and technological contexts in which they operate.

There are several reasons why Asics and Mizuno constitute appropriate and interesting sites of study. First, the sporting industries are, almost by definition, post-industrial and have contributed significantly to our understanding of the ways in which corporations operate in such a context.[7] Nike, for example, has in many ways become the prototypical post-industrial firm that, notwithstanding its ethically problematic manufacturing practices, is viewed by many as the benchmark for how to operate in a global context. In particular, Nike's executives have been responsible for developing and exploiting a new business model that is centred upon two key strategies: intensive, celebrity-based marketing and global outsourcing. In so doing, they have radically altered the bases of competition in the industry.

Second, given that both firms have long histories, they have had extensive exposure to traditional forms of Japanese management. Mizuno was founded in 1906 by Rihachi Mizuno and developed as, in particular, baseball, golf and skiing surged in popularity in Japan. Asics, originally called Onitsuka, was founded in 1949 by Kihachiro Onitsuka providing, most famously, Onitsuka Tiger running shoes. The firm subsequently merged with two Japanese sportswear manufacturers in 1977 to become a general sporting goods company, Asics. Both firms also survived the economic recession of the 1990s which proved so disastrous to many Japanese firms and which, according to Schaede, 'mark[ed] a structural transition towards a postindustrial society'.[8] Therefore, the firms constituted interesting sites in which traditional modes of operating would likely be influenced by pressures to fit with a global, post-industrial context.

Third, both Asics and Mizuno are truly transnational corporations that have significant production and sales operations overseas. They are thus exposed to many of the commercial pressures that others in the industry face. Finally, while much has been written on western sporting goods companies, most notably Nike and to a lesser degree Adidas and Reebok, there remains a dearth of knowledge pertaining to the management practices of Japanese sporting goods firms. Consequently, there is an opportunity for the study of Asics and Mizuno to contribute to our understanding of management in the sporting goods industry in a similar way that others have informed operating practices in the automobile and electronics industries.

The data upon which our study is based were collected from a number of sources, the majority of which were Japanese. These data were subject to a textual analysis from which themes emerged that allowed us to locate the evolving practices of Asics and Mizuno within particular historical, cultural, and industrial contexts.[9] The remainder of the paper is structured in the following way. First we examine the pervasive cultural influences that have impacted Japanese corporations. From here we develop a more specific group of practices that have characterized traditional Japanese management. We then explore the ways in which managerial preferences and practices evolved at Asics and Mizuno as the firms had to cope with changing contextual pressures, followed by a contrast of practices at the firms to examine why particular managerial differences emerged. Our interest, specifically, and theoretical location of our work, stems from a desire to better comprehend the global–local nexus where westernization, if not globalization, of management becomes evident in newly adapted practices but is also simultaneously resisted and eventually hybridized with traditional forms of Japanese management.[10] We finish with some brief concluding comments.

Cultural influences on Japanese management

For those scholars who have asserted the importance of cultural underpinnings in understanding the differences between Japanese and western management practices, a significant disjuncture concerned the different emphases on individualism and collectivism.[11] For example, Ouchi argued that collectivism was a core value for Japanese corporations whereas individual incentives brought great success to American firms.[12] Comparing the construction of the self between Japanese and American citizens, Tolich, Kenny, and Biggart argued that, 'An American adult defines him or herself and then enters into relations with others; in Japan, self-definition is a product of relationships not an *a priori* construct'.[13] A famous Japanese expression that highlights this characteristic of Japanese society is: 'The nail that sticks up gets hammered down' (*deru kui wa utareru*).[14] Thus, historically, the individual who has tried to stand out has tended to be met with disapproval rather than praise.

In a similar vein, Japanese people have traditionally placed more importance on their association with groups than their American counterparts. This is particularly apposite within corporations, viewed by Japanese workers as an arena to reflect one's identification with the collective, and a context in which constructed organizational norms reinforce the employee's identification with the organization.[15] In this respect, Nakane argued that *kaisha* (corporation) was considered to be the group to which one primarily belonged and dedicated one's life, almost like a family in the western sense.[16] This notion of firm-as-family, denoted by the term *ie* (family), has retained an importance in discussions of Japanese organizations.

In fact, several scholars have argued that *ie* was the traditional and fundamental unit of Japanese organizations.[17] According to Murakami, even though *ie* often means a house in the contemporary usage of the word, traditionally it represented something more like a highly organized family in the western sense.[18] In the *ie* structure, the eldest man was regarded as the most important figure in the organization, with the owner's successor expected to be his eldest son. If the owner had a daughter but no son, leadership of the *ie* normally passed, through an arranged marriage, to the daughter's husband. In either case, the successor was expected to be honoured to preserve the name, fame, culture, custom, philosophy and tradition of the *ie*. In the words of Bhappu, 'the *ie* is the material assets of the family, as well as its prestige, class, and ranking in society'.[19] Bhappu also noted that relationships between individuals in the *ie* were characterized by reciprocity and obligation rather than obedience, emphasis on seniority within the organizational hierarchy, and trust, which was regarded as more important than achievement.[20] The unique structure and relationships offered by *ie* have heavily influenced the organization of corporate Japan.

The significance of *ie* has gradually diminished since Japan ended the *sakoku* (isolation) policy of the mid-nineteenth century and became more open to western influences. However, following World War II, the logic of *ie* still played a critical role in (re)forming Japanese corporations. Indeed, *ie* principles, along with the Japanese values of collectivism and long-term orientation, played prominent roles in shaping traditional Japanese management approaches, which will be exposed in the next section.[21] In this regard, the concept of firm-as-*ie* became a symbol of traditional Japanese society.[22] For instance, *dōzoku* (family-controlled) management, which was derived from the *ie* structure, was pervasive across Japanese firms into the late twentieth century. More recently, western influences on Japanese culture, lifestyle, and interaction have challenged the traditional Japanese way of doing business. Thus, we next explore five culturally unique elements of Japanese management, before examining specifically how management practices have evolved at Asics and Mizuno to fit within a globally competitive context.

Characteristics of Japanese traditional management

In addition to the characteristic of *ie,* we identified five other classical characteristics of traditional Japanese management practices.[23] A crucial point is that these characteristics are strongly interrelated since they all stem from core Japanese values and culture. Due to the limited space of this account, brief explanations are provided for each characteristic in the ensuing section.

Lifetime employment

Lifetime employment has been considered a key part of Japanese management by many scholars.[24] According to Clegg and Kono, 'The lifetime employment system is not a formal contract but a commitment on the side of both . . . management and . . . employees'.[25] In other words, the lifetime employment system is not formally regulated by corporate policies but based on a *de facto* agreement between management and employees. Under this arrangement employees are expected to exhibit sustained loyalty to the firm in return for a lifetime commitment from their employer. This mutual commitment was further strengthened by several interrelated practices: a seniority-based system that saw rewards accrue as the basis of longevity,[26] a lump-sum payment upon retirement,[27] job rotations,[28] team-based operating structures,[29] an inter-firm personnel transfer system,[30] and an employee education program.[31] Lifetime employment enables the company to cultivate multi-skilled and firm-specific human resources developed through on-the-job training and job rotations.[32] Knowledge sharing facilitated by job rotations, team-based structures, and intra-firm personnel transfer systems further helps effective diffusion of new and accumulated knowledge across the organization.

Enterprise unions

Unlike their western counterparts, unions in Japan evolved into firm-specific forms encompassing both blue-collar and white-collar employees.[33] Fruin credited the success of enterprise unions to their universality and inclusiveness.[34] In such organizations, distinctions between the blue-collar and white-collar workers were minimized, and 'us' became everyone within a firm, including management, while 'them' referred to people outside a firm.[35] In this respect, enterprise unions reinforce the notion of firm-as-family or firm-as-*ie*.[36] To this end, unions are expected to contribute to the tradition, success and reputation of the corporation through the hard work of their members, consultation with firm leaders, and participation in information forums at corporate, plant, and subunit levels.

Production systems

Japanese production systems are usually known by terms such as 'just-in-time management', 'total quality control', or 'lean production'. These concepts were pioneered by Toyota and have been heavily studied.[37] If one investigates the structures and functions of the system, it is not difficult to understand how Japanese values have influenced the process of building the organizational system. Other Japanese corporations have also focused on manufacturing high-quality products through their sophisticated production systems. As Clegg and Kono noted, successful Japanese transnational corporations such as Sony, Panasonic and Toshiba have invested significant resources in developing their production systems in order to achieve long-term growth rather than short-term profit.[38] In short, whether it be in the automobile, electronics, or other industries, a cornerstone of Japanese workers' competitive positioning is their pride in developing a highly efficient production system.

Keiretsu

The *keiretsu*, or inter-corporate network, has also been heavily associated with Japanese corporate success and has become a significant discussion topic in both academic and popular press outlets. According to Gerlach and Lincoln, a *keiretsu* is an industrial grouping formed by 'the strategic forging of long-term intercorporate relationships across a broad spectrum of markets: banks and insurance companies in the capital markets, *sogo shosha* (general trading companies) in primary goods markets, and subcontractors in component parts markets'.[39]

There are two types of *keiretsu*: horizontal *keiretsu* – a network across industries; and vertical *keiretsu* – a network of supply chain partners.[40] The most prominent horizontal *keiretsu* such as Mitsubishi, Mitsui and Sumitomo were originally formed as *zaibatsu* (family-owned conglomerates) before World War II.[41] *Zaibatsu* were considered to possess more definite *ie* structures and principles than contemporary Japanese organizations. Although the *zaibatsu* were legally dissolved by the Allied forces after World War II, the firms in each *zaibatsu* remained loosely connected through mutual stockholding around a major bank thereby forming what became known as horizontal *keiretsu*.[42] With its roots in *zaibatsu* and origins in single-family firms, it is little surprise that the influence of *ie* and Japanese traditional culture has lingered on in the ways in which *keiretsu* still underpins Japanese approaches to business. Likewise, vertical *keiretsu* were supported by trust building with long-term relationships, employee transfer across *keiretsu* members, and reciprocal shareholding.[43] Those practices are consistent with the Japanese values of collectivism and long-term corporate orientation.

Transfer of Japanese managerial practices overseas

In light of increased economic globalization and rapid technological advances, both western and Japanese managers have sought to exploit opportunities to gain low-cost production and penetrate new global markets. Despite complex cultural differences, scholars in several countries have supported the strong application and positive impact of Japanese management practices on overseas subsidiaries.[44] Most such studies have been conducted on overseas transplants in the automobile and electronics industries. Since Japanese production systems required specifically skilled and trained workers to be effective, Japanese corporations have had to transfer not just Japanese production methods, but also Japanese management concepts. This further explains how a production system is not just a stand-alone management practice but, rather, is integrated with other values and practices central to traditional Japanese management approaches.

Management at Asics and Mizuno

Having identified what we considered to be the most entrenched of traditional Japanese management values and practices, we turned our attention to analysing the evolution of management at Asics and Mizuno. In our analysis, the emergence of alternative managerial practices was generally tied to growing global competition. To survive, Japanese corporations had to negotiate global forces by shifting their positions in various dichotomies between, for example, global and local, individualism and collectivism, marketing and manufacturing, global outsourcing and domestic production, profit maximization and collective responsibility, and conceptually the west and Japan. Here, Nike serves as a reference point for western management since the company has been well known for its marketing capability, which has been regarded as a hallmark of western management, represented by mantras such as 'marketing is everything'.[45] This contrasts with Japanese values that have traditionally been associated with manufacturing excellence, technological capability, and ongoing improvements in efficiency and effectiveness through programs such as 'just-in-time management', 'total quality control', and 'lean production'.[46]

Evolution of Japanese management: the influence of traditional values

It is apparent that traditional Japanese management practices play a defining role at both Asics and Mizuno. This is consistent with a recent analysis by Abegglen who suggested that:

> Over the past half-century of dramatic economic and technological change, has Japan's employment system changed? Basically, it has not. The underlying values on which it was built ... remain the foundation. Key practices – an emphasis on continuity, on group integrity, and on egalitarianism – remain in effect.[47]

However, what is also evident is that, compared to practices exhibited during most of the latter half of the twentieth century, the traditional approach to management has undergone some significant alterations at both firms. It is plausible to assume that traditional management has been heavily influenced by western cultures and practices; however, the foundations of Japanese traditional management have played a significant role and continue to differentiate the firms from their western counterparts. Our analyses proffered several key ways in which the traditional management styles have retained prominence within both firms.

First, even though the corporations had to downsize during the economic downturn of the 1990s, the principle of lifetime employment was supported by intensive employee education that allowed individuals to be reassigned, and voluntary early retirement packages with higher-than-usual lump-sum payments to compensate for the years not worked. This emphasis on retaining workers is demonstrated in the longevity of those employed at Asics and Mizuno (see Table 1).

Second, job rotations and team-based designs are emphasized. Third, cooperative, company-based unions – ASSIST in the case of Asics, Mizuno Union for Mizuno – continue to work in harmony with the firms' management teams. This is exemplified by

Table 1. Average age and tenure (in years) at Asics and Mizuno in 2006.

	Board of directors		Employees	
	Average age	Average tenure	Average age	Average tenure
Asics	61.3	38.8	40.9	17.5
Mizuno	54.1	30.4	41.2	18.4

Sources: Asics Yūka Shōken Hōkokusho 2006; Mizuno Yūka Shōken Hōkokusho 2006.

ASSIST's concept that 'we make *our* company an excellent company'.[48] Fourth, both corporations continue to commit to 'manufacturing' and 'high-quality' production with an emphasis on craftsmanship. Fifth, the *keiretsu* concept continues to play integral roles for both firms through interdependent relationships with banks and suppliers. Finally, the desire to transmit traditional values and operating practices to their overseas subsidiaries is embodied in the corporate philosophies 'Asicsism'[49] and 'Mizunoism'.[50] However, there were also several ways in which traditional management practices were either heavily modified, or supplanted, by a perceived need to more closely meet the demands of global competition. It is to these that we now turn.

Evolution of Japanese management: emergence of alternative practices

Shifts from the seniority-based system

As we noted earlier, an integral component of traditional Japanese management was a payment and promotion system based on seniority. In the *ie* structure, seniority was more important than achievement such that power was usually associated with elders. This emphasis on seniority was consistent with lifetime employment because 'a seniority-based system is efficient only on the assumption that with each passing year the worker acquires skill and experience, thereby enhancing his or her value to the firm'.[51] However, this approach, which effectively curtailed the potential effectiveness of younger talented workers, was found to be too rigid by Asics and Mizuno. At Asics the problems with the seniority-oriented approach had long been recognized with the firm, in fact Asics was one of the first firms in Japan to curtail this system. Company founder, Kihachiro Onitsuka, regarded employee education and development as critical to corporate success. Thus, in 1956 he built an employee-training facility called the Tiger Dormitory (*taigā ryō*) where employees were required to stay for at least one year after joining the firm. Onitsuka foresaw the inefficiency of a seniority-based system and wanted to develop young talent so his firm could compete with other more established footwear companies. Onitsuka suggested that:

> As I founded the corporation, I also built a dormitory near my home to cultivate young employees. At the dormitory, I held training or study sessions every night. Meanwhile, I terminated the seniority-based system soon after I built the dormitory. I executed both the cultivation of capable employees and the active promotion of those talents to executives simultaneously by training employees through workshops and evaluating them through interviews.[52]

As Onitsuka later noted, it was unusual for Japanese corporations to terminate the seniority-based system at this time.[53] Kiyomi Wada, the current chairman of Asics, further explained the stance of the firm:

> We evaluate employees based on their abilities, not on their ages. However, it does not mean that simply being young brings you a chance but rather means highly-motivated employees are given priority. I believe that it is not an ideal company if it does not have employee development from the bottom up.[54]

In fact, the Onitsuka Tiger brand, which vanished after the corporate merger to create Asics in 1977, was revived in 2002 by a small project team consisting of young employees who appreciated the emerging trend of consumers' identification with lifestyle brands.[55] In 2005, sales of Onitsuka Tiger had reached approximately 10 billion yen per year. This established Asics reputation across youth markets as a company that was heavily focused upon design, not simply functionality. This turnaround would have been less – if not impossible – if Asics had persisted with the rigid seniority-based system and curtailed the potential of young employees to envision and develop new projects.

In contrast, Mizuno started a shift from a seniority- to a merit-based system when it employed a yearly salary system for managers in 1996.[56] Mizuno's commitment to this was displayed in its human resource philosophy that noted a desire for a 'thorough implementation of a results-oriented, performance oriented environment...[with] compensation based on skill and ability'.[57] Like other Japanese corporations such as Matsushita, Sanyo, and Sanwa Bank, Mizuno realized the necessity of employing a merit-based system during the economic recession of the 1990s, when senior executives recognized that it was unlikely to be able to survive global competition without the cultivation of young talented employees.[58] Lincoln and Nakata similarly observed that 'growing numbers of [Japanese] companies are explicitly weighting ability and performance over tenure and age in wage and promotion decisions'.[59] Therefore, although a seniority-based system supported 'a logic of motivation and control' under the lifetime employment model,[60] it appeared to be inconsistent and inefficient for Japanese corporations in the post-industrial era.

This shift from a seniority to merit-based reward system exemplifies the growing influence of western management practices on Japanese firms. This point is verified by Onitsuka's statements made over 20 years ago:

> From now on, we should adopt the positive characteristics of western individualism into Japanese *unmei kyōdōtai* management [see below] and build the new Japanese management. Especially, as globalization within a company prevails, Japanese management alone would eventually vanish. Hence, the necessity for these types of modifications will increase more and more. At Japanese companies, the proverb 'the nail that sticks up gets hammered down' states that talented people tend not to be rewarded properly and leave the companies while the remaining people in the company tend to be ordinary. It is expected that only companies which successfully cultivate individual talent and stimulate corporate vitality would be able to flourish in the future.[61]

This shift symbolizes the decay of *ie* principles and traditional values not only in the sporting goods industry but also in contemporary Japanese society as a whole. Thus, westernization of culture and society further rendered a rigid seniority-based system as incompatible with progressive Japanese management approaches in response to global competition.

Marketing and branding emphasis

It has become conventional wisdom that corporations have to excel in marketing and branding in order to flourish in today's global marketplace. This approach has been most heavily exemplified by Nike, as explained by founder and chairman Philip Knight: 'For years, we thought of ourselves as a production-oriented company.... But now we understand that the most important thing we do is market the product'.[62] While Adidas, Reebok, and other western firms adopted the Nike mantra,[63] Asics and Mizuno almost completely ignored it. There are three main reasons why Asics and Mizuno did not compete in the so-called 'sign wars', [64] and in particular the battle for celebrity associations. First, executives at Asics and Mizuno were unwilling to commit to the same levels of expenditure as their western counterparts for celebrity endorsements. For example, Onitsuka claimed that he convinced Ethiopian athlete Abebe Bikila – 'the barefoot marathon runner' – to wear his firm's shoes after he won the 1960 Olympic gold medal. However, when he won the gold medal at the Tokyo Olympics in 1964,

Abebe could not wear Onitsuka Tiger because he had a monetary contract with another company [Puma] in the west. While it was already common in the west to have such contracts, it was unthinkable in Japan to pay money to athletes due to strict regulations relating to amateurism.[65]

As Onituka noted, this reluctance to embrace a commercial attitude, including expenditure on endorsement deals, is partially explained by the way that amateurism was highly valued across Japanese sport and society. Furthermore, although it has been dynamically changing over decades, intensive commercialization was often inconsistent with Japanese traditional values and less welcome in Japanese society. Represented by famous sayings, which praise values of modesty and self-restraint, such as *chinmoku wa kanenari* (silence is golden), *kuchi wa wazawai no moto* (out of mouth comes evil), *nō aru taka wa tsume o kakusu* (still waters run deep), excessively extravagant advertising and promotion may be seen less to raise positive brand images than to draw negative feelings of discord with traditional cultural values in the eyes of Japanese consumers. Consequently, Asics and Mizuno were restricted for many years from offering monetary contracts to athletes, placing them at a disadvantage with respect to their western counterparts when it came to trying to secure endorsements from high-profile athletes.

Second, the nationalities of endorsers should not be ignored. It is likely easier for American companies such as Nike to contract with American athletes and Japanese corporations Asics and Mizuno to contract with Japanese athletes. This was particularly the case before the start of the rapid globalization of sport, sporting organizations, and the sports media in the late 1980s that rendered national barriers less meaningful. Thus, Japanese sporting goods corporations were geographically and culturally disadvantaged in the west-centred sporting context. In other words, the global diffusion of sports, sporting organizations, and athletes has been predominantly from the west to the rest, so much so that Japanese sports and athletes, with some notable exceptions (e.g. judo and karate; Ichiro Suzuki and Hidetoshi Nakata), have had to endure marginal status.[66] This was exemplified by the 'natural' association that led to American footwear companies such as Nike and Reebok developing particularly strong links with the National Basketball Association's global movement.[67]

Third, and perhaps most importantly, as Nike and other western firms invested heavily in marketing, so Asics and Mizuno focused upon manufacturing and employee education. In line with the cultural values traditionally espoused in Japanese industry, Asics and Mizuno emphasized the high quality of their manufacturing processes and end products and were largely blind to the potential of branding and marketing. This 'manufacturer's mindset' at both corporations delayed their shift towards more marketing-intensive management. This fact was captured in remarks from the presidents of Asics and Mizuno. Onitsuka lamented, 'We invested much in production lines and succeeded in the athletic footwear category but lost to Nike in marketing'.[68] Likewise, Akito Mizuno, the president of Mizuno, admitted, 'The weakness of our company is marketing. We had a strong belief that 'superior products satisfy customers' all these years'.[69]

As global competition intensified, so came the realization among those at Asics and Mizuno that there was a need to shift towards more marketing-intensive management in order to compete with their western counterparts. In 1994, Asics established a marketing department as a distinctive function to coordinate marketing activities across all other departments and opened an office for marketing research in Aoyama, considered to be at the cradle of new Japanese trends.[70] As noted above, the revival of Onitsuka Tiger in 2002 symbolized this dynamic corporate paradigm shift from a strict concentration on craftsmanship and functionality to a diversification into market-driven casual and fashionable products by using old designs in accordance with the 'retro' boom. At Mizuno, a marketing director position was not created to coordinate branding across all departments until 1997.[71] In 2005, Mizuno's reluctance to compete in the lifestyle market ended when the company introduced the Mizuno Women's Factory Project.[72]

Globalization of production and distribution

Globalization of production and distribution by Asics and Mizuno was enhanced by intensified global competition. In order to compete with rivals, both corporations needed to shift manufacturing overseas for lower production costs and expand their business in international markets for further growth. Since some scholars have drawn attention to Nike's commodity chain,[73] a particularly interesting point here is the comparison of modes of production at Asics and Nike. Asics and Nike were two of the earliest athletic companies to shift production overseas and underwent quite similar production movements: broadly from Japan to South Korea in the 1970s and to China and Southeast Asia in the 1980s and 1990s[74] in the chase for ever cheaper labour. In Japan, the rapid increase in production costs and appreciation of the yen made shifting production particularly attractive during the 1970s and 1980s.[75] Onitsuka recalled:

> As our brand became more global and overseas sales were increased, we recognized that our new challenge was internationalization of production and sales. In short, it required the establishment of operating bases overseas. The biggest reason for our shift overseas was the rapid increase in cost of production in Japan and the rise of the yen. The price of our products was so inflated that overseas distributors could not handle our products.[76]

In 1969, Asics built a manufacturing subsidiary with 52 employees in Taiwan, its first overseas production site.[77] The choice of Taiwan emanated from the personal experience of Onitsuka who stated: 'When I visited Southeast Asian countries to inspect organizations for overseas industries in 1968, I thought the climate and culture of Taiwan would be the most suitable.'[78] Other Japanese firms also began to shift production abroad. Taiwan and South Korea were particular favourites given their cultural and geographic proximity to Japan. Subsequently, Asics shifted manufacturing activities to South Korea and then China:

> As production costs in Taiwan gradually rose, we shifted the production base to South Korea where we collaborated with a Korean maker to produce Onitsuka's products. However, it was immediately followed by an increase in production costs, so we shifted again to the current location in China. We built a factory in Jiangsu which was one hour inland from Shanghai, and employed about 1000 workers to manufacture shoes and clothing.[79]

On the other hand, Nike contracted with Nissho Iwai, a Japanese trading firm, and its manufacturing contractor Nippon Rubber Company to replace Asics as a shoe producer after Nike's relationship with Asics ended in dispute in 1971.[80] As Asics, 'Nippon Rubber decided to relocate much of its production operations from Japan to Taiwan and South Korea'.[81] Thus, shifts in Nike's production practices reflected trends among Japanese corporations to move production to Taiwan and South Korea. Nike's production system was further developed when the company found other firms in Taiwan and South Korea with which to subcontract.

To clarify a key point here, Asics has owned several manufacturing subsidiaries in Japan and one major overseas manufacturing subsidiary, Jiangsu Asics Co., Ltd., in China.[82] In a similar vein, Mizuno has owned several domestic manufacturing subsidiaries and overseas manufacturing subsidiaries, including Mizuno Corporation of Hong Kong Ltd., Shanghai Mizuno Corporations Ltd., and Thai Sports Garment Co., Ltd.[83]

Conversely, Nike, which started by importing athletic shoes from Asics forerunner, Onitsuka, has never owned any of its factories, with the exception of two short-lived production facilities built in Maine and New Hampshire in 1977. As Onitsuka explained:

> Nike is a trading company and Asics is a maker. Therefore, Nike does not have its own factories. Instead, resources are invested in product development and marketing. For example, Nike captured the consumers' minds with the strategy of using Tiger Woods as Nike's exclusive promotional vehicle in exchange for an enormous amount of money, which really represented the American way of doing business. Furthermore, Nike mass-produces its goods by fully exploiting cheap labor in developing countries, mostly in Southeast Asia. On the other hand, Asics prioritizes technical skill the most. Although we also have production bases overseas, we manage those factories on our own.[84]

The commitment to manufacturing and product quality has been recurrently expressed by the presidents from both corporations over generations. Wada has pointed out the need for Asics' employees to,

> go back to the starting point and rediscover the importance of adhering to the fundamentals of manufacturing, which is essential as a maker. Then, we could strengthen our brand which focuses on the arena of competition sports. We continue to put an emphasis on technology and functionality, which are our brand values. We need to develop and provide the products which only Asics can create.[85]

Similarly, Masato Mizuno, the third president of Mizuno, stated: 'Although we could provide extravagant advertising with costly investment, we think that the most important thing is to convey the message that we provide high-quality, functionally sound products to consumers.'[86] In an interesting contrast to Asics' and Mizuno's adherence to the manufacturer's mindset, Knight stated: 'There is no value in making things any more. The value is added by careful research, by innovation and by marketing'.[87] This antithesis in managerial mentality between the 'manufacturer's mindset' and the 'marketer's mindset' appeared to be a fundamental difference that guided Asics and Mizuno on the one hand and Nike on the other to employ different managerial approaches. Further, it can be argued that the manufacturer's mindset still dominates Japanese corporate paradigms, as Akito Mizuno has argued, that 'The only way for Japanese corporations to survive in global competition is *monozukuri* (manufacturing or craftsmanship)'.[88]

Fulfilment of corporate social responsibility

Corporate Social Responsibility (CSR) has, according to one commentator at least, emerged as an operating framework by which transnational corporations 'should strive to make a profit, obey the law, be ethical, and be a good corporate citizen'.[89] A frenzy of criticism by media workers and human rights activists about Nike's exploitation of workers in economically developing countries in the late 1990s raised awareness of CSR in the sport and leisure industry. As Nike initially responded to the criticism with resistance, the firm's brand image was severely harmed to the extent that even Philip Knight admitted that 'Nike products have become synonymous with slave wages, forced overtime, and arbitrary abuse'.[90] Even though criticism remains fierce among activists, Nike has attempted to convince the public that the corporation has worked towards improvement in worker's conditions by setting labour standards for members of its supply chain, conforming to third-party monitoring, establishing a department for CSR, and publishing CSR reports.[91]

For Asics and Mizuno, the perceived need to engage in overt CSR-related activities was not apparent among the firms' executives. This is evidenced by the fact that they took longer to establish CSR teams and present CSR reports than their western competitors:

Nike (CSR team – 1998, CSR report – 2001), Adidas (CSR team – 1998, CSR report – 2001), Asics (CSR team – 2004, CSR report – 2005) and Mizuno (CSR team – 2004, CSR report – 2004).[92] Perhaps more importantly, Asics and Mizuno have failed to gain as much credit as their western competitors for improving workers' conditions overseas. For example, while Reebok participated in the accreditation process by the Fair Labor Association in 2001, as did Nike and Adidas in 2002, Asics entered the process in 2005 and Mizuno has yet to join.[93] Oxfam International has also criticized Mizuno, calling for the company to 'engage in dialogue and cooperation with independent trade unions and labour rights groups in order to establish ways of improving respect for these rights in the company's supply chain'.[94] This delayed action in publicizing CSR activities can probably in large part be attributed to cultural differences. As traditional Japanese values have emphasized modesty and humility, dramatizing corporate images by promoting CSR activities is less culturally acceptable than the valued attitude of '*fugen jikkō*' (actions speak louder than words).

However, it is noteworthy that Asics and Mizuno have demonstrated significant environmental awareness. In fact, compared to the CSR reports by Nike and Adidas, those by Asics and Mizuno have less information about the improvement of working conditions in production facilities but place greater emphasis on the preservation of the environment. In particular, Mizuno's efforts toward preserving the natural environment have been notable, exemplified by the 'Conservation of Resources and Environmental Wave towards the 21st Century' (CREW21) initiative established in 1991. Furthermore, Masato Mizuno has actively participated in international-level organizations to promote environmental initiatives as a director of the World Federation of the Sporting Goods Industry (1991) and later as a member of the sport and environment commission of the International Olympic Committee (1996).[95] In an interview for a Japanese business journal, Masato Mizuno explained that environmental conservation:

> is an obligation as a human being. It is beyond the pursuit of profit. In the U.S., it is said that products sell well when they are described as environmentally friendly. It would be shameful if the world we live in revolves only around mercenary motives. I always tell people to stop merely pretending to care for the environment.[96]

His statement implies crucial points of difference between Japanese and western (in particular American) business. Japanese corporate executives appear to claim that care for the natural environment is a collective responsibility rather than a strategic play for enhancing return on investment. For instance, Mizuno's implementation of CREW21 was much earlier than its competitors. The development of environmentally friendly hybrid automobiles has similarly been led by Toyota and other Japanese automakers.[97] Thus, it can be argued that the emphasis on environmental responsibility is reflective of traditional Japanese values and has become a natural fit with public calls for firm leaders to exhibit greater levels of CSR. By contrast, the eventual adoption of standards designed to publicly certify a commitment to improved labour practices represents a need to strategically position the firms as being in line with global industry standards.

Contrasting Asics and Mizuno

While we have found several key similarities in the ways in which leaders at Asics and Mizuno have contoured traditional management approaches to take account of the post-industrial context in which they are competing, there are also some significant differences between the firms. These also shed light on the varying ways in which managers at these organizations have responded to a changed competitive context.

Mizuno's dōzoku management

Authority at Mizuno has been dominated by the Mizuno family for over 100 years with Rihachi Mizuno (1906–1969), Kenjiro Mizuno (1969–1988), Masato Mizuno (1988–2006), and Akito Mizuno (2006–present) providing an unbroken family line of leaders. Mizuno has been a good example of a thriving corporation that has pursued *dōzoku* management. As previously mentioned, *dōzoku* management, derived from the *ie* structure, reflects the traditional Japanese way of organizing. Advantages and disadvantages of *dōzoku* management were discussed by the presidents from Mizuno and Asics. Masato Mizuno provided his analysis of *dōzoku* management in an interview in 1998:

> Since I grew up seeing what my grandfather and father were doing, I gained much preliminary knowledge about management. I think that it was one of my advantages. A disadvantage would be that it is easy to become the emperor who had no clothes on [referring to the Danish fairy tale, The Emperor's New Clothes]. For example, it would be easy to abuse the authority, listen to only good news, and spoil employees by accepting marginal performance.[98]

In sum, a perceived advantage of *dōzoku* management is strong control by family members who are supposed to be the most trustworthy and by a sustained exposure to the business that ingrains a strong understanding within subsequent generations. Two disadvantages are that presidents of second or later generations tend to not have experienced the early growing pains, and associated experience, usually endured by the founder, and that preferencing family members prevents non-family members from contributing optimally to the success of the business. Despite its historic relevance *dōzoku* management has eroded among Japanese corporations, as Masato Mizuno himself acknowledged: 'The top company in an industry as listed on the stock exchange should not pursue *dōzoku* management . . . A person who has talent or strong leadership should become a president.'[99] Nevertheless, for the time being at least, *dōzoku* management remains prominent at Mizuno.

Asics' unmei kyōdōtai management

Onituska declared his departure from *dōzoku* management at the company's 10th anniversary ceremony in 1959, a highly unusual move for a Japanese leader at the time. In practice, he terminated the two common practices in *dōzoku* management: employment of family members and the seniority-based system. This move by Onitsuka was triggered when:

> Accidentally, I obtained shorthand notes of the instruction given by Konosuke Matsushita, an executive officer of Matsushita Electric Industrial Co., Ltd., for his workers at the 15th anniversary (1932) of the company and learned a lot from them. This was the beginning of so-called 'Matsushitaism' for me.[100]

Briefly, Matsushitaism referred to a corporate philosophy of the firm as a public entity. In this sense, Matsushita was arguing that firm leaders should not be single-minded in their pursuit of profit, but should also seek ways to improve people's lives.[101] Inspired by such an approach, Onitsuka came to believe that Asics should function as a public organization and should not be monopolized by a single individual or family. Onitsuka analysed *dōzoku* management thus:

> I do not deny the advantages of *dōzoku* management, but the advantages – such as that family members are trustful and able to keep a secret – tend to end up with the employment of only family members [for president and executive positions]. However, as the sole family strengthens the control over management, teamwork would be disturbed and employees would only care about currying favor with the family. Especially under an incompetent family, the talents of employees would not show up.[102]

When he declared the departure from *dōzoku* management, he also introduced his new management philosophy and style, *unmei kyōdōtai* (a united entity sharing a common destiny) management. The idea was that the three entities of management, employees and shareholders would work together through long-term, if not permanent, interdependent relationships to achieve organizational goals.[103]

In launching *unmei kyōdōtai* management, Onitsuka outlined three fundamental management principles. First, corporate and managerial information, including profit distribution was disclosed to the employees; second, 70% of corporate shares, previously fully owned by the founder, were distributed to employees; and third, a merit-based system was introduced to foster a fairer reward structure.[104] In 2006, Wada affirmed that this philosophy had played, and would continue to play, a central role in Asics' management approach:

> Kihachiro Onitsuka, the founder of ASICS and the current chairman, has often noted that shareholders, employees, and business partners form a united entity of three parts that share a common destiny. I concur with this view, and I am confident that our longstanding philosophy and practices will continue serving to underpin growth.[105]

Thus, while *dōzoku* management represents a traditional form of Japanese social organization based on the *ie* structure, *unmei kyōdōtai* management is derived from the continuously dominant Japanese values of collectivism and long-term orientation. In this respect, we see traditional, but different, Japanese values retaining a strong hold on Asics and Mizuno as their leaders contended with a changing managerial context.

Velocity of adjustment to post-industrial conditions

Throughout the two case studies, it was apparent that Asics responded to post-industrial challenges faster than Mizuno. Indeed, employment of the merit-based system for the purpose of talent cultivation was undertaken by Asics approximately 40 years earlier than other Japanese corporations including Mizuno. Even though it was considerably later than Nike and other western competitors to prioritize marketing initiatives and penetrate the rapidly growing lifestyle category, Asics certainly acted earlier than Mizuno. Asics revived Onitsuka Tiger in 2002 and quickly turned it into a globally recognizable 'retro' lifestyle brand, particularly in Europe and Asia; Mizuno has yet to make a global impact in the category.

Further, Asics has developed a global production and distribution system faster and more aggressively than Mizuno. Asics' overseas production reached 50% of total production in 1988[106] and had increased to 60% by 2007;[107] by contrast, Mizuno's overseas

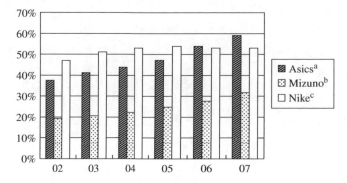

Figure 1.   Ratio of overseas sales (per year, 2002–2007).
Sources: [a]*Asics Yūka Shōken Hōkokusho 2003–2007*; [b]*Mizuno Yūka Shōken Hōkokusho 2003–2007*; [c]*Nike, Inc. Annual Report 2003–2007.*

production remained at 40% of total production in 2000.[108] Further, in 2007, Asics accounted for 59% of its total sales from overseas while those for Mizuno were at 31%. A comparison of overseas sales ratios for Asics, Mizuno and Nike is provided in Figure 1.

From these findings, it appears that Asics has adapted to a post-industrial global context more successfully than Mizuno. In fact, this view is supported by their recent financial reports. First, although Asics was founded later and has spent a long time catching up to Mizuno, it has outperformed Mizuno in total sales since 2005. A comparison of global sales between both corporations is indicated in Figure 2. Second, Asics has outperformed Mizuno with fewer employees. In 2007, Asics had 4230 employees[109] while Mizuno had 6129 employees.[110] This points to the overall effectiveness of Asics' management in the global economy. Third and most strikingly, Asics has performed much better in net income than Mizuno in recent years (see Figure 3).

Both corporations suffered substantially from the economic downturn of the 1990s. However, Asics recovered more quickly by responding more effectively to the challenges inherent in a global, post-industrial industry. It is perhaps an oversimplification to assume that the disparities in recent economic success and velocity of adjustment to the post-industrial conditions between two corporations are single-handedly caused by the difference of *dōzoku* and *unmei kyōdōtai* management styles. Yet, given the importance of cultural influence on their management and the need to hybridize Japanese management with western values, cultures, and practices to compete in this post-industrial

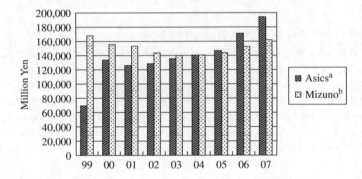

Figure 2.   Global sales of Asics and Mizuno (per year, 1999–2007).
Sources: [a]*Asics Yūka Shōken Hōkokusho 2003–2007*; [b]*Mizuno Yūka Shōken Hōkokusho 2003–2007*.

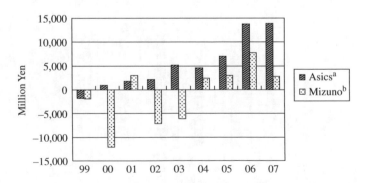

Figure 3.   Net incomes of Asics and Mizuno (per year, 1999–2007).
Sources: [a]*Asics Yūka Shōken Hōkokusho 2003–2007*; [b]*Mizuno Yūka Shōken Hōkokusho 2003–2007*.

era, these differences in managerial styles are likely to have played a critical role in shaping their contrasting paths.

Conclusion

This study of Japanese sporting goods corporations Asics and Mizuno has revealed some interesting ways in which traditional Japanese management approaches have been modified to fit within a post-industrial global context. First, the strong links between culture and management are clearly apparent in both organizations. While Japanese traditional management systems and practices have been influenced by western cultures and practices, the core values remain, on the whole, intact underpinning major differences in the managerial approach to their western counterparts. In a similar vein, Mizuno's *dōzoku* management and Asics' *unmei kyōdōtai* management, while clearly differing in their emphases, do highlight the impact of the cultural context in which the firms exist.

Second, western-influenced management practices, identified as the shift from a seniority to a merit-based system, an increased emphasis on marketing and branding, the globalization of production and distribution, and pressures to exhibit CSR, became necessary for Japanese corporations to survive in a global context. This adaptation of Japanese management to western values, culture and practices has cohered with current shifts in Japanese society, which is itself witnessing a tension between maintaining Japanese traditions while embracing western values and cultural practices.

Third, a 'manufacturer's', as opposed to a 'marketer's', mindset has prevailed in today's management at Asics and Mizuno. This is vastly different from Nike which was transformed from a production-centred to a marketing-centred company. As such, Asics and Mizuno continue to prioritize manufacturing and employee education whereas Nike has more focused on the creation of emotional ties with consumers through intensive marketing. Not only did the western-oriented sporting context position Japanese sporting goods corporations in a geographically and culturally distant position, the long-term blindness to global market trends largely due to the manufacturer's mindset and Japanese values against intensive commercialization further hindered Asics and Mizuno from creating the ties with consumers on a global scale that Nike – and to a lesser extent Adidas, Reebok and other western firms – was able to profit from with its heavy investment in endorsement contracts.

Finally, the differences between Asics and Mizuno were also exposed. From our findings, it is plausible to conclude that Asics' departure from *dōzoku* management and transformation to *unmei kyōdōtai* management formed the core management philosophy and practices which drove Asics to adapt to a post-industrial global context more successfully than Mizuno. In other words, Asics' leadership appears to have discovered a more successful formulation of hybridizing Japanese management styles with western values, cultures and practices than did Mizuno. However, this is a conclusion that requires further verification from future investigation.

This study also offers intriguing implications for Japanese and western management. First, differences appear to be diminishing as managers in Japanese and western firms seek to develop ever more effective global management practices by learning from each other. However, despite intense forces of globalization,[111] differences remain in managerial elements which strongly reflect national cultures and values. In this study, Asics and Mizuno have managed to retain key Japanese values and indeed actively spread 'Asicsism' and 'Mizunoism' while emerging as global corporations. It will be interesting to note, in the years ahead, how, or indeed if, residual national markers are retained by Asics, Mizuno or their western counterparts.

Acknowledgements

We would like to thank Ronald Mower, Mizuki Takahashi, and Sayaka Tokunaga for their invaluable help and comments on earlier drafts of this essay.

Notes

[1] See Bell, *The Coming of Post-Industrial Society*.

[2] E.g. Castells, *The Rise of the Network Society*; Maguire, *Global Sport*; Sampler, 'Redefining Industry Structure'; Silk and Andrews, 'Beyond a Boundary?'.

[3] E.g. Abegglen and Stalk, *Kaisha, The Japanese Corporation*; Dore, *Taking Japan Seriously*; Fruin, *The Japanese Enterprise System*; Ouchi, *Theory Z*; Pascale and Athos, *The Art of Japanese Management*; Vogel, *Japan as Number One*.

[4] Donnelly, 'The Local and the Global'.

[5] E.g. Abo, *Hybrid Factory*; Liker, *The Toyota Way*; Oaklander, *The Canon Case*; Womack, Jones and Roos, *The Machine*.

[6] E.g. Abegglen, *21st-Century Japanese Management*; Vogel, *Japan Remodeled*.

[7] E.g. Amis, 'Beyond Sport'; Goldman and Papson, *Nike Culture*; Grainger and Jackson, 'Sports Marketing'; Jackson, Batty and Scherer, 'Transnational Sport Marketing'.

[8] Schaede, 'What Happened to the Japanese Model?', 277.

[9] Textual extracts are crucial because: 'As well as providing evidence for particular claims, quotations provide color, add interest and enhance the legitimacy and credibility of the account' (Amis, 'Interviewing', 131). In this sense, the data for this study were predominantly qualitative and gathered from various sources. These included books (e.g. Onitsuka, 1987, 1991, 2000, 2001; Matsui, 2004), corporate publications (e.g. Adidas: *Annual Report 2006, Social and Environmental Report 2005*; Asics: *Annual Report 2003–2007, CSR Report 2006–2007, Yūka Shōken Hōkokusho (Securities Report) 2003–2007*; Fair Labor Association, *2006 Annual Public Report*; Mizuno: *Kessan Tanshin, Renketsu (Consolidated Financial Settlement) 2000–2004, CSR Report 2006–2007, Fact Book 2007, Yūka Shōken Hōkokusho 2003–2007*; Nike: *FY04 Corporate Responsibility Report, FY05-06 Corporate Responsibility Report, Annual Report 2003–2007, Proxy Statement 2006*; Oxfam International, *Offside!*, websites (e.g. www.adidas-group.com, www.ambc.co.jp, www.asics.co.jp, www.asicsamerica.com, www.cleanclothes.org, www.mizuno.co.jp, www.mizunousa.com, www.nike.com, www.reebok.com), articles in trade and business journals (e.g. Adweek, Aera, Atlanta Business Chronicle, Footwear News, Fortune, Industry Week, Knight Ridder Tribune Business News, Business Week, Mainichi Economist, Nikkei Business, Nikkei Information Strategy, Nikkei Marketing Journal, Time, Women's Wear Daily), and Japanese newspapers (e.g. Asahi Shimbun, Kobe Shimbun, Mainichi Shimbun, Nihon Sen-I Shimbun, Nikkan Kogyo Shimbun, Nikkei, Nikkei Sangyo Shimbun, Sankei Shimbun). Japanese sources were translated by the first author with the interpretations subsequently reviewed by two other native Japanese speakers who are fluent in English. Conclusions emerged, were challenged, and subsequently settled upon following numerous meetings among the authors.

[10] For the global–local, homogenization–heterogenization, and universality–particularity debates, see, for example, Andrews et al., 'Jordanscapes'; Appadurai, 'Disjuncture and Difference'; Robertson, *Globalization*, 'Glocalization'.

[11] Dore, *Taking Japan Seriously*; Nakane, *Japanese Society*; Ouchi, *Theory Z*; Tolich, Kenny, and Biggart, 'Managing the Managers'.

[12] Ouchi, *Theory Z*.

[13] Tolich, Kenny, and Biggart, 'Managing the Managers', 592.

[14] Gregersen and Black, 'Multiple Commitments upon Repatriation', 212.

[15] Aoki, *Information, Incentives, and Bargaining*.

[16] Nakane, *Japanese Society*.

[17] Bhappu, 'The Japanese Family'; Fruin, *The Japanese Enterprise System*; Murakami, 'Ie Society'; Nakane, *Japanese Society*.

[18] Murakami, 'Ie Society'.

[19] Bhappu, 'The Japanese Family', 410.

[20] Ibid.

[21] Bhappu, 'The Japanese Family'; Hofstede, 'Management Scientists Are Human'.

[22] Murakami, 'Ie Society'.

[23] There are arguments over defining which practices are more 'Japanese' and important than others (see, for example: Clegg and Kono, 'Trends in Japanese Management'; Hayashi, 'A Historical Review'; Ito, 'Japan and the Asian Economies'; McCormick, 'Whatever Happened'). We have focused on those practices that are most entrenched and have the broadest impact within Japanese industry.

[24] Fruin, *The Japanese Enterprise System*; Lincoln and Kalleberg, *Culture, Control, and Commitment*; Pil and MacDuffie, 'Transferring Competitive Advantage'; Yuzawa, 'Japanese Business Strategies'.

[25] Clegg and Kono, 'Trends in Japanese Management', 276.

[26] E.g. Lincoln and Nakata, 'The Transformation'.

[27] E.g. Aoki, *Information, Incentives, and Bargaining*.

[28] E.g. Ito, 'Japan and the Asian Economies'; Monden, *Toyota Production System*.

[29] E.g. Kawamura, 'Characteristics'; Liker, Fruin, and Adler, 'Bringing Japanese Management Systems'.

[30] E.g. Ouchi, *Theory Z*.

[31] E.g. Hatvany and Puick, 'Japanese Management Practices'.

[32] Aoki, *Information, Incentives, and Bargaining*.

[33] Nishiguchi, *Strategic Industrial Sourcing*.

[34] Fruin, *The Japanese Enterprise System*.

[35] Nishiguchi, *Strategic Industrial Sourcing*.

[36] Kenny, 'Transplantation?'; Pil and MacDuffie, 'Transferring Competitive Advantage'.

[37] E.g. Liker, *The Toyota Way*; Womack, Jones and Roos, *The Machine*.

[38] Clegg and Kono, 'Trends in Japanese Management'.

[39] Gerlach and Lincoln, 'The Organization of Business Networks', 493.

[40] Banjeri and Sambhaya, 'Vertical Keiretsu'; Johnston and McAlevey, 'Stable Shareholdings'; McGuire and Dow, 'The Persistence and Implications'.

[41] Ito, 'Japan and the Asian Economies'.

[42] Aoki, *Information, Incentives, and Bargaining*.

[43] Dyer and Ouchi, 'Japanese-Style Partnerships'.

[44] E.g. Abo, *Hybrid Factory*; Adler, 'Hybridization'; Beechler, 'International Management Control'; Liker, Fruin, and Adler, 'Bringing Japanese Management Systems'; Oliver and Wilkinson, *The Japanization of British Industry*.

[45] McKenna, 'Marketing Is Everything'.

[46] It is worthwhile to note that Nike underwent the start-up period under tremendous Japanese influences, in particular Asics management. It is evident since Nike started as Blue Ribbon Sports by importing athletic footwear from Onitsuka in 1964 and Philip Knight initially learned the athletic footwear business from Kihachiro Onitsuka (Onitsuka, *Nenji, inori, tsuranuku*). In this sense, although today's Nike well represents the western style of management, it can be argued that the construction process of Nike management was driven less by western traditional business models than by hybridization of western and Japanese ideas.

[47] Abegglen, *21st-Century Japanese Management*, 89.

[48] *Asics CSR Report 2006*, 22, emphasis added.

[49] Onitsuka, *Shigokoro*, 243.

[50] *Nihon Keizai Shimbun*, 12 April 1989, 1.

[51] Lincoln and Nakata, 'The Transformation', 47.

[52] *Asics CSR Report 2006*, 4.

[53] Onitsuka, *Watashi*.

[54] *Nihon Sen-I Shimbun*, 23 January 2003, 8.

[55] *Nikkei Information Strategy*, 24 December 2005.

[56] *Nihon Keizai Shimbun*, 3 May 1996, 10.

[57] *Mizuno CSR Report 2006*, 9.

[58] *Yomiuri Shimbun (Osaka)*, 10 May 1998.

[59] Lincoln and Nakata, 'The Transformation', 48.

[60] Ibid., 47.

[61] Onitsuka, *Shigokoro*, 249–50.

[62] Willigan, 'High-Performance Marketing', 92.

[63] Klein, *No Logo*.

[64] Goldman and Papson, *Sign Wars*. Asics and Mizuno were more concerned about competitions over domestic market shares and thus sought to secure contracts with renowned Japanese

athletes such as Ichiro Suzuki, Kosuke Kitajima and Naoko Takahashi. Even so, Asics and Mizuno have been left behind western counterparts in the development of their brands through, in particular, celebrity endorsements.

65 Onitsuka, *Nenji, inori, tsuranuku*, 109.
66 See also Maguire, *Global Sport*.
67 Jackson and Andrews, 'Between and Beyond the Global'.
68 Onitsuka, *Nenji, inori, tsuranuku*, 140.
69 *Nihon Sen-I Shimbun*, 22 August 2006, 1.
70 *Nikkei Sangyo Shimbun*, 17 May 1994, 18.
71 *Nikkei Marketing Journal*, 21 October 1999, 12.
72 *Nihon Sen-I Shimbun*, 10 February 2005, 1.
73 Frenkel, 'Globalization'; Harrison, 'The Dark Side'; Korzeniewicz, 'Commodity Chains'.
74 Korzeniewicz, 'Commodity Chains'.
75 Kawamura, 'Characteristics'.
76 Onitsuka, *Nenji, inori, tsuranuku*, 124–5.
77 Onitsuka, *Shigokoro*.
78 Onitsuka, *Nenji, inori, tsuranuku*, 125.
79 Ibid., 125–6.
80 Strasser and Becklund, *Swoosh*.
81 Harrison, 'The Dark Side', 492.
82 *Asics Yūka Shōken Hōkokusho* 2007.
83 *Mizuno Yūka Shōken Hōkokusho* 2007.
84 Onitsuka, *Nenji, inori, tsuranuku*, 140. Asics and Mizuno also have utilized foreign subcontractors, for instance, the Taiwanese-owned Pou Chen Group, the world's largest athletic footwear manufacturer (Clean Clothes Campaign: http://www.cleanclothes.org/companies/asics.htm#top).
85 *Nihon Sen-I Shimbun*, 23 January 2003, 8.
86 *Nihon Sen-I Shimbun*, 21 January 2004, 6.
87 Quoted in Klein, *No Logo*, 197.
88 *Nihon Sen-I Shimbun*, 16 May 2006, 4. The notion of *monozukuri* is important for understanding the Japanese way of manufacturing and the 'manufacturer's mindset'. *Monozukuri* cannot be simply translated into manufacturing in the western sense but rather reflects traditional Japanese craftsmanship values, spirit, and a traditional desire to make high-quality goods.
89 Carroll, 'The Pyramid', 43.
90 Knight, 'Global Manufacturing', 637.
91 Zadek, 'The Path to Corporate Responsibility'.
92 These data were collected from: *Nike FY04 Corporate Responsibility Report*; *Adidas Group Social and Environmental Report, 2005*; *Asics Annual Report 2005*; *Asics CSR Report 2006, 2007*; *Mizuno CSR Report 2006, 2007*.
93 Fair Labor Association, 2006 *Annual Public Report*.
94 Oxfam International, *Offside!*
95 *Nikkan Kogyo Shimbun*, 16 November 1998, 19.
96 *Nikkei Marketing Journal*, 9 July 1998, 28.
97 Stewart and Raman, 'Lessons from Toyota's Long Drive'.
98 *Nikkei Business*, 22 June 1998, 92–4.
99 *Nikkei Sangyo Shimbun*, 20 July 1991, 12.
100 Onitsuka, *Nenji, inori, tsuranuku*, 73.
101 For the Matsushita philosophy and spiritual values, see Pascale and Athos, *The Art of Japanese Management*.
102 Onitsuka, *Shigokoro*, 97.
103 Onitsuka, *Ashikkusu*.
104 Onitsuka, *Nenji, inori, tsuranuku*.
105 *Asics Annual Report*, 2006, 4.
106 *Asahi Shimbun*, 6 March 1988, 13.
107 *Kobe Shimbun*, 29 March 2008.
108 *Nihon Keizai Shimbun*, 1 May 2000, 12.
109 *Asics Yūka Shōken Hōkokusho* 2007.
110 *Mizuno Yūka Shōken Hōkokusho* 2007.
111 See Holt, Quelch, and Taylor, 'How Global Brands Compete'; Quelch, 'The Return'.

References

Abegglen, J.C. *21st-Century Japanese Management: New Systems, Lasting Values*. New York: Palgrave Macmillan, 2006.

Abegglen, J.C., and G. Stalk. *Kaisha, The Japanese Corporation*. New York: Basic Books, 1985.

Abo, T. *Hybrid Factory: The Japanese Production System in the United States*. Oxford: Oxford University Press, 1994.

Adidas Group Social and Environmental Report 2005. Retrieved from: http://www.adidas-group.com/en/investor/_downloads/pdf/SOE/SOE_2005_e.pdf.

Adler, P.S. 'Hybridization: Human Resource Management at Two Toyota Transplants'. In *Remade in America: Transplanting and Transforming Japanese Management Systems*, edited by J.K. Liker, W.M. Fruin and P.S. Adler, 75–116. Oxford: Oxford University Press, 1999.

Amis, J. 'Beyond Sport: Imaging and Re-imaging a Transnational Brand'. In *Sport and Corporate Nationalisms*, edited by M.L. Silk, D.L. Andrews and C.L. Cole, 143–65. Oxford: Berg, 2005.

Amis, J. 'Interviewing for Case Study Research'. In *Qualitative Methods in Sports Studies*, edited by D.L. Andrews, D.S. Mason and M.L. Silk, 104–38. Oxford: Berg Publishers, 2005.

Andrews, D.L., B. Carrington, S.J. Jackson and Z. Mazur. 'Jordanscapes: A Preliminary Analysis of the Global Popular'. *Sociology of Sport Journal* 13, no. 4 (1996): 428–57.

Aoki, M. *Information, Incentives, and Bargaining in the Japanese Economy*. New York: Cambridge University Press, 1988.

Appadurai, A. 'Disjuncture and Difference in the Global Cultural Economy'. *Theory, Culture and Society* 7 (1990): 295–310.

Asics Annual Report 2006. Retrieved from: http://www.asics.com/investors/index_G.html.

Asics CSR Report 2006 and 2007. Retrieved from: http://www.asics.co.jp/environment/index.html.

Asics Yūka Shōken Hōkokusho 2003–2007. Retrieved from: http://www.asics.co.jp/ir/index.html.

Banjeri, K., and R. Sambhaya. 'Vertical Keiretsu and International Market Entry: The Case of the Japanese Automobile Ancillary Industry'. *Journal of International Business Studies* 27, no. 1 (1996): 89–113.

Beechler, S. 'International Management Control in Multinational Corporations'. *ASEAN Economic Bulletin* 9, no. 2 (1992): 149–68.

Bell, D. *The Coming of Post-Industrial Society: A Venture in Social Forecasting*. New York: Basic Books, 1973.

Bhappu, A.D. 'The Japanese Family: An Institutional Logic for Japanese Corporate Networks and Japanese Management'. *The Academy of Management Review* 25, no. 2 (2000): 409–15.

Carroll, A.B. 'The Pyramid of Corporate Social Responsibility: Toward the Moral Management of Organizational Stakeholders'. *Business Horizons* 34 (1991): 39–48.

Castells, M. *The Rise of the Network Society*. Cambridge, MA: Blackwell Publishers, 1996.

Clegg, S., and T. Kono. 'Trends in Japanese Management: An Overview of Embedded Continuities and Disembedded Discontinuities'. *Asia Pacific Journal of Management* 19, no. 2–3 (2002): 269–85.

Donnelly, P. 'The Local and the Global: Globalization in the Sociology of Sport'. *Journal of Sport and Social Issues* 20, no. 3 (1996): 239–57.

Dore, R.P. *Taking Japan Seriously*. Stanford: Stanford University Press, 1987.

Dyer, J.H., and W.G. Ouchi. 'Japanese-Style Partnerships: Giving Companies a Competitive Edge'. *Sloan Management Review* 35, no. 1 (1993): 51–63.

Fair Labor Association. *2006 Annual Public Report*. Retrieved from: http://www.fairlabor.org/all/2006PublicReport.pdf, 2006.

Frenkel, S.J. 'Globalization, Athletic Footwear Commodity Chains and Employment Relations in China'. *Organization Studies* 22, no. 4 (2001): 531–62.

Fruin, W.M. *The Japanese Enterprise System: Competitive Strategies and Cooperative Structures*. Oxford: Oxford University Press, 1992.

Gerlach, M.L., and J.R. Lincoln. 'The Organization of Business Networks in the United States and Japan'. In *Networks and Organizations: Structure, Form, and Action*, edited by N. Nohria and R.G. Eccles, 491–520. Boston: Harvard Business School Press, 1992.

Goldman, R., and S. Papson. *Sign Wars: The Cluttered Landscape of Advertising*. New York: Guilford Press, 1996.

Goldman, R., and S. Papson. *Nike Culture: The Sign of the Swoosh*. London: SAGE Publications, 1998.

Grainger, A., and S.J. Jackson. 'Sports Marketing and the Challenges of Globalization: A Case Study of Cultural Resistance in New Zealand'. *International Journal of Sports Marketing & Sponsorship* 2, no. 2 (2000): 111–25.

Gregersen, H.B., and J.S. Black. 'Multiple Commitments upon Repatriation: The Japanese Experience'. *Journal of Management* 22, no. 2 (1996): 209–29.

Harrison, B. 'The Dark Side of Flexible Production'. *National Productivity Review* 13, no. 4 (1994): 479–501.

Hatvany, N., and V. Pucik. 'Japanese Management Practices and Productivity'. *Organizational Dynamics* 9, no. 4 (1981): 5–21.

Hayashi, M. 'A Historical Review of Japanese Management Theories: The Search for a General Theory of Japanese Management'. *Asian Business & Management* 1, no. 2 (2002): 189–207.

Hofstede, G. 'Management Scientists Are Human'. *Management Science* 40, no. 1 (1994): 4–13.

Holt, D.B., J.A. Quelch, and E.L. Taylor. 'How Global Brands Compete'. *Harvard Business Review* 82, no. 9 (2004): 68–75.

Ito, T. 'Japan and the Asian Economies: A "Miracle" in Transition'. *Brookings Papers on Economic Activity* 2 (1996): 205–72.

Jackson, S.J., and D.L. Andrews. 'Between and Beyond the Global and the Local: American Popular Sporting Culture in New Zealand'. *International Review for the Sociology of Sport* 34, no. 1 (1999): 31–42.

Jackson, S.J., R. Batty, and J. Scherer. 'Transnational Sport Marketing at the Global/Local Nexus: The Adidasification of the New Zealand All Blacks'. *International Journal of Sports Marketing & Sponsorship* 3, no. 2 (2001): 185–201.

Johnston, S., and L. McAlevey. 'Stable Sharcholdings and Japan's Bubble Economy: An Historical Overview'. *Strategic Management Journal* 19 (1998): 1101–7.

Kawamura, T. 'Characteristics of the Japanese Production System and Its International Transfer Model'. In *Hybrid Factory: The Japanese Production System in the United States*, edited by T. Abo, 26–57. Oxford: Oxford University Press, 1994.

Kenny, M. 'Transplantation?: A Comparison of Japanese Television Assembly Plants in Japan and the United States'. In *Remade in America: Transplanting and Transforming Japanese Management Systems*, edited by J.K. Liker, W.M. Fruin and P.S. Adler, 256–93. Oxford: Oxford University Press, 1999.

Klein, N. *No Logo: Taking Aim at the Brand Bullies*. New York: Picador, 1999.

Knight, P. 'Global Manufacturing: The Nike Story Is Just Good Business'. *Vital Speeches of the Day* 64, no. 20 (1998): 637–40.

Korzeniewicz, M. 'Commodity Chains and Marketing Strategies: Nike and the Global Athletic Footwear Industry'. In *Commodity Chains and Global Capitalism*, edited by G. Gereffi and M. Korzeniewicz, 247–61. Westport, Conn.: Greenwood Press, 1994.

Liker, J.K. *The Toyota Way: 14 Management Principles from the World's Greatest Manufacturer*. New York: McGraw-Hill, 2004.

Liker, J.K., W.M. Fruin, and P.S. Adler. 'Bringing Japanese Management Systems to the United States: Transplantation or Transformation?'. In *Remade in America: Transplanting and Transforming Japanese Management Systems*, edited by J.K. Liker, W.M. Fruin and P.S. Adler, 3–35. Oxford: Oxford University Press, 1999.

Lincoln, J.R., and A.L. Kalleberg. *Culture, Control, and Commitment: A Study of Work Organization and Work Attitudes in the U.S. and Japan*. Cambridge, UK: Cambridge University Press, 1990.

Lincoln, J.R., and Y. Nakata. 'The Transformation of the Japanese Employment System Special Issue: Dynamics of Asian Workplaces'. *Work and Occupations* 24, no. 1 (1997): 33–55.

Maguire, J. *Global Sport: Identities, Societies, Civilizations*. Cambridge, UK: Polity Press, 1999.

Matsui, H. *Sekai saisoku no kutsu o tsukure!: Jōshiki o kutsugaese! Suetsugu Shingo o sasaeru Mizuno sutaffu tachi no chōsen*. Tokyo: Kobunsha, 2004.

McCormick, K. 'Whatever Happened to "the Japanese Model"?'. *Asian Business & Management* 3, no. 4 (2004): 371–93.

McGuire, J., and S. Dow. 'The Persistence and Implications of Japanese Keiretsu Organization'. *Journal of International Business Studies* 34 (2003): 374–88.

McKenna, R. 'Marketing Is Everything'. *Harvard Business Review* 69, no. 1 (1991): 65–79.

Mizuno CSR Report 2006 and 2007. Retrieved from: http://www.mizuno.co.jp/csr/pdf/index.html.

Mizuno Yūka Shōken Hōkokusho 2003–2007. Retrieved from: http://www.mizuno.co.jp/about/finance/yuho/index.html.

Monden, Y. *Toyota Production System: Practical Approach to Production Management*. Atlanta, Ga.: Institute of Industrial Engineers, 1983.

Murakami, Y. 'Ie Society as a Pattern of Civilization: Response to Criticism'. *Journal of Japanese Studies* 11, no. 2 (1985): 401–21.

Nakane, C. *Japanese Society*. Berkeley: University of California Press, 1970.

Nike FY04 Corporate Responsibility Report. Retrieved from: http://www.nike.com/nikebiz/nikeresponsibility/pdfs/color/Nike_FY04_CR_report.pdf, 2005.

Nishiguchi, T. *Strategic Industrial Sourcing*. New York: Oxford University Press, 1994.

Oaklander, H. 'The Canon Case'. *Japan Forum* 9, no. 2 (1997): 149–53.

Oliver, N., and B. Wilkinson. *The Japanization of British industry: New developments in the 1990s*. Oxford: Blackwell, 1992.

Onitsuka, K. *Ashikkusu Onitsuka Kihachiro no keiei shinan*. Tokyo: Chichi Publishing Co., Ltd., 2000.

Onitsuka, K. *Nenji, inori, tsuranuku: Motomeru kokoro ga seikō o michibiku*. Osaka: Brain Center Inc., 2001.

Onitsuka, K. *Shigokoro ga nai kara mina ga ikiru*. Tokyo: Nippon Jitsugyo Publishing, 1987.

Onitsuka, K. *Watashi no rirekisho – Onitsuka Kihachiro*. Tokyo: Nikkei Inc., 1991.

Ouchi, W.G. *Theory Z: How American Business Can Meet the Japanese Challenge*. Reading, MA: Addison-Wesley Publishing Company, Inc., 1981.

Oxfam International. *Offside! Labor Rights and Sportswear Production in Asia*. Retrieved from: http://www.oxfam.org/en/files/offside_labor_report/download, 2006.

Pascale, R., and A.G. Athos. *The Art of Japanese Management: Applications for American Executives*. New York: Simon and Schuster, 1981.

Pil, F.K., and J.P. MacDuffie. 'Transferring Competitive Advantage across Borders: A Study of Japanese Auto Transplants in North America'. In *Remade in America: Transplanting and Transforming Japanese Management Systems*, edited by J.K. Liker, W.M. Fruin and P.S. Adler, 39–74. Oxford: Oxford University Press, 1999.

Quelch, J. 'The Return of the Global Brand'. *Harvard Business Review* 81, no. 8 (2003): 22–3.

Robertson, R. *Globalization: Social Theory and Global Culture*. London: Sage, 1992.

Robertson, R. 'Glocalization: Time-Space and Homogeneity-Heterogeneity'. In *Global Modernities*, edited by M. Featherstone, S. Lash and R. Robertson, 25–44. London: Sage, 1995.

Sampler, J.L. 'Redefining Industry Structure for the Information Age'. *Strategic Management Journal* 19 (1998): 343–55.

Schaede, U. 'What Happened to the Japanese Model?'. *Review of International Economics* 12, no. 2 (2004): 277–94.

Silk, M., and D.L. Andrews. 'Beyond a Boundary?: Sport, Transnational Advertising, and the Reimagining of National Culture'. *Journal of Sport & Social Issues* 25, no. 2 (2001): 180–201.

Stewart, T.A., and A.P. Raman. 'Lessons from Toyota's Long Drive'. *Harvard Business Review* 85, no. 7/8 (2007): 74–83.

Strasser, J.B., and L. Becklund. *Swoosh: The Unauthorized Story of Nike and the Men Who Played There*. New York: HarperBusiness, 1993.

Tolich, M., M. Kenny, and N. Biggart. 'Managing the Managers: Japanese Management Strategies in the USA'. *Journal of Management Studies* 36, no. 5 (1999): 587–607.

Vogel, E.F. *Japan as Number One: Lessons for America*. Cambridge, MA: Harvard University Press, 1979.

Vogel, S.K. *Japan, Remodeled: How Government and Industry Are Reforming Japanese Capitalism*. Ithaca: Cornell University Press, 2006.

Willigan, G.E. 'High-Performance Marketing: An Interview with Nike's Phil Knight'. *Harvard Business Review* 70, no. 4 (1992): 90–101.

Womack, J., D.T. Jones, and D. Roos. *The Machine That Changed the World*. New York: Rawson Associates, Macmillan, 1990.

Yuzawa, T. 'Japanese Business Strategies in Perspective'. In *Japanese Business Success: The Evolution of a Strategy*, edited by T. Yuzawa, 1–22, New York: Routledge, 1994.

Zadek, S. 'The Path to Corporate Responsibility'. *Harvard Business Review* 82, no. 12 (2004): 125–32.

Sport business and social capital: a contradiction in terms?

Ramón Spaaij[a] and Hans Westerbeek[b,c]

[a]La Trobe Refugee Research Centre and School of Social Sciences, Faculty of Humanities and Social Sciences, La Trobe University, Victoria, Australia; [b]Institute of Sport, Exercise and Active Living, Victoria University, Melbourne, Australia; [c]Free University of Brussels, Brussels, Belgium

Sport's potential for the creation and maintenance of social capital is well established. The role that sport business organizations (can) play in social capital formation nevertheless remains unclear and underspecified. This article seeks to establish a link between the activities executed by sport business organizations and the different species of social capital that these activities may generate. It is first argued that sport business organizations, like any other organizations, engage to varying extents in activities that are related to their social responsibilities. These activities can lead to the production of bonding, bridging and linking social capital. We extend this discussion by arguing that, dependent on the orientation of the sport business organization (profit seeking or surplus seeking), they will try to exploit opportunities in different markets for social capital that, in one way or another, will advance their business objectives. A differentiated approach to the relationship between sport business and social capital is therefore necessary.

Introduction

At first glance sport business appears at odds with, if not diametrically opposed to, the often-praised concept of social capital. Sport business organizations are essentially concerned with maximizing economic capital. As such, they tend to be regarded as emblematic of the neoliberal capitalist movement or, as Andrews notes, 'an important arm of the global capitalist order'.[1] Social capital, on the other hand, highlights the benefits that accrue from meaningful social relationships based on social trust and generalized reciprocity. While the former is seen by critics as maintaining or exacerbating social inequalities, the latter is often advocated as a vehicle for reducing such inequalities and for enhancing community spirit and well-being. In this article, we critically examine these arguments by addressing the capacity of sport business to contribute to social capital. Acknowledging the opportunities for social change and social reform that are (re)presented by, and through, contemporary sport,[2] we seek to identify the ways in which sport business organizations promote or erode the creation and transference of social capital.

This article is divided into three parts. The first part provides a definition of sport business and examines the main features of contemporary sport business. In the second part we critically examine the concept of social capital and its applications to sport. The final part of this article considers the role of sport business in the promotion of corporate social responsibility and social capital. It discusses two case studies that highlight different means and forms of civic engagement available to sport business organizations: Nike and the Homeless World Cup. In doing so, we seek to establish a link between the activities executed by sport business organizations and the different species of social capital that these activities may generate.

Defining sport business

For the purpose of this paper we define sport as activities that require physical exertion and that are structured and standardized according to internationally agreed rules and regulations.[3] We depart from the formal, more restrictive definition of sport in separating organized (competitive) sport from sporting activities that are mainly non-competitive and played during leisure time as recreational activities. Hence, we propose a separation between organized sport and unorganized sport in order to describe the two principal markets that sport organizations, or organizations that produce sport products, aim to do business in. In regard to business we refer to definitions provided in the online Compact Oxford English dictionary where 'business' is described as 'a commercial activity' or as 'a commercial organization' and 'commercial' in turn is defined as 'making or intended to make a profit'. Finally, 'profit' is defined as 'a financial gain' or as an 'advantage; benefit'. Although many organizations that operate in the sport industry are not seeking profit to distribute to investors or shareholders, they are seeking to make a financial surplus that is used in the process of further popularizing and professionalizing the sport itself. We therefore propose a separation between sport organizations that seek a profit and sport organizations that seek to make a surplus. We feel that, increasingly, surplus-seeking sport organizations operate as if they were a profit-seeker in order to acquire and access competitive funding resources. Hence, they also operate as sport business organizations. Organizations that use sport as a platform of communication – most commonly known as sport sponsors – are not considered to be sport business organizations as their core production and delivery of goods and services does not centre on sport.

The above definitions allow us to come up with the following examples of profit-seeking sport business:

- sporting goods manufacturing and sales companies (e.g. Nike);
- sport consulting companies (e.g. TEAM marketing);
- sport event companies (e.g. IMG);
- non-government media companies (e.g. News Corporation);
- privately or shareholder owned sporting franchises or teams (e.g. Manchester United).

Some examples of surplus-seeking sport business are:

- international and national sport governing bodies (e.g. IOC);
- government-owned media companies (e.g. BBC);
- government departments for sport policy and development (e.g. Australian Sports Commission);
- elite sport development and training institutes (e.g. Australian Institute of Sport);
- development organizations that use sport as the principal platform (e.g. Homeless World Cup).

With this broad conception of sport business in mind, we will now turn our attention to some of the key debates in regard to the concept of social capital and its applications to sport.

Social capital: concept and applications

Social capital is a contested concept. It has become a kind of catch-all label that groups together a wide range of issues and applications. There is no single, generally accepted definition of social capital. Bourdieu's approach has particularly influenced the way in which the concept is used in this article.[4] Bourdieu's usage of social capital 'is designed to address the way in which social capital is part of a wider set of structural relations and subjective beliefs that are bound up with inequalities of resources, and hence with inequalities of power'.[5] These inequalities are key to understanding the ways in which different species of capital are generated in and through sport in particular social contexts. However, Bourdieu's approach is slightly sketchy and incomplete. For example, his theory remains rather one-dimensional as it acknowledges almost exclusively the social capital of the privileged.[6] To correct this imbalance, we draw selectively on other approaches to social capital, including those developed by Robert Putnam, Alejandro Portes and Nan Lin.

Social capital is generally viewed to stand for 'the ability of actors to secure benefits by virtue of membership in social networks or other social structures'.[7] Social capital refers to a kind of 'resource to action' that is produced by, and invested in, social interactions and relationships by social actors for their individual and mutual benefit.[8] Social capital is relational rather than being the exclusive property of any one individual. It is mainly a public good in that it is shared by a group, and it is produced by societal investments of time and effort, but in a less direct fashion than is economic or cultural capital. Social capital is, in Bourdieu's view, 'the sum of the resources, actual or virtual, that accrue to an individual or a group by virtue of possessing a durable network of more or less institutionalized relationships of mutual acquaintance and recognition'.[9] For Bourdieu,[10] social capital is not independent from other forms of capital, but can actually help to facilitate economic and cultural capital.

Lin identifies four explanations as to why social connections may enhance the outcomes of actions:

–   they may facilitate the flow of *information*, providing a social agent (i.e. individual, group, organization) with useful information about opportunities and choices otherwise not available;
–   they may exert *influence* on those (e.g. recruiters or supervisors of an organization) who play a critical role in decisions (e.g. hiring or promotion) involving the social agent;
–   they may be conceived as certifications of the individual's *social credentials*, some of which reflect the individual's accessibility to resources through social networks and relations;
–   they are expected to *reinforce identity* and recognition, providing not only emotional support but also public acknowledgement of one's claim to certain resources.[11]

These four elements may explain why social capital works in instrumental and expressive actions not accounted for in economic or cultural capital. At the heart of the concept are norms of trust and generalized reciprocity.[12] Trust refers to the extent to which there are shared beliefs that people will take account of the interests of others in their actions. Reciprocity corresponds to the extent to which there are expectations that good deeds done will ultimately be returned. Trust, belief in reciprocity, norms and commitments can be measured as attitudes of individuals. However, social capital exists in relationships; it is present to the extent that these attitudes are held in common.[13]

In recent years, this approach to social capital has been stretched considerably to include the formation or loss of social capital at the level of entire communities or nations. In macro-level approaches, the concept of social capital is inflated to become an attribute of the 'community' itself. From this perspective, the benefits of social capital accrue not so much to individuals as to the collectivity as a whole.[14] At the wider community level, social capital is seen to contribute to social cohesion and harmony, economic and social development, lower crime rates and more effective democratic procedures.[15] This conceptual stretch was initiated by Robert Putnam in his studies of social and civic engagement in the United States and Italy.[16] Putnam's work has been well cited in the literature and has helped place social capital as a central policy concern for national governments as well as international organizations, such as the World Bank and the Asian Development Bank.[17]

Putnam argues that, as the only changeable form of capital, policy should be aimed at increasing social capital: 'precisely because poor people (by definition) have little economic capital and face formidable obstacles in acquiring human capital (that is, education), social capital is disproportionately important to their welfare'.[18] Putnam found that although the United States appears rich in terms of its associations and civic life, these are rapidly eroding. He suspected a gradual demise of American 'community'. For Putnam, the touchstone of social capital is the principle of generalized reciprocity: 'I'll do this for you now, without expecting anything immediately in return and perhaps without even knowing you, confident that down the road you or someone else will return the favor'.[19] Social connections are an important means by which mutual obligations are fostered. This conceptual stretch made it possible to speak of the social capital possessed by communities or nations and the consequent structural effects on their development.

In order to accommodate the range of outcomes associated with social capital, it is necessary to recognize its multidimensional nature.[20] A popular distinction is between 'bonding' and 'bridging' social capital.[21] Bonding social capital refers to ties between like people in similar situations, such as immediate family, close friends and neighbours. Bonding social capital is viewed to promote homogeneity, and emphasizes the building of strong ties. Putnam notes that bonding social capital 'is good for undergirding specific reciprocity and mobilizing solidarity'.[22] At the same time, bonding social capital, by creating strong in-group loyalty, may also create strong out-group antagonism. Dense social connections that reinforce homogeneity are more likely to build high social walls and be less tolerant of diversity. It should therefore be remembered that social capital also has a 'downside' and can be linked to various forms of social exclusion.[23]

In contrast to bonding social capital, bridging social capital refers to more distant ties with like persons, such as loose friendships and work colleagues. Bridging social capital can generate broader identities and reciprocity. Bridging networks are viewed to be 'better for linkage to external assets and for information diffusion'.[24] Bridging is nevertheless essentially a horizontal metaphor, implying connections between people who share broadly similar demographic characteristics. A potentially negative aspect of this type of social capital is that the social connections tend to be weaker and are generally more fragile. Putnam emphasizes that bonding and bridging social capital 'are not "either-or" categories ... but "more or less" dimensions along which we can compare different forms of social capital'.[25] He contends that both forms of social capital are necessary, and can have powerful positive effects. Putnam argues that the 'right mix' is required for benefits to accrue. Further, bonding and bridging are not interchangeable and there are often tensions and trade-offs between the two forms.

A major limitation of Putnam's approach is its failure to adequately address power and resource inequalities. DeFilippis has made the important point that in Putnam's analysis 'social capital becomes divorced from other forms of capital, stripped of power relations, and imbued with the assumption that social networks are win-win relationships and that individual gains, interests, and profits are synonymous with group gains, interests, and profits'.[26] Putnam reduces social inequalities to the logical outcome of social contacts and social cohesion rather than being the result of exploitation and shortage of opportunities. Once social inequality becomes synonymous with disintegration, solving social inequality is just a matter of building more social bridges and connections.[27]

Considering this major limitation, it could be argued that social capital also has a vertical dimension, which has been termed 'linking' (or 'scaling') social capital. Linking social capital is concerned with relations between individuals and groups in different social strata.[28] Linking social capital reaches out to unlike people in dissimilar situations, such as those who are entirely outside the community, thus enabling members to leverage a far wider range of resources than are available within the community.[29] The notion of linking social capital is extended by Woolcock to include the capacity of individuals and communities to leverage resources, ideas and information from formal institutions beyond the immediate community.[30] Woolcock argues that it is different and changing combinations of bonding, bridging and linking social capital that are responsible for the range of outcomes we observe in the literature. He contends that the poor typically have a close-knit and intensive stock of bonding social capital that they leverage to 'get by', a modest endowment of the more diffuse and extensive bridging social capital typically deployed by the non-poor to 'get ahead', and almost no linking social capital enabling them to gain sustained access to formal institutions such as banks, insurance agencies and the courts. In the following section, we will examine the role that sport plays in the creation and maintenance of these different types of social capital.

Sport and social capital

The notion of social capital has informed several recent studies of sport.[31] Conversely, for those interested in social capital, sport has gradually become a more serious avenue of inquiry. A significant part of Putnam's landmark study of civic and social engagement in the United States focused on a tendency amongst an increasing number of people not to participate in traditional sports clubs.[32] At the same time, he notes the growing popularity of a few 'new' sports, such as in-line skating, snowboarding and soccer, with relatively high levels of participation. The associational nature of sport participation, and particularly sports clubs, is often seen as a forum for the creation of social capital. Jarvie argues that the 'promise in the notion of social capital is that sport and other associational activity can make a contribution to building up levels of trust in sport, culture and society and consequently contributing to democracy, community spirit and a weakening public domain.'[33]

There is strong evidence that sport provides opportunities for the development of bonding social capital. Research by Hague and Mercer in the Scottish town of Kirkcaldy demonstrates how the local football team helped to create a sense of identity and strong attachment to the locality.[34] However, some studies also point to the negative consequences of bonding social capital in sport, reflecting a more general debate on the 'downside' of social capital. Strong bonds within sports clubs can make them homogeneous in their membership and relatively hostile toward outsiders. Engagement in sport in some parts of rural Australia, for example, is sharply divided according to class, status and ethnicity. Dempsey's account of social life in a rural Australian town demonstrates the gender inequality in the creation of social capital in and through sport.[35] He points out that the greater importance given to men's over women's work is extended into non-work time, in which women are expected to subjugate their leisure activities in deference to those of their male 'breadwinner'. Women tend to find it considerably more difficult to attend training sessions or participate in sporting fixtures.

In addition, some scholars have argued that sport can foster bridging and/or linking social capital.[36] For example, Harris suggests that sport can be used to foster new friendships and social connectivity across class, religious and ethnic boundaries.[37] This can include players, coaches, volunteers and spectators, and can ultimately lead to increases in norms of trust and reciprocity.[38] Sport engagement is thus regarded as stimulating bridges or links between different groups and social networks. Yet, as Jarvie notes, 'the explanatory power of the relationship between sport and the promise of renewed forms of social capital needs to carry with it a cautionary note'.[39] For instance, there is some research that indicates that sport facilitates relatively few bridging links for minority ethnic groups.[40] The notion that sport is said to increase social capital therefore becomes problematic when it is accepted as a general or universal truth.[41] Moreover, and more importantly for the present purpose, the role that sport business organizations play, or can play, in the creation of different forms of social capital remains unclear and underspecified. It is to this theme that we now turn.

Conceptualizing corporate social responsibility and social capital in and through sport

Sport business organizations, like other business organizations, no longer submit to the classical view that they are only answerable to shareholders and that their only commitment is to the maximization of profits. Businesses today are expected to look beyond self-interest and recognize that they belong to a larger group, or society, that expects responsible participation.[42] Although many forces appear to have shaped the debate on corporate social responsibility (CSR) and corporate citizenship, the increasing globalization of business has made it an international concern. Transnational corporations seek to exploit the opportunities of globalization and capital mobility to exempt themselves from labour regulations. There is growing recognition of the widening gap between the transnational character of corporate activity and the availability of transnational regulatory structures that may be effectively used to monitor and restrain corporations irrespective of any specific territory in which they may happen to operate at a given moment.[43] Critics have raised questions of growing social inequalities, corruption, environmental degradation, unfair wages and unsafe working conditions. Alongside legal action, activists around the globe have launched numerous campaigns of public shaming to pressure transnational corporations to adopt responsible business practices.[44]

The fundamental strategy adopted by transnational corporations in the wake of various 'production scandals' that threaten their corporate image has been to become active players in the area of CSR.[45] To varying degrees, sport organizations have assumed a social responsibility orientation based on the recognition, albeit often in utilitarian terms, of their responsibilities to a multitude of 'stakeholders'. CSR can be defined as 'the adoption by a business of a strategic focus for fulfilling the economic, legal, ethical, and philanthropic responsibilities expected of it by its stakeholders'.[46] In a similar vein, Marsden and Andriof describe CSR as the satisfaction of the expectations of all societal stakeholders to maximize the company's positive impact on its social and physical environment, while providing a competitive return to its financial stakeholders.[47] The stakeholder concept personalizes social or societal responsibilities by delineating the specific groups or persons business should consider in its CSR orientation and activities. It puts 'names and faces' on the societal members or groups who are most important to business and to whom it must be responsive.[48]

From a stakeholder perspective, CSR requires organizations to consider the interests of investors, suppliers, consumers, employees, community members and the environment in discharging their profit-directed activities. New conceptions of CSR are integrated into the old models of how to successfully manage a business enterprise and how to ensure its reputation. It is increasingly recognized that having a reputation of being an ethical organization respected for its environmental and social performance is 'good for business'. In other words, CSR is positively associated with return on investment, return on assets, and sales growth.[49] Increased organizational costs caused in the short term by improved social performance would be more than offset by the long-term benefits for the organization.[50] This viewpoint is summarized in Figure 1.

The deployment of CSR in and through sport offers substantial potential for community return. The use of sport as a vehicle for contributing to corporate efforts toward social responsibility can be seen as a distinct opportunity for both the organizations in charge of sport and those that seek to use sport in their efforts to make contributions to communities. Smith and Westerbeek argue that corporations will begin to realize that sport offers powerful social structures for the disadvantaged and disenfranchised to gain a firmer foothold in a ruthlessly commercial world that the corporations have been instrumental in constructing.[51] They predict that future sport business will

> provide opportunities for corporate enterprises to recognise and deliver their local and global community obligations. This will mark a change in the deployment of some corporate resources. Community sport and social sport programmes will be amongst the beneficiaries of this corporate citizenship.'[52]

A recent article in the *Wall Street Journal* suggests that the trend among corporate enterprises to look beyond their business legacy and undertake philantrophic, community-building projects already extends to global sport business.[53] The article discusses the

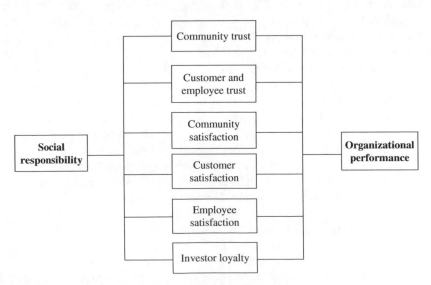

Figure 1.   The role of social responsibility in corporate performance.
Note: Adapted from Thorne McAlister, Ferrell and Ferrell, *Business and Society*, 20.

Manchester United Foundation, an independent body of Manchester United Football Club established in 2006. According to the *Wall Street Journal*, Manchester United counts over 330 million fans around the world and in 2007 netted a record $310 million in revenue, making it the richest club in the world. The Foundation, which receives funding from the club and raises its own money, centres its mission on improving football facilities, creating opportunities for youth and 'building communities'. Long before the Foundation formally began operations, Manchester United worked with UNICEF, the United Nations affiliated food and health assistance organization. The United for UNICEF campaign was launched in 1999. Projects range from China, where efforts are made to prevent trafficking in children and protect them from exploitation, to South Africa, where the focus is on raising HIV/AIDS awareness. The Manchester United Foundation is keen to lend Manchester United's well-known name to such projects. The *Wall Street Journal* also notes that many sports organizations bear in mind that over the long term their investment in community-building ventures tends to produce greater brand recognition, loyalty and revenues.[54]

The link between CSR and social capital is evident in this analysis. The social infrastructure of certain local communities is regarded to have been eroded, leading to a loss of social capital in the Putnamian sense. This viewpoint implicitly assumes that communities contain valuable social resources which might be lost if not managed and cultivated. Moreover, the very institutions that rely on communities and their constituents to achieve economic prosperity are often the very same ones that are driving their marginalization. This observation, coupled with the slipperiness of the notion of 'community' and the ongoing debate as to whether the loss of civic engagement and generalized reciprocity is specific to the United States, indicates the complexity of relationship between sport business and social capital. Among other important questions, the question is raised how far sport business organizations have actually come in contributing to the creation of social capital. Identifying the (grassroots) operations of sport business organizations and the resulting processes of social inclusion and exclusion then becomes a central task. As we indicated earlier in this paper, organizations that use sport organizations to deploy CSR, but do not produce sport themselves, are excluded from the analysis as we do not consider them to be a sport business organization.

Below we further explore the links between sport business organizations, CSR and social capital by means of two brief case studies: Nike's responses to anti-sweatshop campaigns, and a review of the Homeless World Cup, an organization set up to effect positive social change through sport. Rather than providing an exhaustive overview of social responsibilities of sport business organizations, we use these case studies to identify different modes of deploying CSR and social capital through sport. Figure 2 shows the general contours of this model, of which the case studies are only two practical examples.[55]

Nike's corporate social responsibility

Nike is probably the best example of a sport business organization that has an extreme focus on making a profit for shareholders. It is an example of sport business in the purest sense of the word, and of an organization at the vanguard of corporate innovation and marketing best practice. Nike has been in the spotlight of public interest and scrutiny more than any other sport organization. Nike has become one of the most vilified companies in the world after being subjected to anti-sweatshop campaigns that to this day continue to keep the organization on its toes. In 2005, Nike released a report on the working conditions in the 700 factories that produce its footwear and clothing. The report detailed admissions

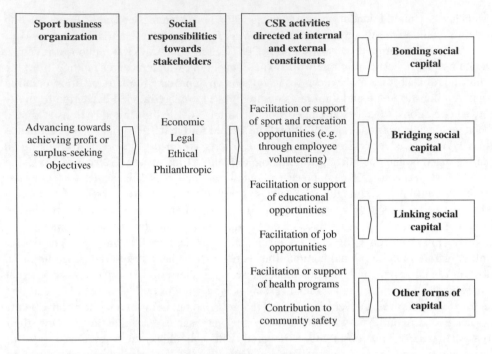

Figure 2.   Social capital formation through sport business.

of 'abusive treatment', physical and verbal, including forced overtime and restricted access to water in more than a quarter of its South Asian plants. Wages were below the legal minimum in about one quarter of factories. Michael Posner, the executive director of Human Rights First, described the report as 'an important step forward' but added: 'The facts on the ground suggest there are still enormous problems with these supply chains and factories ... what is Nike doing to change the picture and give workers more rights?'[56]

If Nike was not going to formulate its own corporate citizenship principles and policies, then the global campaign against their cheap labour practices has certainly forced the organization to do so.[57] Social responsibility is now a strategic component of its global strategy, and Nike has been a proactive partner in setting up independently monitored covenants, such as the The Fair Labour Association Charter Agreement, to which (at the time) sport business organizations such as Adidas and Reebok also signed up. Although it was the Australian-based organization Oxfam Community Aid Abroad that forced Nike to review its practice of sourcing cheap labour in a number of Asian countries, the company seems to have taken comprehensive action to improve its overall operation and its reputation as a world leading sporting goods company. Nike currently provides public information on www.nikebiz.com where a dedicated link provides access to the organization's most recent (2005–06) Corporate Responsibility Report. The 163-page report describes how, for Nike, corporate responsibility is now a catalyst for growth and innovation. The opening statement on www.nikebiz.com/responsibility/ explains that Nike:

> believe in the power of sport to unleash potential. That's why we will invest a minimum of $315 million in grants, product donations and in-kind support through 2011 to give excluded youth greater access to sport ... We'll provide Nike product, resurface old playing fields, fund community-based programs. These impacts come as we've evolved how we frame, define and

approach corporate responsibility. We see corporate responsibility as an integral part of how we can use the power of our brand, the energy and passion of our people, and the scale of our business to create meaningful change. So we've set aggressive business targets that embed our corporate responsibility goals into the company's long-term growth and innovation strategies because we believe there's no better way to achieve them than to tie them directly to our business.[58]

In its 'Let Me Play' programme Nike uses as an indicator of success 'social impact', and as a target it aims to design metrics around programmes for excluded youth around the world. The company's most recent approach to engaging with communities is best expressed in its statement regarding sport for social development:

In the past, we disbursed funds, product donations and in-kind support through a traditional philanthropy model. Our approach was more reactive than proactive, providing checks rather than building partnerships and making one-time contributions to a wide variety of projects and organizations rather than building long-term work through focused strategies. In [the financial year 2005–06] we reviewed and refocused our social investment strategies in line with our broader strategic thinking about social change and how we can help bring about social change through innovation. We refined our approach during that period, giving us a clearer set of principles, which include:

- a belief in cross-sector collaboration and partnerships as the best model of viability and scalability;
- a focus on bringing our core competencies and assets to the table in support of our partners;
- a focus on building models that are not reliant on any one partner's support and can ultimately thrive after Nike's input;
- recognition of our role in supporting high-risk, innovative initiatives through seed funding;
- supporting our partners' need to access capacity building as part of how we enable self sufficiency and sustained models of social entrepreneurship.[59]

In its corporate responsibility report Nike also outlines that:

As a company focused on young people, we considered how we could apply our core competencies to tackle some of the issues. We see clearly how sport brings health and fitness benefits. We also see further reaching benefits, including building teamwork, leadership, self-esteem, inclusion and confidence. A growing number of examples demonstrate how sport can be used to address the world's most pressing challenges, as represented by the Millennium Development Goals that cover issues as diverse as gender equity and HIV/AIDS. Although we recognize that sport by itself will not solve the world's challenges, we believe that sport and Nike's role as a funder of innovation and advocacy can help spark real change on the ground. To do so, we focus on leveraging our core business competencies, including funding, research and development, innovation, marketing, employees, products and partners.[60]

A current example of Nike's CSR activities of this kind is the organization's involvement in the Brazilian-led *Vencedoras* programme. *Vencedoras* uses a sport-based methodology that incorporates soccer and classroom activities to help girls transform sport-related skills such as teamwork, communication, discipline and a focus on results into practical employment skills. The programme provides employability, vocational, and entrepreneurial skills training in conjunction with practical work experiences, professional mentorship and community service opportunities. More than 1400 young women between the ages of 17 and 24 from economically disadvantaged communities in Brazil will participate. The Nike Foundation, a non-profit organization supported by Nike, invests $1.85 million over three years in the programme. *Vencedoras* ultimately aims to serve as a model for economic empowerment of young women in Brazil and around the world, 'empowering adolescent girls and young women to change themselves, their families, and communities everywhere'.[61] This aim reflects the Nike Foundation's commitment to 'tackling the barriers girls face at life transitions' and accelerating 'girls' economic empowerment'.[62]

There will remain strong critics of Nike's profit-driven business practices. Based on the organization's public communication and assumed leadership role in improving the workplace practices of its contractors, and on its investment in sustainable production and community-based sport programmes, it is nevertheless possible to consider Nike a sport business organization at the forefront of deploying CSR activities through sport. As such, it may contribute to building social capital. One specific way in which this appears to occur is through the organization's involvement in the Homeless World Cup (HWC). The co-founder and President of the HWC, Mel Young, argues that 'Nike is an example of a sport business that has fully integrated its corporate social responsibility activities with its core business. They support the Homeless World Cup as a citizen, not as a company. Sure, they will take the opportunity to expose their logo where they can, but their support is not "in your face" and they do it in light of their commitment to their social responsibility.'[63]

The Homeless World Cup

Mel Young is a leading social entrepreneur as recognized by the Schwab Foundation for Social Entrepreneurship. In 1993 he co-founded The Big Issue, a weekly magazine sold by homeless people on the streets of the UK. On the back of this success he co-founded the International Network of Street Papers, a global network of over 80 street papers sold in every continent, with a combined annual circulation of over 30 million.[64] The idea for the Homeless World Cup was conceived by Young and Austrian Harald Schmied when they were seeking a means for homeless people to communicate with each other across national borders. With football as an existing platform of international communication, the idea to create a world cup for homeless people seems logical yet surprisingly creative. They organized the first cup with 18 participating nations in Graz, Austria in 2003. Five years after the first HWC, 56 nations were represented at the event in Melbourne, Australia.

Rather than setting up a solid competition and qualification structure and slowly expand the event to multiple participants, Young and Schmied decided to invite anyone who wanted to participate and grow the event from the bottom up.[65] Through corporate and host city support homeless people and their support team are flown into the host city to participate in an event that focuses on togetherness, participation and engagement. All teams continue to play until the day of the final where different cups are presented to play-off winners at all levels of competition. In 2008 the first HWC for females was contested among eight teams. In Australia the road towards the HWC has sparked the emergence of street soccer programmes for homeless people in 30 different locations. Worldwide the HWC organization now supports grassroots football programmes in more than 60 nations involving more than 30,000 homeless people. The HWC headquarters in Edinburgh and the organization aims to 'be the most reputable organization to use sports as a means for social inclusion, involving one million players by 2012'. Part of the organization is the HWC Foundation and in order to achieve its main aim the HWC subscribes to underpinning principles such as:

- Responsiveness and commitment to social impact;
- Accountability by measuring our social impact;

- Focusing on core competencies and partnering with the best organizations in specific areas as a key driving force;
- Enabling grass root programs to deliver, reach their full potential and be inspired and able to grow.[66]

Based on a survey among participants conducted at the event in Copenhagen in 2007 it is argued on the HWC website that the HWC is creating a profound level of change. More than 94% of participants say that the HWC has a positive impact on their lives and 77% make significant changes in their lives as a direct result of their involvement, such as coming off drugs and alcohol, moving into homes, jobs, education or becoming coaches and players.[67] According to co-founder Mel Young, it only took them five years and six events to achieve street football competitions in more than 60 countries in which more than 30,000 homeless people participate. In countries such as Australia and The Netherlands there are weekly competitions, where homeless people now have a regular purpose to get together, to play, to talk, and have something to look forward to. They not only engage with each other, but also with the many volunteers and professionals who assist in organizing the competitions.

Social capital markets in the sport industry

Where Nike is a good example of a sport business organization driven by the profit imperative, the HWC provides an insight into the workings of a sport business organization that seeks surplus resources in order to better advance its aims towards social inclusion and social development. Both Nike and the HWC, as two quite different types of sport business organizations, fit the model presented in Figure 2: they either seek profit or surplus funding; they are obliged to deliver on their social responsibilities to different stakeholders; they engage in what can be defined as CSR activities directed at internal and external constituents; and through these CSR activities they may create one or more species of social capital.

It is in the focus on stakeholders, and in the type(s) of social capital that they are most likely to generate, that Nike and the HWC significantly differ. As a profit seeker, Nike's focus remains on delivering economically to its main stakeholders: shareholders. The HWC, on the other hand, is a surplus-seeking organization which focuses on ethical and philanthropic responsibilities towards a much broader and more diffuse range of stakeholders. In order to further theorize this vital difference we argue that to some degree social capital is a scarce and valuable resource and as such there is a competitive marketplace where different types of social capital may be traded. We have conceptualized that marketplace in Figure 3. As an extension of Figure 2, where social capital is an undifferentiated outcome of activities of all sport business organizations, in Figure 3 we return to our earlier definition of sport business organizations and argue that the type of social capital that is most effectively produced depends on the type of sport business organization that seeks to generate it as part of its business process.

Following our earlier discussion of the multidimensional nature of social capital it can be argued that where social capital is an intended or unintended outcome of CSR activities (see Figure 2), the types of social capital produced depend largely on two factors: firstly, on the organization's business objectives; and secondly, on the networks that the organization has available, is likely to tap and/or actively seeks to establish. In other words, sport business organizations aim to exploit opportunities in different markets for social capital that, in one way or another, will advance their business objectives.

		Sport	
		Organized sport	**Unorganized sport**
BUSINESS	**Profit-seeking sport business**	FOCUS ON linking social capital PART OF CSR (hidden marketing message)	FOCUS ON bonding/bridging social capital PART OF community engagement (altruism?)
	Surplus-seeking sport business	FOCUS ON bridging social capital PART OF social responsibilities (core business)	FOCUS ON bonding social capital PART OF CSR (hidden marketing message)

Figure 3.   A typology of social capital markets in the sport industry.

For a profit-seeking sport business organization it is critical to maximize the return on its investment of resources when partnering with organized sport. For example, Nike, as a profit seeker, has entered into a partnership with the HWC (a surplus seeker) as part of its corporate responsibility strategy. Nike can be viewed as contributing to the creation of linking social capital by building relations between individuals and groups in different social strata where socially disadvantaged people, such as homeless people, can start leveraging opportunities that would not have been available to them without the event and its corporate supporter. Although Nike may argue that its CSR activities are part of wider community responsibility, it can still be contended that Nike will benefit from its seemingly altruistic commitment to the homeless community (the actual relationship is with organized sport, not with the homeless community!). It is likely that the perceptions about the Nike brand will be positively reinforced through its association with the HWC. This is why altruism as the driving force of involvement is question-marked at the level of profit-seeking support of unorganized sport, as exemplified next.

Nike's involvement in *Vencedoras* is a good example of sport business organizations' potential contribution to bonding or bridging social capital (as well as cultural capital). It can be argued that through CRS activities (i.e. creating local football facilities) Nike invests in bonding social capital by means of strengthening ties between like people in similar situations, such as families and local community members. Like the Manchester United Foundation noted earlier, the company also invests in the formation of bridging social capital by contributing to broader flows of information and opportunities for reciprocity, for example through sport development workers or health care professionals associated with sponsored projects. The bridging networks that are formed may enhance linkage to external assets and allow for more effective information diffusion, social credentials and skills development. It can be argued that, notwithstanding the potential 'downsides' mentioned earlier, increases in bonding and bridging social capital can provide valuable resources for both individual community members and disadvantaged communities as a whole, and also for the profit-seeking organization that invests in its creation. It not only improves the organization's public image, but communities that are richer in social capital may also be more likely to generate economic resources that could be spent on consumer goods and services. Hence, altruism in the strictest sense of the word is unlikely to apply to profit-seeking sport business organizations that become involved as sponsors, CSR partners or 'philanthropists' in either organized or unorganized sport.

For a surplus-seeking sport business, such as a national or international sport governing body, it is part of the organization's social responsibilities to maintain active links with local communities and to contribute to the development of individual (sport organization) members. It can be argued that bridging networks have been the backbone of successful membership-based sport organizations since their very inception. To operate in the market for bridging social capital (by definition this involves relationships beyond family, close friends and neighbours) is essential for surplus-seeking sport business organizations as it is at the core of their service provision. Membership of a sports club can generate broader identities and reciprocity, as well as social networks that allow linkage to external assets and are used for wider information diffusion. As noted earlier, sports club members continue to broadly share similar demographic characteristics. However, surplus-seeking sport business organizations also are forced to compete fiercely for the favours of existing and new members and, as such, are increasingly engaging in activities that will make them looked upon favourably by the community at large. Not only is this communicated as part of their wider responsibilities to the community, but it also positions them favourably in the minds of potential funding agencies, and potential members or what some sport organizations now would refer to as 'customers'. This is why we propose that surplus-seeking sport business organizations engage in CSR-like activities in order to broaden their market reach, and to position themselves for more favourable access to market resources and customers. Much like Nike's hidden marketing message through association with the HWC, FIFA will invest in grassroots football projects around the world to ensure that football rather than competing sport offerings are considered to be the number one choice of consumers.

Conclusion

In this article, we have sought to locate sport business within contemporary debates on sport's potential for the creation and maintenance of social capital. We have done so by examining the CSR activities deployed by transnational sport business organizations and the different species of social capital that these activities may produce. We have argued that through acting on their social responsibilities directed at internal and external constituents, sport business organizations can make contributions to the creation and transference of bonding, bridging and linking social capital. However, we have also shown that sport business organizations aim to exploit opportunities in different markets for social capital that, in one way or another, will advance their business objectives. A differentiated approach to the relationship between sport business and social capital is therefore necessary. The type(s) of social capital produced depend largely on two factors: firstly, on the organization's business objectives, and secondly, on the networks that the organization has available, is likely to tap and/or actively seeks to establish.

The case studies on Nike and the HWC suggest that the deployment of CSR in and through sport offers substantial potential for community return. The use of sport as a vehicle for contributing to corporate efforts toward social responsibility can be seen as a distinct opportunity for both the organizations in charge of sport and those that seek to use sport in their efforts to make contributions to communities. The question here, of course, is the extent to which sport business organizations actually commit to such efforts. CSR activities continue to be mainly self-regulated and non-enforceable; there are no formalized CSR regulations at the supranational level. Many sport business organizations, critics would claim, appear to be involved in CSR principally for goodwill and reputation, and for furthering business objectives (i.e. financial gain). Moreover, it could be argued that efforts to deploy CSR activities aimed at contributing to social capital and community development operate on a very limited scale when compared to the massive financial profit these sport business organizations produce.

Arguably, it does not really matter whether the production of social capital is largely dependent on first generating an economic profit or surplus, as long as corporate governors realize that economic gains will ultimately be higher if the stock of social capital is increased as well. A strong focus on the financial success of organizations is reasonable given their need to survive in a competitive business environment, but improved knowledge of the relationship between social gains and economic success may well lead to increasing investment in the achievement of social outcomes. This is likely to be beneficial for both profit seekers and those organizations that aim to reinvest surplus in the advancement of non-profit objectives.

Notes

[1] Andrews, 'Sport in the Late Capitalist Moment', 3.
[2] Jarvie, Sport, *Culture and Society*, 343.
[3] Compare Shilbury, Deane and Kellett, *Sport Management in Australia*.
[4] Bourdieu, 'Forms of Capital'.
[5] Field, *Social Capital and Lifelong Learning*, 19.
[6] Ibid., 21.
[7] Portes, 'Social Capital', 6.
[8] Hogan and Owen, 'Social Capital, Active Citizenship', 81.
[9] Bourdieu and Wacquant, *An Invitation to Reflexive Sociology*, 119.
[10] Bourdieu, 'Forms of Capital'.
[11] Lin, *Social Capital*, 19–20.
[12] Putnam, *Bowling Alone*.
[13] Black and Hughes, *Identification and Analysis*, 37.
[14] Portes, 'Two Meanings of Social Capital', 3.
[15] Field, *Social Capital*.
[16] Putnam, 'Bowling Alone'; Putnam, 'Prosperous Community'.
[17] For example: Grootaert, *Social Capital*; Dasgupta and Serageldin, *Social Capital*; Asian Development Bank, *Social Capital*.
[18] Putnam, *Bowling Alone*, 318.
[19] Ibid., 134.
[20] Woolcock, 'Place of Social Capital'.
[21] Gittell and Vidal, *Community Organizing*, 10; Putnam, *Bowling Alone*, 22–3.
[22] Putnam, *Bowling Alone*, 22.
[23] Portes and Landolt, 'Downside of Social Capital'; Field, *Social Capital*.
[24] Putnam, *Bowling Alone*, 22.
[25] Ibid., 23.
[26] DeFilippis, 'Myth of Social Capital', 800.
[27] Blokland, 'Waarom de Populariteit van Putnam Zorgwekkend is', 107–8.
[28] Healy and Côté, *The Well-being of Nations*, 42.
[29] Woolcock, 'Social Capital and Economic Development', 13–4.
[30] Woolcock, 'Place of Social Capital'.
[31] For example: Seippel, 'Sport and Social Capital'; Coalter, 'Sports Clubs'; Persson, 'Social Capital'; Nicholson and Hoye, *Sport and Social Capital*.
[32] Putnam, *Bowling Alone*.
[33] Jarvie, *Sport, Culture and Society*, 335.
[34] Hague and Mercer, 'Geographical Memory'.
[35] Dempsey, *A Man's Town*.
[36] For example: Janssens, 'Education through Sport'; Coalter 'Sport-in-development'.
[37] Harris, 'Civil Society'.
[38] Tonts, 'Competitive Sport', 139.
[39] Jarvie, *Sport, Culture and Society*, 335.

[40] Veldboer, Boonstra and Krouwel, 'Eenheid en Verdeeldheid op het Veld'.

[41] Jarvie, Sport, *Culture and Society*, 335.

[42] Thorne McAlister, Ferrell and Ferrell, *Business and Society*, 4.

[43] Shamir, 'Corporate Social Responsibility', 95–6.

[44] See for example Klein, *No Logo*; Starr, *Naming the Enemy*; Starr, *Global Revolt*.

[45] Shamir, 'Corporate Social Responsibility', 100.

[46] Thorne McAlister, Ferrell and Ferrell, *Business and Society*, 4.

[47] Marsden and Andriof, 'Towards an Understanding'.

[48] Carroll, 'Pyramid of Corporate Social Responsibility', 43; Carroll, 'Corporate Social Responsibility', 290.

[49] Thorne McAlister, Ferrell and Ferrell, *Business and Society*, 23.

[50] Norris and Innes, *Corporate Social Responsibility*.

[51] Smith and Westerbeek, *Sport Business Future*, 5; see also Westerbeek and Smith, *Sport Business*.

[52] Ibid.

[53] 'The Business of Sport: Beyond the Playing Field', *Wall Street Journal*, January 8, 2009.

[54] Ibid.

[55] The model builds on Smith and Westerbeek, 'Sport as a Vehicle '. The four general types of social responsibilities outlined in Figure 2 are derived from Carroll, 'Pyramid of Corporate Social Responsibility'.

[56] *The Sydney Morning Herald*, 16 May 2005.

[57] Litvin, *Empires of Profit*; Sage, 'Sporting Goods Industry'; Rodríguez-Garavito, 'Nike's Law'.

[58] Nike, 'Nike Responsibility', http://www.epl.org/library/strategic-plan-00.html (accessed 2 December 2008).

[59] Nike, *Innovate for a Better World*, 78.

[60] Ibid., 76.

[61] Partners of the Americas, 'Goals for Girls', 2.

[62] Nike, *Innovate for a Better World*, 90.

[63] Mel Young, interview by the author, December 2008.

[64] Homeless World Cup, 'Mel Young: Serial Social Entrepreneur', http://www3.homelessworldcup.org/content/founder-biography-1 (accessed 2 December 2008).

[65] Mel Young, interview by the author, December 2008.

[66] Homeless World Cup, 'Mission', http://www3.homelessworldcup.org/content/mission (accessed 7 December 2008).

[67] Homeless World Cup, 'Mel Young: Serial Social Entrepreneur', http://www3.homelessworldcup.org/content/founder-biography-1 (2 accessed December 2008).

References

Andrews, D.L. 'Sport in the Late Capitalist Moment'. In *The Commercialisation of Sport*, edited by T. Slack, 2–28. London: Routledge, 2004.

Asian Development Bank. *Social Capital, Local Capacity Building, and Poverty Reduction*. Manila: Asian Development Bank, 2001.

Black, A., and P. Hughes. *The Identification and Analysis of Indicators of Community Strength and Outcomes*. Canberra: Australian Government Department of Family and Community Services, 2001.

Blokland, T. 'Waarom de Populariteit van Putnam Zorgwekkend is'. *Beleid en Maatschappij* 29, no. 2 (2002): 101–9.

Bourdieu, P. 'The Forms of Capital'. In *Handbook of Theory and Research for the Sociology of Education*, edited by J. Richardson, 241–58. New York: Greenwood, 1986.

Bourdieu, P., and L. Wacquant. *An Invitation to Reflexive Sociology*. Chicago: University of Chicago Press, 1992.

Carroll, A.B. 'Corporate Social Responsibility'. *Business and Society* 38 (September 1999): 268–95.

Carroll, A.B. 'The Pyramid of Corporate Social Responsibility: Toward the Moral Management of Organizational Stakeholders'. *Business Horizons* 34 (July–August 1991): 39–48.

Coalter, F. 'Sport-in-development: Development For and Through Sport?'. In *Sport and Social Capital*, edited by M. Nicholson and R. Hoye, 39–67. Oxford: Elsevier Butterworth-Heinemann, 2008.

Coalter, F. 'Sports Clubs, Social Capital and Social Regeneration: "Ill-defined Interventions with Hard to Follow Outcomes"?'. *Sport in Society* 10, no. 4 (2007): 537–59.

Dasgupta, P. and Serageldin, I., eds. *Social Capital: A Multifaceted Perspective*. Washington, DC: World Bank, 1999.

DeFilippis, J. 'The Myth of Social Capital in Community Development'. *Housing Policy Debate* 12, no. 4 (2001): 781–806.

Dempsey, K. *A Man's Town: Inequality between Men and Women in Rural Australia*. Melbourne: Oxford University Press, 1992.

Field, J. *Social Capital*. London: Routledge, 2003.

Field, J. *Social Capital and Lifelong Learning*. Bristol: Policy Press, 2005.

Gittell, R., and A. Vidal. *Community Organizing: Building Social Capital as a Development Strategy*. London: Sage, 1998.

Grootaert, C. *Social Capital: The Missing Link?* Washington, DC: World Bank, 1998.

Hague, E., and J. Mercer. 'Geographical Memory and Urban Identity in Scotland: Raith Rovers FC and Kirkcaldy'. *Geography* 83, no. 2 (1998): 105–16.

Harris, J. 'Civil Society, Physical Activity and the Involvement of Sports Sociologists in the Preparation of Physical Activity Professionals'. *Sociology of Sport Journal* 15, no. 2 (1998): 138–53.

Healy, T., and S. Côté. *The Well-being of Nations: The Role of Human and Social Capital*. Paris: OECD, 2001.

Hogan, D., and D. Owen. 'Social Capital, Active Citizenship and Political Equality in Australia'. In *Social Capital and Public Policy in Australia*, edited by I. Winter, 74–104. Melbourne: Australian Institute of Family Studies, 2000.

Janssens, J., ed. *Education through Sport: An Overview of Good Practices in Europe*. Nieuwegein: Arko Sports Media, 2004.

Jarvie, G. *Sport, Culture and Society*. London: Routledge, 2006.

Klein, N. *No Logo: Taking Aim at the Brand Bullies*. New York: Picador, 2000.

Lin, N. *Social Capital: A Theory of Social Structure and Action*. Cambridge: Cambridge University Press, 2001.

Litvin, D. *Empires of Profit: Commerce, Conquest and Corporate Responsibility*. New York and London: Texere, 2003.

Marsden, C., and J. Andriof. 'Towards an Understanding of Corporate Citizenship and How to Influence It'. *Citizenship Studies* 2, no. 2 (1998): 329–52.

Nicholson, M. and Hoye, R., eds. *Sport and Social Capital*. Oxford: Elsevier Butterworth-Heinemann, 2008.

Nike. *Innovate for a Better World:Nike: FY05-06 Corporate Responsibility Report, 2006*. http://www.nikeresponsibility.com/pdfs/bw/Nike_FY05_06_CR_Report_BW.pdf (accessed 28 November 2008).

Norris, G., and J. Innes. *Corporate Social Responsibility: Case Studies for Management Accountants*. Amsterdam: Elsevier, 2005.

Partners of the Americas. "Goals for Girls: Empowering Young Girls through Soccer". Newsletter July–September 2008. Washington: Partners of the Americas, 2008.

Persson, T. 'Social Capital and Social Responsibility in Denmark: More than Gaining Public Trust'. *International Review for the Sociology of Sport* 43, no. 1 (2008): 35–51.

Portes, A. 'Social Capital: Its Origins and Applications in Modern Sociology'. *Annual Review of Sociology* 24, no. 1 (1998): 1–24.

Portes, A. 'The Two Meanings of Social Capital'. *Sociological Forum* 15, no. 1 (2000): 1–12.

Portes, A., and P. Landholt. 'The Downside of Social Capital'. *The American Prospect* 7, no. 26 (1996): 18–22.

Putnam, R. 'Bowling Alone: America's Declining Social Capital'. *Journal of Democracy* 6, no. 1 (1995): 65–78.

Putnam, R. *Bowling Alone: The Collapse and Revival of American Community*. New York: Simon & Schuster, 2000.

Putnam, R. 'The Prosperous Community: Social Capital and Public Life'. *The American Prospect* 4, no. 13 (1993): 35–42.

Rodríguez-Garavito, C.A. 'Nike's Law: The Anti-Sweatshop Movement, Transnational Corporations, and the Struggle over International Labour Rights in the Americas'. In *Law and*

Globalization from Below: Towards a Cosmopolitan Legality, edited by B. de Sousa Santos and C.A. Rodríguez-Garavito, 64–91. Cambridge: Cambridge University Press, 2005.

Sage, G.H. 'The Sporting Goods Industry: From Struggling Entrepreneurs to National Businesses to Transnational Corporations'. In *The Commercialisation of Sport*, edited by T. Slack, 29–51. London: Routledge, 2004.

Seippel, Ø. 'Sport and Social Capital'. *Acta Sociologica* 49, no. 2 (2006): 169–83.

Shamir, R. 'Corporate Social Responsibility: A Case of Hegemony and Counter-Hegemony'. In *Law and Globalization from Below: Towards a Cosmopolitan Legality*, edited by B. de Sousa Santos and C.A. Rodríguez-Garavito, 92–113. Cambridge: Cambridge University Press, 2005.

Shilbury, D., J. Deane, and P. Kellett. *Sport Management in Australia*. 3rd ed. Melbourne: Strategic Sport Management, 2006.

Smith, A., and H. Westerbeek. 'Sport as a Vehicle for Deploying Corporate Social Responsibility'. *The Journal of Corporate Citizenship* 25, no. 1 (2007): 43–54.

Smith, A., and H. Westerbeek. *The Sport Business Future*. Basingstoke: Palgrave, 2004.

Starr, A. *Global Revolt: A Guide to the Movements against Globalization*. London: Zed Books, 2005.

Starr, A. *Naming the Enemy: Anti-corporate Movements Confront Globalization*. London: Zed Books, 2000.

Thorne McAlister, D., O.C. Ferrell, and L. Ferrell. *Business and Society: A Strategic Approach to Social Responsibility*. Boston: Houghton Mifflin Company, 2007.

Tonts, M. 'Competitive Sport and Social Capital in Rural Australia'. *Journal of Rural Studies* 21, no. 2 (2005): 137–49.

Veldboer, L., N. Boonstra, and A. Krouwel. 'Eenheid en Verdeeldheid op het Veld: De Januskop van Sport'. In *De Mixfactor: Integratie en Segregatie in Nederland*, edited by L. Veldboer, J.W. Duyvendak, and C. Bouw, 71–80. Amsterdam: Boom, 2007.

Westerbeek, H., and A. Smith. *Sport Business in the Global Martketplace*. Basingstoke: Palgrave, 2003.

Woolcock, M. 'The Place of Social Capital in Understanding Social and Economic Outcomes'. *Isuma: Canadian Journal of Policy Research* 2, no. 1 (2001): 1–17.

Woolcock, M. 'Social Capital and Economic Development: Towards a Theoretical Synthesis and Policy Framework'. *Theory and Society* 27, no. 2 (1998): 151–208.

Sport-for-development: going beyond the boundary?

Fred Coalter

Department of Sports Studies, University of Stirling, Stirling, UK

Recent policy statements by the United Nations relating to sport-for-development have gone beyond simple sports participation to emphasize the supposed importance of sport as an element of civil society. Reflecting changes in the wider aid paradigm, emphasis has been placed on sport's potential contribution to social cohesion and the development of social capital. However, such statements are vague and lack theoretical and policy coherence. This article reviews theories of social capital and, via a case study of the Mathare Youth Sport Association, explores the extent to which certain elements of sport-for-development organizations can contribute to certain types of social capital (bonding, bridging and linking). It also examines the extent to which various types of social capital can contribute to aspects of development and at the same time illustrates the potential limitations of overly romanticized, communitarian views based on limited and untheorized notions of bonding capital.

The United Nations, sport and playing on everybody's team

In November 2003 the General Assembly of the United Nations adopted a resolution affirming its commitment to sport as a means to promote education, health, development and peace. Following this, the United Nations declared 2005 to be the Year of Sport and Physical Education, via which 'the United Nations is turning to the world of sport for help in the work for peace and the effort to achieve the Millennium Development Goals'.[1] These goals include universal primary education, promoting gender equality and empowering women, combating HIV/AIDS and addressing issues of environmental sustainability. The wide-ranging contribution expected of sport is stated clearly.[2]

> The world of sport presents a natural partnership for the United Nations' system. By its very nature sport is about participation. It is about inclusion and citizenship. Sport brings individuals and communities together, highlighting commonalities and bridging cultural or ethnic divides. Sport provides a forum to learn skills such as discipline, confidence and leadership and it teaches core principles such as tolerance, cooperation and respect. Sport teaches the value of effort and how to manage victory, as well as defeat. When these positive aspects of sport are emphasized, sport becomes a powerful vehicle through which the United Nations can work towards achieving its goals.

Many of these statements of desired outcomes are derived from traditional and widespread ideologies of 'sport' – the development of discipline, confidence, tolerance and respect – although robust generic evidence for such claims is limited.[3] In addition to a relatively weak generic evidence base, in the emerging policy area of sport-for-development we are also faced with a widespread lack of evidence for the effectiveness of some of the core claims.[4] In part this reflects the recent establishment of many of the organizations and programmes and the widespread lack of expertise and resources to undertake monitoring and evaluation of aid-dependent organizations which often have insufficient funds to deliver their programmes. However, it also reflects the widespread failure to specify precisely the nature of the desired outcomes and to develop measurable indicators. In turn this reflects what Kruse has referred to as 'an intuitive certainty ... that there is a positive link between sport and development'.[5] These beliefs, apparently shared by many funders and sport-for-development organizations are reinforced by the fact that the rhetorical label of sport-for-development 'is intriguingly vague and open for several interpretations'.[6]

This vagueness is reflected in the wide diversity of organizations and approaches included in what has been rather grandiosely labelled the 'sport-for-development-and-peace movement'.[7] Kidd admits that it is a 'movement' only in the loosest of senses – it is 'still in its infancy, woefully underfunded, completely unregulated, poorly planned and coordinated and largely isolated from mainstream development efforts' (with regard to the later point see also Levermore[8]). For example, Kidd suggests that there are three broad, overlapping, approaches: (1) traditional sports development in which the provision of basic sports coaching, equipment and infrastructure are the central concern; (2) humanitarian assistance in which fund-raising in sport is used to provide forms of aid assistance, frequently for refugees (e.g. the early work of Olympic Aid, some of the subsequent work of Right to Play and the work of the British charity Sport Relief); (3) the 'sport-for-development-and-peace' movement which covers a very wide variety of organizations and loose coalitions (e.g. Kidd points to the fact that there are 166 such organizations listed on the International Platform on Sport and Development).[9] Levermore proposes an alternative classification based on a more disaggregated approach to the desired outcomes of sport-for-development organizations: conflict resolution and inter-cultural understanding; building physical, social and community infrastructure; raising awareness, particularly through education; empowerment; direct impact on physical and psychological health and general welfare; economic development and poverty alleviation.[10] Coalter suggests a simpler approach based on the relative emphasis given to sport to achieve certain objectives: traditional forms of provision for *sport,* with an implicit assumption or explicit affirmation that sport has inherent developmental properties for participants; *sport plus,* in which sports are adapted and often augmented with parallel programmes in order to maximize their potential to achieve developmental objectives; *plus sport* in which sport's popularity is used as a type of 'fly paper' to attract young people to programmes of education and training (a widespread approach for HIV/AIDS prevention programmes), with the systematic development of sport rarely being a strategic aim.[11]

Sport, social capital and civil society

However, the varied, vague and 'mythopoeic' nature of sport and sport-for-development is more evident when we examine the even more ambitious claims for sport's *institutional* contribution to the development of aspects of civil society.[12] For example, in launching the International Year of Sport and PE the United Nations stated that although it had previously collaborated with a range of organizations in the commercial, public and voluntary sectors, 'what was missing, however, was a systematic approach to an important sector in civil society: sport'.[13] This is followed by the assertion of the need to 'ensure that this powerful and diverse element of civil society becomes an active and committed force in the global partnership for development'.[14]

In an earlier document the United Nations stressed the centrality of volunteering in sport and argued that it contributes to 'social welfare, community participation, generation of trust and reciprocity, and the broadening of social interaction through new networks.

Consequently, volunteerism creates social capital, helping to build and consolidate social cohesion and stability'.[15] Further, while the concept of *social capital* is not explicitly stated, it is clearly implied by the statement that,

> Local development through sport particularly benefits from an integrated partnership approach to sport-for-development involving a full spectrum of actors in field-based community development including all levels of and various sectors of government, sports organisations, NGOs and the private sector. Strategic sport-based partnerships can be created within a common framework providing a structured environment allowing for coordination, knowledge and expertise sharing and cost-effectiveness.[16]

Consequently, there is a need to promote partnerships which enable resource mobilization 'both for and through sport' as 'effectively designed sports programmes ... are a valuable tool to initiate social development and improve social cohesion'.[17]

This emphasis on the potential role of sport in civil society (partnerships, social development, social cohesion, coordination, sharing of knowledge and expertise) reflects a broader shift in the 'aid paradigm'. This new aid paradigm is illustrated in the World Bank's increased emphasis on the potential of social capital, community and social relations to contribute to various types of social development and economic growth.[18] Woolcock and Narayan argue that the new emphasis on civil society and social capital reflected a recognition that the concentration of development policy on the economic dimension was too narrow, often dismissing various aspects of traditional social relations and networks as being obstacles to development, rather than potential resources.[19] In fact, Portes and Landholt suggest that the new emphasis represented an attempt to repair the damage done by previous policies, with their emphasis on market forces increasing income disparities, atomization and the erosion of communal normative controls.[20] In such circumstances the notion of social capital holds 'the promise of a ground-up alternative to the top-down policies promoted by international financial organisations in the recent past'.[21] The hope is that, where national and local states are weak, or not interested, organizations in civil society and the degrees of trust and reciprocity they are presumed to engender, can provide informal social insurance, can increase community participation and strengthen democracy and can facilitate various types of social development and economic growth.[22]

This broad shift from an emphasis on top-down economic aid to an increased emphasis on aspects of civil society and bottom-up community development, from economic capital to social capital, permitted the sport-for-development lobby (led by such organizations as Right-to-Play) to argue for sport's utilitarian contributions to aspects of the new aid paradigm. For example, Hognestad illustrates that the Norwegian government's 'Action Plan for the eradication of poverty in the South 2015' emphasizes the connections between poverty and cultural conditions and the significance of securing cultural rights as an important part of the fight against poverty.[23]

Consequently the relatively new emphasis on sport-for-development and the rather vague and ambitious claims for its potential contribution to development, may be understood within the context of this new aid paradigm.[24] Just as in the UK, where new Labour's emphasis on social inclusion and active citizenship has increased the social policy role of sport, so a new emphasis on social relationships and networks within development programmes has lead to an increased concern with social capital and sport's potential contribution to its development.[25] However, Van Rooy suggests that within development policy the concept of *civil society* has become an 'anaytical hatstand' on which donors can opportunistically hang a range of ideas around politics, organization and citizenship.[26] In this regard it is noticeable that in the various documents referred to above, the concepts of civil society, social capital and even 'sport' remain untheorized and are intriguingly vague and open for several interpretations.[27]

Social capital and development

The concept of social capital is not new and has its roots in the classic concerns of sociology and political science with aspects of social cohesion and associational life.[28] Although its precise meaning and relevance to 'development' are disputed, a useful general definition of social capital is that it refers to social networks based on social and group norms, which enable people to trust and cooperate with each other and via which individuals or groups can obtain certain types of advantage.

There are three main sources of theories of social capital: two sociologists – Bourdieu and Coleman; and one political scientist – Putnam.[29] Although all three would broadly accept the above definition, there are significant differences in their use of the term (related to their assumptions about the nature of society, human motivation and social relationships). In terms of our concerns with sport-for-development, Coleman and Putnam are the most relevant.

Coleman, social capital and human capital

Although Coleman is rarely quoted in discussions relating to social capital and sport-for-development, his concerns with the relationship between social capital and the development of human capital (education, employment skills and expertise) are clearly relevant. Coleman views social capital as largely neutral aspects of social structure and social relationships which facilitate actions and he stresses the conscious actions of individuals in the development and use of social capital. In this context social capital is:

> the set of resources that inhere in family relations and in community social organisation and that are useful for the cognitive or social development of a child or young person. These resources differ for different persons and constitute an important advantage for children and adolescents in the development of their human capital.[30]

Johnston and Percy-Smith illustrate that Coleman identified three aspects of relations of social capital: (1) obligations, expectations and trustworthiness of structures; (2) information channels; (3) norms and effective sanctions, which facilitate 'closure' of such networks and ensure that obligations are met and 'freeloaders' are expelled.[31] The importance of such sanctions and norms lies in the expectation of reciprocity and the fact that an individual's 'investment' (e.g. time, effort, helping others) is made not for altruistic purposes, but in the strong expectation that it will pay future dividends. Coleman refers to the decline (and eventual disappearance) of 'the voluntary and spontaneous social organisation that has in the past been the major source of social capital available to the young'.[32] In this regard Portes notes that Coleman laments the decline of the 'close or dense ties' associated with 'primordial' institutions based on the family and emphasizes the need to replace these with 'rationally devised material and status incentives'.[33]

Within this context it is worth noting that many sport-for-development organizations place a strong emphasis on the need for young people to remain in education and some provide both social and financial support for them to do so. Further, there is a widespread emphasis on the development of various aspects of human capital (e.g. transferable social and organizational skills), trust and collective responsibility, accompanied in many cases by rationally devised material and status incentives. However, it is Putnam's version of social capital which tends to inform the rather vague assertions within the policy rhetoric of sport-for-development.[34]

Putnam and social capital

Putnam's appeal to policy makers is that he is more clearly interested in the role of organized voluntary associations and *collective outcomes* (unlike Coleman's more individualistic focus). From his perspective social capital can be regarded as a public good, which serves to bind communities together. Social capital is viewed as an essentially neutral resource which is a property of collectives – communities, cities, regions. For Putnam 'the core idea of social capital is that social networks have value ... [it refers to] connections between individuals – social networks and the norms of reciprocity and trustworthiness that arise from them'.[35]

Communities with high levels of social capital are viewed as being characterized by three main components – strong social networks and civic infrastructure which are characterized by strong social norms (i.e. informal and formal rules about personal and social behaviour and associated sanctions), which both support and reinforce mutual trust and reciprocity among members of a community. Putnam views the civic engagement, associational life and volunteering associated with social capital as important because they improve the efficiency of communities and societies by facilitating coordinated actions, reducing transaction costs (e.g. high levels of trust facilitate commerce via less dependency on formal contractual agreements) and enabling communities to be more effective in pursuit of their collective interests.[36] Its potential value for development is indicated by Woolcock and Narayan who, summarizing Fukuyama, state that 'social capital includes norms and values that facilitate exchanges, lower transaction costs, reduce the cost of information, permit trade in the absence of contracts and encourage responsible citizenship and the collective management of resources'.[37]

Putnam distinguishes between two types of social capital – bonding and bridging.[38] The former refers to networks based on strong social ties between similar people – people 'like us' – with relations, reciprocity and trust based on ties of familiarity and closeness. Putnam refers to this as a type of 'sociological superglue', whose function is to enable people to 'get by' and which works to maintain a strong in-group loyalty and reinforce specific identities.[39] Woolcock and Narayan, social scientists writing for the World Bank, identify this as a rather romanticized *communitarian perspective* within the development literature.[40] From this perspective social capital is equated with local clubs, associations and civic groups and is viewed as 'inherently good, the more the better, and its presence always has a positive effect on a community's welfare'.[41] Nevertheless, many writing within the development literature acknowledge that for many people living in highly deprived communities, such networks are a key resource and an important means of cooperation and survival.

It is clear that this communitarian vision is the one which underpins many of the assertions about sport-for-development. Certainly, aspects of bonding social capital could be regarded as part of the historic role of sports clubs – like-minded people (often from similar economic circumstances, age ranges, educational backgrounds, sex, social class, race and religion) coming together to produce and consume a common interest – a particular sport.[42] If we move beyond the simple use of the terms 'sport' and 'participation', and begin to conceptualize the issues around more formal clubs and organizations, it is clear that, to varying degrees, they are capable of developing forms of bonding social capital that provide a basis for resource mobilization *for* sport and, to a certain, extent *through* sport.[43] To illustrate and explore some of these issues we turn to a case study of the Mathare Youth Sport Association (MYSA).

The Mathare Youth Sport Association

Mathare, in north east Nairobi, is one of the largest and poorest slums in Africa, with a population of about 500,000 living in an area of two kilometres by 300 metres (1.2 miles by 0.2 miles). It is a maze of low, rusted iron-sheeting roofs with mud walls. Housing is wholly inadequate, with most houses measuring about eight feet by six feet and holding up to 10 people. Few houses have running water, open gutters of sewage run throughout, the road infrastructure is extremely poor, refuse and litter dominate the area and the local authority provides few services.[44]

MYSA was established by Bob Munro (a Canadian United Nations environmental development officer) in 1987 as a small self-help project to organize soccer. The concentration on soccer is explained by the extremely high levels of local interest, low-skill entry levels and basic facility and equipment costs. It is now the largest youth sports organization in Africa, with more than 1000 teams and 17,000 members. MYSA's teams range from under 10 to 18 years of age, organized in 16 zones – the biggest league in Africa. MYSA also has two male semi-professional teams, Mathare United A and B.[45] These teams were established for two reasons: firstly, to provide the top of the development pyramid and provide motivation and role models for the junior players; secondly, it was hoped to develop players and benefit from transfer fees which could be used to provide economic security for the broader MYSA programme (of which more later). In light of the analysis to be presented below it is essential to remember that MYSA is a highly successful sports development programme – in 2009 Mathare United supplied 11 players for Kenya's African Nation's Cup squad, plus its manager and its coach. They also won the Kenyan Premier League title.

Producing citizens

MYSA initially attracted young males who played on waste ground in the slums with footballs made of recycled plastic bags and twine. The attraction of MYSA was threefold: firstly, access to real footballs (not to be underestimated in conditions of such poverty); secondly, organized and structured games, which simulated the professional game; thirdly, an ordered and protective environment, which was especially important for the many street children attracted to MYSA. However, it soon developed into a much more complex and ambitious *sport plus* project, whose ultimate ambition is to produce citizens – 'the leaders needed for building the new Kenya'.[46]

Consequently, soccer is an entry point to a comprehensive, interdependent programme, in which all elements are mutually reinforcing in order to produce a form of social capital. Some of these elements are outlined by Munro as follows:

1. To link sport to community service.
2. Youth are owners and decision-makers. They are elected from zonal league committees to Sports Council/Community Service Council and then to the MYSA Executive Council. A recently formulated constitution requires equal gender representation and in a recent election, a 12-year-old girl was elected chair of her local committee. (Commenting on the role of women in MYSA Brady and Kahn state: 'Girls' participation can begin to change community norms about their roles and capacities. In this way, sports may be a catalyst for the transformation of social norms.'[47])
3. To help youth to help themselves by helping others. Reflecting a key component of bonding social capital, Munro argues that 'when you are poor cooperation and sharing are crucial for survival'.

4. To help young leaders to stay in school. This is achieved via a points-based educational scholarship system, with points being awarded for volunteer activities (coaching, refereeing, community service).[48]

These various philosophies and practices clearly reflect components of the definitions of social capital – social networks based on social and group norms which enable people to trust and cooperate with each other and via which individuals or groups can obtain certain types of advantage. Further, this is clearly a form of *bonding social capital* as it is based on strong social ties of familiarity and closeness between people who share very similar social, cultural and economic circumstances – many members refer to MYSA as a 'family'. This is reinforced by the fact all full and part-time employees are recruited from MYSA members (who appear to possess a deep sense of responsibility to act as positive role models). These basic elements are part of an over-arching philosophy of mutual self-help and a number of specific practices and activities which serve formally to reinforce certain values and attitudes.

The sense of involvement, responsibility and values of active citizenship are reinforced by member-involvement in decision making at all levels, with a strong emphasis on mutual self-help – stated succinctly by Munro as 'you do something, MYSA does something. You do nothing, MYSA does nothing'. This ethic of reciprocity, which serves as a form of closure thereby reducing the problem of freeloaders, is especially important in a society where there is widespread corruption, including in soccer (to which we will return).[49]

Sport plus

However, from the perspective of sport-for-development, it is essential to understand that MYSA does not depend on any simple view of 'sports participation' to maximize the possibility of achieving the desired outcomes. For example, the rules of soccer have been amended and during games anyone other than the captain who speaks to an official can be sent off (a substitute player is permitted). However, punishment is accompanied by learning as the player then has to referee six junior matches to put him or herself in the place of a referee before being permitted to play again. In addition, a green card is awarded to the most sporting player and this is accompanied by the practical award of educational scholarship points – fairness brings its rewards. As part of its commitment to helping young leaders to stay in school, MYSA has about 400 annual leadership awards (it also provides small libraries and study rooms to compensate for the lack of study space in overcrowded dwellings). Although schooling is free up to the age of 14, many schools require pupils to wear uniforms (prohibitive for those living in poverty) and in the post-14 schools, fees are required. The awards are paid to the school of the winners' choice and are used to pay for tuition, books and uniforms. Points towards these awards are also linked to volunteer, peer-leadership and coaching work. It is interesting that older players often accumulate these points for their younger brothers or sisters. This clearly illustrates an aspect of social capital emphasized by most theorists – that the social relations/networks provide access to certain significant resources and advantages.

A more general commitment to community service is compulsory for all members of MYSA, including the semi-professionals in Mathare United. The aim of the work is to increase environmental awareness and entails a 'clean up', in which teams from the various zones clear drains, cut grass and remove litter. Although this work makes little overall impact on the overwhelming environmental problems of Mathare, the core value being emphasized here is that of collective responsibility and reciprocity – 'if you get something from the community you must put something back into the community'.[50] The extent of programme integration and re-enforcement of values is emphasized by the fact that each completed clean-up project earns a soccer team three points towards its league standings – success is a combination of sporting talent and social responsibility.

Rather than reflecting Putnam's somewhat 'organic' view of social capital, the MYSA approach seems to be closer to Coleman's 'rationally devised material and status incentives', needed to compensate for the weakening of family, community and local government structures. It can also be viewed as illustrating aspects of Coleman's perspective about the relationship between social capital and the development of human capital and his greater emphasis on the more conscious and self-interested aspects of social capital and their importance for children's education and development.[51] For example, initial parental resistance to girls' participation in some sport-for-development projects is often overcome once parents realize the educational and other benefits to be obtained via membership. Further, issues of reciprocity and trust are clearly and regularly articulated and reinforced within the organization, rather than simply assumed (or illustrated via sanctions for transgression).

Consequently, MYSA's importance goes well beyond any simple definition of 'sport', or the traditional functions of most sporting organizations.[52] In effect, it operates in a number of areas in civil society, seeking to compensate for major failures of the local and national states' welfare provision – facilitated and given coherence by soccer and soccer-related programmes. Although MYSA is a particularly sophisticated example of a sport-plus organization, it is based on an approach which is characteristic of many sport-for-development organizations – the development and use of volunteer *youth peer leaders, educators and coaches.*

Volunteering plus

In traditional sports development programmes leaders and coaches are regarded simply as *inputs* – qualified sports development officers who use their professional expertise to develop programmes for local communities. However, by adopting a youth peer leader approach, many sport-for-development organizations involve young men and women at various levels of planning, implementation and decision making, providing important experience of control, empowerment and a sense of collective responsibility (via the much emphasized and important status of 'role models'). In other words, *people* are a major product of many such organizations, one that is central to their sustainability and precedes the programmes whose impacts are often the subject of evaluation.

Consequently, volunteer peer leaders, teachers and coaches are at the centre of such organizations and programmes. In addition to being a vital resource for the sustainability of the organizations and an attractive cost-reducing value-addition for aid agencies, the use of peer leaders is based on sound educational and learning theory. It is argued that because young people's attitudes are highly influenced by their peers' values and attitudes, peer educators are less likely to be viewed as 'preaching' authority figures and more likely to be regarded as people who know the experiences and concerns of young people).[53] Further, Payne et al., illustrate that, to be effective, role models must be embedded, based on the development of supportive, longer-term trusting relationships.[54] In line with social learning and self-efficacy theory, evidence suggests that major factors underpinning the effectiveness of role models are the characteristics of the model and their *perceived similarity to the learner.*[55] Learning is more likely to occur when the learners perceive that they are capable of carrying out the behaviour (self-efficacy expectancy), think that there is a high probability that the behaviour will result in a particular outcome (outcome expectancy) and if the outcome is desirable – all of which are reinforced via peer education and associated reward systems. In addition, Saavedra emphasizes the special importance of female role models in sport-for-development organizations, most of which seek to confront traditional, exploitative and often abusive social relations.[56] Munro illustrates the importance placed on role models by asking rhetorically: 'role models for youth: is anything more important in development?'.[57] He argues that in most African countries the poor are the majority and youth constitute the majority of that poor majority and that 'among the many debilitating aspects of poverty is that the poor, and especially the youth, lack confidence and belief in themselves'. Consequently, 'after food, water, shelter, health and education, nothing is more important for future development than providing good role models for our youth'.[58]

However, although accepting the theoretical legitimacy of the peer educator approach, Kruse points to the lack of research on the nature and quality of such processes, arguing that there is a lack of information about the quality of the exchanges in particular contexts (a key issue for social capital), the extent to which peer leaders and coaches are given sufficient training, the extent of supervision and support provided after initial training and their effectiveness.[59] In this regard, Nicholls argues that 'the necessary support for peer educators is not always available in the resource-poor and donor-driven world of development through sport'. Consequently, although there is a strong theoretical underpinning for such an approach, there is an urgent need for empirical research relating to both educational and social capital outcomes.[60]

Social capital: motivation and differential distribution

In this regard, a better understanding of how such organizations actually work might be to adopt a less romanticized, communitarian view, of the *organization* and explore the potential range of motivations – from those motivated by civic/democratic/moral values, to more Coleman-like instrumentalism.[61] Clearly there is a substantial ethos of altruism, sense of belonging and collective responsibility among most youth peer leaders – values and attitudes presumed to underpin volunteerism and central to Putnam's civic virtues. However, in many cases this is accompanied and reinforced by rationally devised material and status incentives – access to educational scholarships, foreign travel to competitions (a major incentive), status within the organizations and community – which appear to be closer to Coleman's more instrumental and self-interested approach, whose attraction and power are wholly understandable in conditions of extreme poverty. The nature of motivations and incentives has clear implications for the design and use of sport-for-development programmes and for our understanding of the nature and strength of the social capital that they might produce.

Motivation and meaning also raise another important issue when discussing social capital and sport-for-development – the possible differential distribution of benefits – referred to by Fukuyama as the 'radius of trust'.[62] For example, where an organization's social capital produces positive externalities (e.g. via MYSA's clean-up activities and educational scholarships) then the radius of trust can be larger than the group – an outcome clearly implied by much policy rhetoric in sport-for-development. However, while it is clear that there are collective benefits as a result of the ability of the organization to mobilize and maximize the use of sporting resources (e.g. access to limited playing space), there is also likely to be a differential distribution of social capital and its benefits *within* the organization – perhaps the collective strengths of social capital inevitably benefit some more than others. Fukuyama suggests that it is also possible that trust-based and cooperative norms are strongest among the leadership and permanent staff.[63] For example, those most actively involved in the organization and the provision of opportunities will be those most likely to benefit via the development of their human capital and increased employability.[64] An example is provided by a small qualitative study of the Edusport organization in Zambia in which Mwaanga illustrates that the level and intensity of participation were key moderators of programme effectiveness – not surprisingly the youth peer leaders were more likely to benefit than general participants.[65] They are the most committed, have gone through the various training programmes, have experience of decision making and perceptions of control and status and are highly conscious of their positions (and responsibilities) as role models.

Such comments should not be taken as criticisms – to produce a cadre of highly committed and responsible youth peer leaders (especially female) in such difficult economic and cultural circumstances is clearly a major achievement. Rather, the comment relates solely to the need to understand better how such organizations work and the nature and limits of bonding capital produced in sport-for-development initiatives – the extent to which they can, in the words of the United Nations, mobilize resources 'both for and through sport' and 'improve social cohesion'.[66]

Is bonding enough?

MYSA clearly indicates the potential of sport-for-development organizations to compensate for certain aspects of the wider failures of national and local states, weak civic structures and disintegrating families. Such organizations have the potential to develop forms of social capital by providing young men and women with rare opportunities to participate in decision making, confront exploitative gender relations, encourage and support ambition, recognize the value of education, develop relationships based on trust and reciprocity and provide opportunities for the development of aspects of human capital.

However, many academics and policy makers concerned with social capital and various forms of community development express certain reservations about the limitations of *bonding social capital* – especially for contributing to wider policies of social and economic regeneration. Clearly it can play a significant role in local social regeneration – for example, as an essential first step towards building collective confidence, cohesion and cooperation. However, concerns have been expressed about certain socio-cultural aspects of bonding social capital, what Putnam has referred to as its 'dark side' – acting to impose conformity and downward levelling, excluding outsiders and maybe even providing the basis for anti-social activities.[67] It is possible that while such capital can assist in community bonding, it may lead to 'defensive communities' (or organizations) – linking disadvantaged individuals together, but effectively excluding them from the wider society and its resources and opportunities and effectively restricting routes out of poverty and exclusion.[68] Consequently, Woolcock and Narayan refer to bonding social capital as a 'double-edged sword', with strong group loyalties and collectively enforced obligations potentially serving to 'isolate members from information about employment opportunities, foster a climate of ridicule towards efforts to study and work hard, or siphon off hard-won assets' (e.g. via the enforcement of collective obligations on small entrepreneurs to make charitable gifts, or fund festivals or celebrations, thereby reducing their ability to reinvest in their businesses).[69] However, it is possible to argue that many sport-for-development organizations, with their emphasis on gender equity, education, personal development and social responsibility, are seeking to confront and replace potentially negative bonding social capital with much more positive forms – a task which sometimes leads to confrontation with wider community power and economic interests.

While many sport-for-development organizations may manage to promote the positive aspects of bonding social capital, there is a broader danger that 'equating social capital with the resources acquired through it can easily lead to tautological statements' – in other words such networks can be 'resource poor', both internally and externally.[70] Portes and Landholt emphasize that 'it must be recognised that local-level cooperation alone cannot overcome macro-structural obstacles to economic stability, autonomous growth, and accumulation'.[71] Therefore, Portes and Landholt conclude that although the development of forms of social capital is a very attractive proposition for aid agencies, because they can increase the yield of aid and investment (e.g. via volunteer labour and greater openness and accountability),

> One must not be over-optimistic about what enforceable trust and bounded solidarity can accomplish at the collective level, especially in the absence of material resources. Social capital can be a powerful force promoting group projects but . . . it consists of the ability to marshal resources through social networks, not the resources themselves. When the latter are poor and scarce, the goal achievement capacity of a collectivity is restricted, no matter how strong the internal bonds . . . social capital are not a substitute for the provision of credit, material infrastructure and education.[72]

For example, Woolcock and Narayan point to the limitations of civil society organizations where there is 'rampant corruption, frustrating bureaucratic delays, suppressed civil liberties, vast inequality'.[73] Although the example is not directly analogous, it is worth noting the case of MYSA. The establishment of the semi-professional Mathare United was part of a strategy to achieve some degree of financial sustainability. It was hoped that by developing players their transfer fees could be used to provide economic security for the broader MYSA programme. However, reflecting wider aspects of corruption in Kenyan sport, football agents, in association with the Kenyan Football Federation, undermined this strategy by depriving MYSA of its legitimate share of two transfer fees. This was in addition to clear examples of match fixing, systematic siphoning-off of match fees and a failure to distribute FIFA youth development funds (for a full detailed analysis, see Munro[74]). Although after much conflict certain resolutions have been found to some of these issues, they serve to illustrate what Woolcock and Narayan term the *institutional view* of the role of social capital in development – that civil society organizations are not simple substitutes for the state and can only really thrive to the extent that the state actively encourages them. In other words, in the absence of what they refer to as 'civic and government social capital' such well-intentioned efforts will have limited general impact.[75]

Going beyond the boundary

The limitations of even positive bonding social capital can be partially moderated by the development of other forms of social capital – *bridging social capital* and *linking social capital*. The former refers to weaker social ties between different types of people – more colleagues than family and friends. This is less of a glue than 'a sociological WD40'[76] and facilitates 'getting ahead' via, for example, the diffusion of information and employment opportunities. The notion of linking social capital is proposed by Woolcock, a social scientist concerned with development. Whereas bonding and bridging social capital are concerned with types of horizontal relationships, linking social capital refers to vertical connections between different social strata, including those entirely outside the community (thereby offering access to wider networks and the potential to leverage a broader range of resources).[77] In fact, Skidmore, Bound and Lownsborough suggest that broader policies to promote community participation in governance are frequently concerned with linking capital, the theory being 'that being involved in the governance of services, participants build relationships with public institutions or officials which give their community access to valuable external resources like money, support or political leverage'.[78]

In this regard it is worth noting Seippel's distinction between *connected* sports organizations (i.e. members have ties to members of other associations) and *isolated* organizations, which focus solely on their sport and local community.[79] The latter are a vehicle for the mobilization of resources *for* sport and may achieve certain intermediate impacts supposedly associated with participation in sport (self efficacy, confidence) and develop certain forms of bonding social capital (with varying 'radii of trust').

The United Nations' aspiration for an integrated approach to sport-for-development 'involving a full spectrum of actors in field-based community development including all levels of and various sectors of government, sports organizations, NGOs and the private sector', clearly relates to *connected clubs*.[80] However, the extent to which clubs can develop both bridging and linking capital will vary by their type, size and location (e.g. isolated or connected, single or multi-sport, urban or rural, competitive or recreational). Nevertheless, in many cases they are part of a wider 'sports community', in which participation in leagues, competitions and governing bodies provides theoretical opportunities for the development of forms of bridging and linking social capital, although the extent to which this is restricted to 'sporting social capital' – i.e. mobilization of resources *for* sport, within the sports community – is an important empirical question in relation to their precise contribution to broader processes of development.

Woolcock and Narayan refer to the combination of bridging and linking social capital as the *networks view,* arguing that 'strong intra-community ties and weak extra-community networks are needed to avoid making tautological claims regarding the efficacy of social capital'.[81] This networks view seems to be closer to Coleman's rather individualistic perspective than to Putnam's more collective views and returns us to the questions relating to the beneficiaries of forms of social capital – with substantial implications for development. For example, Woolcock and Narayan suggest that 'this view minimises the "public good" nature of social groups, regarding any benefits of group activity as primarily the property of the particular individuals involved'.[82] Whereas bonding social capital may provide an essential collective support and insurance network for the poor, for development to occur it needs to be weak enough to permit the (individual) poor to gain access to wider and more formal institutions and a more diverse stock of bridging (and maybe even linking) social capital – MYSA's citizens must leave eventually.

It is clear that many sport-for-development organizations have the potential to gain access to forms of both bridging and linking social capital, although their relationships with national governing bodies and government sports organizations vary widely (in some cases they are antagonistic). In particular, the burgeoning international sport-for-development networks provide access to such networks and the funding and resources which accompany them. However, Renard suggests that there may be a conflict at the heart of these relationships in the new aid paradigm – between largely locally-determined poverty reduction strategies (or in our case, sports development strategies) and externally imposed Millenium Development Goals, which may skew programmes and not reflect local issues and needs.[83] In such circumstances Renard posits two contrasting sets of relationship (which can be regarded as forms of linking social capital).

One set of relationships involves donors and recipients pursuing similar policy objectives, based on consensus and trust. It might be hypothesized that this refers to aid given to existing sporting organizations by sporting organizations in a spirit of relative altruism, in order to promote and develop sport and international sporting solidarity (see Kidd[84]). In current circumstances such aid is nearly always for a *sports plus* approach, but will nevertheless be concerned with sports development and the strengthening of the sporting infrastructure (accompanied by an implicit belief in the positive outcomes associated with sport). Renard's second set of relations is based on the possibility that donors and recipients may have differing agendas. This is more likely to be closer to a *plus sport* perspective, in which sport's 'fly paper' properties are emphasized and sports organizations are funded or even 'constructed', with the purpose of achieving defined, non-sporting social and/or developmental goals.

In this regard concern has been expressed about the possible consequences of external aid to such civil society organizations. Some have argued that the rapid growth in influence of locally non-accountable NGOs represents new forces of neo-colonialism, with their main leadership and strategies being formulated in the West they are viewed as promoting new forms of dependency. With regard to sport, Giulianotti has raised questions about the exporting of overly 'functionalist' views of sport by new 'sports evangelists' and questions the nature of the dialogue between donors and recipients and the extent to which 'empowerment' is a goal.[85] It is certainly the case that donors' frequently unrealistically high, and mostly vague, aspirations for the contribution of sport to development encourages organizations wholly dependent on external aid to include objectives and programme elements in their funding applications which they might not otherwise have contemplated. The necessity to compete for limited resources frequently leads to projects being developed to fit the funding criteria, with the potential to compromise beneficiaries' needs, promote organizational mission drift and the acceptance of donor targets with insufficient implementation capacity.[86]

The nature of such donor/client relationships is important because of a desire to 'promote' forms of social capital, and the more general concerns that 'the essence of social capital is that it consists of activities and relationships freely engaged in by individuals'.[87] For example Fukuyama warns that excessive (state) intervention 'can have a serious negative impact on social capital'[88] and Field refers to Coleman's doubts about the ability of constructed forms of organization to provide the required normative cohesion and network closure central to the effective working of social capital – although this is clearly a matter for empirical investigation.[89] In this regard Sport England accepts that requiring sports clubs to adopt different agendas contains substantial risks and argues that 'any external assistance offered needs to emphasise that it is designed to help them achieve *their* aims'.[90] It is worth leaving the last word on this to Bob Munro (the founder of MYSA) who stated that 'the best thing that happened to MYSA was that nobody was interested for the first five years'.[91] The implication of this is that the absence of aid-dependency (or the availability of aid) permitted the establishment of locally based aims, objectives, principles and processes – whether these are viewed via the lens of Coleman or Putnam.

Conclusions

In considering the contribution of sport-for-development to the formation of social capital, the key theoretical, policy and practical issues relate to the types of social capital being assumed, the precise meaning of resource mobilization 'both for and *through* sport' and the limits of sport-for-development's contributions to broader development strategies.[92]

The case study of MYSA illustrates a number of issues about the danger of decontextualized, overly romanticized, communitarian generalizations about the 'power' of sport-for-development. It seems that it is not simple sports participation that can hope to achieve most desired outcomes, but *sports plus*; it is not 'sport' that achieves many of these outcomes, but *sporting organizations;* it is not sport that produces and sustains social capital, enters into partnerships and mobilizes sporting and non-sporting resources, but certain types of social organization. Further, evidence would suggest that some of these organizations are consciously and systematically organized to maximize the possibility of achieving such outcomes – developing forms of Coleman's rationally devised material and status incentives, rather than depending on Putnam's rather more organic perspective.

Some types of sport-for-development organizations can provide relatively inclusive sports development programmes, enabling many young people to have access to sporting opportunities and some non-sporting resources (e.g. education, foreign travel) that they would not otherwise have had. In some circumstances they offer compensation for certain aspects of weak civic structures, disintegrating families and inadequate education systems. They can develop forms of social and human capital by providing some young people with opportunities to participate in decision making, confront exploitative gender relations, encourage ambition and recognize the value of education, develop relationships based on trust and reciprocity, provide opportunities for the development of aspects of human capital – especially via volunteer youth peer coaches and educators. These possibilities make such organizations an attractive investment for aid agencies, as they increase the yield of aid and investment – you get a lot for your money. However, there is a wide variety of such organizations and in terms of understanding the contribution of sports organizations to development it is essential to distinguish between the social relations characteristic of forms of social capital and the frequently very limited resources associated with them.[93]

The type and strength of social capital (and associated resources) developed will depend on the size and type of organization (e.g. isolated or connected, single or multi-sport, urban or rural, competitive or recreational, single or mixed sex) and their relationships with the 'community' (both local and sporting) – the 'radius of trust'.[94] Further, although there is a tendency to talk about social capital in organizational and collective terms, many commentators – reflecting the perspective of Coleman (and Bourdieu)[95] – raise the issue of the differential distribution of social capital (most especially bridging and linking) within organizations.

A further key issue relates to the nature of the processes involved in the formation and sustaining of different types of social capital. There is broad agreement that prescriptive policy-led attempts to construct social capital may fail, as social capital is based on activities, relationships and norms freely engaged in by individuals. Such an analysis raises significant issues for organizations that are wholly aid-dependent and are encouraged to offer an economy of solutions to a wide range of social, political and economic problems.[96] However, it is also worth noting Coleman's suggestion that 'organisations once brought into existence for one set of purposes can also aid others, thus constituting social capital available for use which are set up for one purpose'.[97] In this regard the wider potential of sport-for-development organizations remains unexplored.

Consequently we are left with questions about how to understand the relationships between forms of sport, forms of organization, types of social capital and forms of development, *or the extent to which such relationships can exist.*[98] Certainly, in the area of sport-for-development we can clearly see the truth of Pawson's assertion that 'social interventions are always complex systems thrust amidst complex systems' – something frequently ignored in policy rhetoric.[99]

Notes

[1] United Nations, *Business Plan.*
[2] United Nations, *Sport as a Tool.*
[3] Coalter, *A Wider Social Role for Sport.*
[4] UNICEF, *Monitoring and Evaluation*; Kruse, 'Review of Kicking AIDS Out'; Botcheva and Huffman, *Grassroot Soccer Foundation.*
[5] Kruse, 'Review of Kicking AIDS Out', 8.

[6] Ibid.

[7] Kidd, 'A New Social Movement', 376.

[8] Levermore, 'Sport'.

[9] Kidd, 'A New Social Movement'.

[10] Levermore, 'Sport'.

[11] Coalter, *A Wider Social Role for Sport*. Mwaanga, *Kicking Aids Out*; Banda and Mwaanga, *Dunking AIDS out*.

[12] Coalter, *A Wider Social Role for Sport*.

[13] United Nations, 'International Year of Sport and Physical Education', www.un.org/sport2005.

[14] Ibid., 7.

[15] United Nations, *Sport for Development and Peace*, 14.

[16] Ibid., 7.

[17] Ibid., 12, 20.

[18] Renard, 'Cracks in the New Aid Paradigm'; World Bank, *Social Capital and Civil Society*; Grootaert et al., 'Measuring Social Capital'.

[19] Woolcock and Narayan, 'Social Capital'.

[20] Portes and Landholt, 'Social Capital'.

[21] Ibid. 530.

[22] World Bank, *Social Capital and Civil Society*, http://web.worldbank.org/wbsite/external/topics/extsocialdevlopment.

[23] Hognestad, 'Norwegian Strategies on Culture'.

[24] Renard, 'Cracks in the New Aid Paradigm'.

[25] Coalter, *A Wider Social Role for Sport*.

[26] Van Rooy, *Global Legitimacy Game*.

[27] Kruse, 'Review of Kicking AIDS Out'.

[28] Portes, 'Social Capital'; Field, *Social Capital*; Johnston and Percy-Smith, 'In Search of Social Capital'; Farr, 'Social Capital'.

[29] Bourdieu, 'Forms of Capital'; Coleman, *Foundations of Social Theory*, 'Social Capital'; Putnam, *Bowling Alone*.

[30] Coleman, *Foundations of Social Theory*, 300.

[31] Johnston and Percy-Smith, 'In Search of Social Capital', 321–34.

[32] Coleman, 'Social Capital', 117.

[33] Portes, 'Social Capital', 10.

[34] Putnam, *Bowling Alone*.

[35] Ibid., 18–9.

[36] Ibid.

[37] Woolcock and Narayan, 'Social Capital', 240; Fukuyama, *Social Capital and Civil Society*.

[38] Putnam, *Bowling Alone*.

[39] Ibid. 23.

[40] Woolcock and Narayan, 'Social Capital'.

[41] Ibid., 229.

[42] Coalter, 'Sports Clubs'.

[43] United Nations, *Sport for Development and Peace*.

[44] Brady and Kahn, *Letting Girls Play;* Willis, 'Sport and Development', 825–49; www.mysakenya.org.

[45] H. Atkins, 'Mathare United: A Model CECAFA Club', available at www.toolkitsportdevelopment.org.

[46] Munro, 'Role Models', 5.

[47] Brady and Kahn, *Letting Girls Play*, 2.

[48] Munro, 'Role Models', 3.

[49] Ibid., 2.

[50] Ibid.

[51] Portes, 'Social Capital', 10.

[52] Coalter, 'Sports Clubs'.

[53] YouthNet, *From Theory to Practice*; Kerrigan, *Peer Education and HIV/AIDS*.

[54] Payne et al., *Sports Role Models*.

[55] Bandura, *Social Learning through Imitation*.

[56] Saavedra, 'Women, Sport and Development'.

[57] Munro, 'Role Models', 4.
[58] Ibid.
[59] Kruse, 'Review of Kicking AIDS Out'.
[60] Nicholls, 'On the Backs of Peer Educators', 170.
[61] Putnam, *Bowling Alone*; Gaskin and Smith, *A New Civic Europe?*; Portes and Landholt, 'Social Capital'.
[62] Fukuyama, *Social Capital and Civil Society*, 2.
[63] Ibid.
[64] Seippel, 'Sport and Social Capital'; Skidmore, Bound and Lownsborough, *Community Participation*.
[65] Mwaanga, 'HIV/AIDS'.
[66] United Nations, *Sport for Development and Peace*, 12, 20.
[67] Putnam, *Bowling Alone*.
[68] Forrest and Kearns, *Joined-up Places?*, 1.
[69] Woolcock and Narayan, 'Social Capital', 231.
[70] Portes, 'Social Capital', 19.
[71] Portes and Landholt, 'Social Capital', 542.
[72] Ibid. 546.
[73] Woolcock and Narayan, 'Social Capital', 235.
[74] Munro, 'Greed vs Good Governance'
[75] Woolcock and Narayan, 'Social Capital'.
[76] Putnam, *Bowling Alone*, 23.
[77] Woolcock , 'Place of Social Capital'.
[78] Skidmore, Bound and Lownsborough, *Community Participation,* viii.
[79] Seippel, 'Sport and Social Capital'.
[80] United Nations, *Sport for Development and Peace*, 21.
[81] Woolcock and Narayan, 'Social Capital', 231.
[82] Ibid. 234.
[83] Renard, 'Cracks in the New Aid Paradigm'.
[84] Kidd, 'A New Social Movement'.
[85] Giulianotti, 'Human Rights'.
[86] Howells, 'Organisational Sustainability'.
[87] Field, *Social Capital*,118.
[88] Fukuyama, *Social Capital and Civil Society*, 18.
[89] Field, *Social Capital*.
[90] Sport England, *Sports Volunteers*,14. Emphasis added.
[91] Personal communication.
[92] United Nations, *Sport for Development and Peace,* 20. Emphasis added.
[93] Kruse, 'Review of Kicking AIDS Out'; Nicholls, 'On the Backs of Peer Educators'; Portes and Lindolt, 'Social Capital'; Coalter, 'Sports Clubs'.
[94] Fukuyama, *Social Capital and Civil Society*.
[95] Coleman; Bourdieu, 'Forms of Capital'.
[96] Howells, 'Organisational Sustainability'.
[97] Coleman, 'Social Capital', 108.
[98] Kruse, 'Review of Kicking AIDS Out'.
[99] Pawson, *Evidence-Based Policy*, 5.

References

Banda, D., and O. Mwaanga. *Dunking AIDS Out: Learning about AIDS through Basketball Movement Games*. Zambia: Edusport Foundation, 2008. http://assets.sportanddev.org/downloads/39_dunking_aids_out_learning_about_aids_through_basketball_movement_games.pdf.

Bandura, A. *Social Learning through Imitation*. Lincoln, NE: University of Nebraska Press, 1962.

Botcheva, L., and M.D. Huffman. *Grassroot Soccer Foundation HIV/AIDS Education Program: An Intervention in Zimbabwe*. White River Junction, VT: Grassroot Soccer Foundation, 2004.

Bourdieu, P. 'The Forms of Capital'. In *Education, Culture, Economy and Society*, edited by A.H. Halsey, H. Launder, P. Brown, and A. Stuart Wells, 46–58. Oxford: Oxford University Press, 1997.

Brady, M., and A.B. Kahn. *Letting Girls Play: The Mathare Youth Sports Association's Football Program for Girls*. New York: Population Council, 2002.

Coalter, F. *A Wider Social Role for Sport: Who's Keeping the Score?* London: Routledge, 2007.

Coalter, F. 'Sports Clubs, Social Capital and Social Regeneration: "Ill-defined Interventions with Hard to Follow Outcomes"?'. *Sport in Society* 10, no. 4 (2007): 537–59.

Coleman, J. 'Social Capital in the Creation of Human Capital'. *American Journal of Sociology* 94 (1988–9): 95–120.

Coleman, J.S. *Foundations of Social Theory*. Cambridge, MA: Belknap Press, 1994.

Farr, J. 'Social Capital: A Conceptual History'. *Political Theory* 32, no. 1 (2004): 6–33.

Field, J. *Social Capital*. London: Routledge, 2003.

Forrest, R., and A. Kearns. *Joined-up Places? Social Cohesion and Neighbourhood Regeneration*. York: YPS for the Joseph Rowntree Foundation, 1999.

Fukuyama, F. *Social Capital and Civil Society*. Washington, DC: George Masson University, The Institute of Public Policy, 1999.

Gaskin, K., and D. Smith. *A New Civic Europe? A Study of the Extent and Role of Volunteering*. London: Volunteer Centre UK, 1995.

Giulianotti, R. 'Human Rights, Globalization and Sentimental Education: The Case of Sport'. *Sport in Society* 7, no. 3 (2004): 355–69.

Grootaert, C., D. Narayan, V.N. Jones, and M. Woolcock. 'Measuring Social Capital: An Integrated Questionnaire'. World Bank working paper no. 18, Washington, 2004.

Hognestad, H. 'Norwegian Strategies on Culture – and Sports Development with Southern Countries'. A presentation to the Sports Research Forum, Australian Sports Commission, Canberra, 13–15 April 2005.

Howells, S. 'Organisational Sustainability for Sport and Development'. A paper presented at the 2nd Commonwealth Sport for Development Conference, Glasgow, 12 June 2008.

Johnston, G., and J. Percy-Smith. 'In Search of Social Capital'. *Policy and Politics* 31, no. 3 (2003): 321–34.

Kerrigan, D. *Peer Education and HIV/AIDS: Concepts, Uses and Challenges*. Washington, DC: Horizons/Population Council, 1999.

Kidd, B. 'A New Social Movement: Sport for Development and Peace'. *Sport in Society* 11, no. 4 (2008): 370–80.

Kruse, S.E. 'Review of Kicking AIDS Out: Is Sport an Effective Tool in the Fight Against HIV/AIDS?'. Draft report to NORAD 2006.

Levermore, R. 'Sport: A New Engine of Development'. *Progress in Development Studies* 8, no. 2 (2008): 183–90.

Munro, B. 'Greed vs Good Governance: The Fight for Corruption-Free Football in Kenya'. A paper presented at Play the Game 2005 – Governance in Sport: The Good, The Bad and The Ugly, Copenhagen. http://www.playthegame.org.

Munro, B. 'Role Models: Is Anything More Important for Future Development?'. Role Models Retreat, Laureus Sport for Good Foundation, Pretoria, South Africa, 23–24 November 2005.

Mwaanga, O. 'HIV/AIDS At-Risk Adolescent Girls' Empowerment through Participation in Top Level Football and Edusport in Zambia'. MSc thesis, Institute of Social Science at the Norwegian University of Sport and PE, Oslo, 2003.

Mwaanga, O. *Kicking Aids Out Through Movement Games and Sports Activities*. Oslo: NORD, 2002. http://assets.sportanddev.org/downloads/5__kicking_aids_out.pdf.

Nicholls, S. 'On the Backs of Peer Educators: Using Theory to Interrogate the Role of Young People in the Field of Sport-in-development'. In *Sport and International Development*, edited by R Levermore and A Beacom, 156–175. Palgrave Macmillan, London, 2008.

Pawson, R. *Evidence-Based Policy: A Realist Perspective*. London: Sage, 2006.

Payne, W., M. Reynolds, S. Brown, and A. Fleming. *Sports Role Models and their Impact on Participation in Physical Activity: A Literature Review*. Victoria: VicHealth, 2003.

Portes, A. 'Social Capital: Its Origins and Applications in Modern Sociology'. *Annual Review of Sociology* 24 (1998): 1–24.

Portes, A., and P. Landholt. 'Social Capital: Promise and Pitfalls of its Role in Development'. *Journal of Latin American Studies* 32 (2000): 529–47.

Putnam, R. *Bowling Alone: The Collapse and Revival of the American Community*. New York: Simon & Schuster, 2000.

Renard, R. 'The Cracks in the New Aid Paradigm'. Discussion paper, Institute of Development Policy and Management, Antwerpen, Belgium, 2006.

Saavedra, M., *Women, Sport and Development*. Sport and Development International Platform, 2005. http://www.sportanddev.org/data/document/document/148.pdf.

Seippel, O. 'Sport and Social Capital'. *Acta Sociologica* 49, no. 2 (2006): 169–83.

Skidmore, P., K. Bound, and H. Lownsborough. *Community Participation: Who Benefits?* York: Joseph Rowntree Foundation, 2006.

Sport England. *Sports Volunteers in England in 2002*. London: Sport England, 2003.

UNICEF. *Monitoring and Evaluation for Sport-based Programming for Development: Sport Recreation and Play*. Workshop report. UNICEF, New York, NY, 2006.

United Nations. *Business Plan International Year of Sport and Physical Education*. New York: United Nations, 2005.

United Nations. *Sport as a Tool for Development and Peace: Towards Achieving the Millennium Development Goals*. Report from the United Nations Inter-Agency Task Force on Sport for Development and Peace Geneva: United Nations, 2005.

United Nations. *Sport for Development and Peace: Towards Achieving the Millennium Development Goals*. New York: United Nations, 2003.

Van Rooy, A., ed. *Global Legitimacy Game: Civil Society, Globalisation and Protest*, London: Palgrave Macmillan, 2004.

Willis, O. 'Sport and Development: The Significance of Mathare Youth Sports Association'. *Canadian Journal of Development Studies* 21, no. 3 (2000): 825–49.

Woolcock, M. 'The Place of Social Capital in Understanding Social and Economic Outcomes'. *ISUMA Canadian Journal of Policy Research* 2, no. 1 (2001): 11–17.

Woolcock, M., and D. Narayan. 'Social Capital: Implications for Development Theory, Research, and Policy'. *The World Bank Research Observer* 15, no. 2 (2000): 225–49.

YouthNet. *From Theory to Practice in Peer Education*. New York: United Nations Population Fund and Youth Peer Education Network, 2005.

Community sports development for socially deprived groups: a wider role for the commercial sports sector? A look at the Flemish situation

Marc Theeboom, Reinhard Haudenhuyse and Paul De Knop

Department of Sports Policy and Management, Vrije Universiteit Brussel, Brussels, Belgium

Since the early 1990s, specific community sports programmes have been set up in Flanders (Belgium) to stimulate participation among socially deprived groups. With only a limited involvement of the traditional sports sector, alternative providers (e.g. youth welfare sector) became active in organizing local initiatives, such as neighbourhood sports. However, despite the multiplicity of sports providers, to date, inequalities in sports participation still exist. The present paper investigates whether or not the commercial sports sector can contribute in developing a sustainable community sports offering for socially deprived youth. Based on examples regarding its involvement in so-called 'street sports', it is argued that the commercial sector entered the domain of community sports providers by using highly accessible activities for this youth. It is yet to be determined if, and under which circumstances, this involvement offers opportunities for a wider role of the commercial sports sector in community sports development.

Introduction

Enabling every individual to participate in sport has been voiced by the Council of Europe in the European Sports Charter, as the primary task of governments. The Charter also states that 'measures shall be taken to ensure that all citizens have opportunities to take part in sport and where necessary, additional measures shall be taken aimed at enabling ... disadvantaged or disabled individuals or groups to be able to exercise such opportunities effectively'.[1] Defenders of this social (counter) movement which originated in the sixties, shifted the long-standing focus of 'performance' (competition and competence) in sports involvement towards a broader 'participation' dimension. The more inclusive and democratic participation in sports was viewed in relation to it generating health benefits and the social integrating effects for both the individual and society. A rhetoric that has more recently been rejuvenated by the European Commission's White Paper on Sport.

The founders of the Sport for All Charter have articulated that sports organizations should be encouraged to establish mutually beneficial arrangements with each other and with potential partners, such as the commercial sector, the media, etc. In this paper, taking Flanders, the Dutch-speaking region of Belgium, as our case study, we set out to determine the opportunities and implications of a wider involvement of the commercial sports sector within a sport-for-all community development context, and more specifically, in relation to socially deprived youth.

Pioneering a sport-for-all policy

Belgium was one of the pioneers in implementing the first European Sport for All Charter. In the late sixties, the Belgian state underwent a number of constitutional reforms in which more autonomy was granted to the regions and language communities (Dutch, French and German speaking). A constitutional reform in 1993 resulted in a federal state, with three levels of government (federal, regional and linguistic community) and a complex division of responsibilities. The Flemish region, with a population of more than six million inhabitants, consists of five provinces. The other Belgian provinces are located in the French-speaking region of Wallonia and in the capital district of Brussels. With the introduction of the so-called 'cultural autonomy' of the communities in 1969, a Ministry of Education and Dutch Culture was installed, with a separate Flemish sports administration.

During the past 40 years, the Flemish Government has actively promoted sport for all, in which the focus has been on the promotion of sports participation for as many people as possible, regardless of age, gender, socio-economic status, ethnic origin, etc. From the early seventies onwards, large-scale promotional campaigns were launched in Flanders to stimulate sports participation among specific target groups such as women, elderly people and people with disabilities. Two decades later, the emphasis shifted towards participation of young people as organized sports were characterized by increased youth drop-out rates and alarmingly low physical fitness levels among youngsters. Sport for all portrayed itself increasingly as a collective movement and the diversification of sports in the Flemish landscape gradually became a fact. However, in the late nineties, the sport focused philosophy slowly dissolved and the movement became synonymous with wider concepts such as physical activity and lifetime fitness.

Although it is difficult to determine the actual effects of the Flemish sport-for-all policy, at present, two-thirds of the population is actively involved in sports.[2] This is distinctly higher than in the sixties, when just over one-fifth of the population older than 12 was 'sport active'. Interestingly, the increase of sports participation in Flanders can be attributed for a large part to the growing number of sports-active women and elderly people. It is indicated that, for the first time in Flanders, women are now almost equally involved in sport compared to men, and older adults are gradually narrowing down the 'participation gap' with youngsters.[3] The high participation rates, however, do not take into account the intensity, frequency or the context of sports participation. When, for example, health criteria (i.e. minimum intensity and duration) are considered, only one-third of the total adult population in Flanders can be regarded as 'sports active'. It is indicated that frequency and intensity of participation also seem to have an effect on group cohesion.[4] Hence, it remains unclear if the increased participation has been paralleled with increased sport-for-all outcomes and benefits that are traditionally attributed to specific sports participation patterns.

Alternative sports providers

Through specific decrees, the Flemish Government now recognizes and supports a number of important sports actors, such as provincial and municipal sports services, sports federations and the school system. These public and private non-profit actors are responsible for an important part of the actual sports provision in Flanders. It is interesting to note, that while the Flemish Government has primarily focused on supporting the traditional sports system (e.g. sports clubs), over the years the increase of sports participation in Flanders appears to be strongly situated in the sports provided outside this traditional system. In this context, diverse structures can be found within different sectors

101

that are providing a sports provision for specific target groups, and more noticeably youth. Schools are, next to the regular physical education curriculum, organizing after-school sports programmes in collaboration with municipal sports services. Youth organizations have systematically included sports activities in their overall approach and municipal sports services have for their part become more active in creating alternative formats for youth sports. Recently, the welfare sector has also showed an increased involvement in trying to generate more accessible sporting opportunities for certain youths.

Sport for all: an evidence-based policy?

Despite the multiplicity of sports providers that are active in Flanders, to date, sport for all is still far from being a reality, as significant inequalities remain with regard to sports participation. Among the non-participants, there is a proportional over-representation of women, 45+, lower educated, unskilled labourers, professional inactives and people with a limited social leisure network. For example, Flemish statistics show that sports participation among the higher educated (80.0%) doubles that of the lower or non-educated people (41.8%).[5] Furthermore, the degree of sports participation among certain groups such as ethnic minorities and disabled persons is also substantially lower than among other segments of the Flemish population.[6]

At present, it remains a reality that specific groups are not making use of what is offered by the more traditional sports providers and are systematically being excluded. A number of barriers exist that can account for these differences in sports participation. These relate to a variation in personal attitudes and knowledge of sports and physical activity, but also to differences in availability of time, means, mobility, etc. In other words, although the degree of sports participation of the Flemish population has increased distinctly over the past decades, sport is far from being democratized in Flanders. This corresponds with what has been indicated elsewhere in that a number of groups in society can profit more than others from the subsidies provided by the Government for sports promotion and from the positive and medical effects that forms of active leisure generate.[7]

In general, two categories of participants can be distinguished that are not, or only to a limited extent, involved in sports. These categories can either be characterized in relation to (1) their (problematic) degree of sports participation (e.g. 'sport inactives' and 'sport underprivileged') or to (2) their (problematic) situation (e.g. socially deprived, ethnic minorities). Over the years, several sports initiatives have been set up in Flanders to reach out to these people. The aims differ according to the specific category. With regard to the first category, the emphasis is on increasing the interest in sports (e.g. through raising the quality of the provision, an increased demand-orientation, improving communication and accessibility of the provision). These strategies have also been used in reaching out to the groups in the second category. For example, in recent years the Flemish Government has encouraged more sports actors to become actively involved in optimizing the accessibility of their sports provision to socially deprived groups in society. In order to do so, a number of specific campaigns (e.g. to increase ethnic minorities in sports clubs), as well as more structural measures (e.g. implementation of specific decrees on local sports policy and participation) have been set up or introduced.

Organized sports

The organized non-profit sports sector (i.e. sports federations and clubs) has always been regarded as one of the keystones of the Flemish sport-for-all policy. It is believed that this sector can have a significant contribution in encouraging as many people as possible to become and stay 'sports active'. Reference here, among other things, is often made to high levels of sports technical expertise and to quality structural networks, which facilitates competition organization and access to adequate sports infrastructure. However, it has been indicated that sports clubs in Flanders are facing a number of problems, which undoubtedly have an impact on the quality of the sports provision they offer. Besides financial and infrastructural problems, there is a lack of qualified sports trainers and coaches (i.e. only 53% of all club trainers have a specific sports pedagogical qualification).[8] And although the possibilities of sports clubs in providing opportunities in relation to the building of social capital have been described by an increasing number of authors in recent years,[9] some argue that the traditional format of sports clubs, which often requires a substantial and active involvement of its members, drives many people away into alternative formats, which in turn are characterized by weaker ties and less obligations.[10]

The focus of the Flemish sports policy on youth sports can be explained by relatively high involvement of young people within organized sports and the assumed educational values that are attributed to organized sports practice. In the nineties this focus changed due to the high dropout rates and the worsening physical fitness of young people. Over the years, an increasing number of sports programmes and initiatives have been set up specifically for the sports stimulation of socially deprived youth. Educators and policy makers were becoming concerned with the moral socialization of young people. This concern stems from the increase in antisocial and delinquent behaviour among youths.[11] Alongside education and work, sport is viewed as an important means of counteracting disintegrating trends.[12] The sports club has been considered as an ideal social structure in this regard.[13]

However, despite a number of specific measures aimed at a greater involvement of organized sports in the sports stimulation of socially deprived groups, until now successful initiatives in this sector remain scarce. Experiences in the 1980s in The Netherlands already showed that sports clubs could not play a significant role in creating equal participation conditions for socially deprived youth.[14] One of the explanations was related to the fact that most sports clubs are not confronted with these groups and therefore do not feel a need to become involved in specific sports stimulation initiatives. In an attempt to further encourage the organized sports sector to take up a more proactive societal role, the Flemish Government has recently passed on a 'participation decree' aimed at increasing the chances of socially excluded groups to participate in sports. This decree has been issued as a policy instrument to counter persistent barriers that are hindering certain groups within Flemish society from actively participating in sport and leisure. To date, however, past practices in Flanders have not been subjected to any systematic evaluation. Consequently, it remains difficult to determine the specific mechanisms and strategies that might be effective in encouraging the organized sports sector to become more involved. The fact that no monitoring and evaluation strategy has been developed in the past hinders an understanding in how and for whom sports stimulation initiatives are supposed to work.

Besides the lack of evaluation, there are also doubts regarding the impact of the organized sports sector in catering for socially excluded groups. As earlier mentioned, sports clubs in Flanders are facing a variety of problems, which will surely affect the quality of their sports provision. It can therefore be expected that services situated 'outside' of their core business (e.g. attracting socially deprived youth), are not given any priority and, most likely, will not be provided in an optimal way. This is in line with Coalter, who stated that attempts to use the organized sports sector to achieve wider policy goals (conditions associated with funding), can undermine their essential (mostly non-altruistic) purpose, qualities and stability. He argued that this might not come as a surprise as 'it is also possible that the resources of national sporting organizations will become so stretched that neither form of sports development can be adequately sustained'.[15] Those sports clubs that do take up a proactive role in trying to create a more social inclusive policy are facing existential challenges. More members – in numbers and difference in backgrounds – will raise the necessity of more (professionalized) volunteers, more and better qualified coaches and a higher demand for accessible and adequate sports facilities.

Some researchers strongly argue that sports clubs might be the source of generating or at least amplifying mechanisms of inclusion as well as exclusion, and that processes of bonding and bridging do not necessarily, nor automatically happen within the structures of a traditional sports club.[16] The unsettled position of the organized sports sector (forced) to play a bigger role in a more inclusive sport-for-all movement paved the way for the development of other sports (delivery) structures.

Community sports for socially deprived youth

The concept of community sports originally arose out of the realization that traditional participation patterns were dominated by advantaged sections of the population and that an alternative approach was needed.[17] As described earlier, specific community sports initiatives for socially deprived groups have been set up in Flanders. The first initiatives were primarily situated within the youth welfare sector.[18] Within these small-scale initiatives, sport has been regarded as a way to build positive social capital using a community development approach with an emphasis on high involvement, expanding empowerment and well-being of participants. However most of the organizations involved, with highly motivated and sports-minded youth welfare workers, were confronted with a lack of sufficient means and adequate sports equipment, limited sports pedagogical skills among their guidance staff, as well as no or limited opportunities to make use of the existing local sports facilities. The Belgian King Baudouin Foundation has played a major role in drawing the attention of other sports actors in Flanders to the need for a community sports development approach in reaching out to socially deprived youth.[19] Gradually, local sports services of (especially) larger municipalities and cities also became involved in the organization of these initiatives as they began to regard this group as a specific target group of their sports policy. Targeting underprivileged youth and focusing on a more instrumental function of sport by local (municipal) sports services has often been triggered by the growing concern among local policy makers regarding the public 'nuisance' caused by specific youth groups in urban deprived areas (e.g. vandalism, offensive behaviour). This difference in perspective has shaped the first initiatives that were set up by local sports services, which mostly emphasized the prevention of 'undesirable' behaviour among these youngsters.

As mentioned earlier, the organized sports sector has never played any significant role in the provision of sports opportunities for underprivileged youth. Instead, somewhat surprisingly, other providers have gradually become involved in the organization of specific community sports initiatives. This is surprising, as most of these 'new' providers are traditionally not linked to sports provisions. Through the years, several of these other providers (e.g. the sector of youth, education, integration, social affairs, prevention) have started to work together, thereby increasing their potential.

Next to sports stimulation to increase levels of sports participation among socially deprived groups, there has also been a growing tendency in Flemish sports policy to focus on the 'instrumental' function of sport, in which sports participation is regarded as a means to increase personal and social development among specific groups. The underlying notion is that sporting outcomes (e.g. skill development) facilitated by a certain degree of an organized sports involvement, might eventually lead to intermediate changes at the individual level (e.g. pro-social development), which in turn might lead to broader societal changes (e.g. social cohesion). Research in Flanders has suggested that (club) sports activity is negatively correlated with antisocial attitudes, such as ethnocentrism, individualism, political distrust, traditionalism and feelings of insecurity.[20] But the underlying processes that instigate these changes are unknown and seldom formulated. In a more general context, it has been indicated that, to date, many functions and meanings attributed to sport lack a sound empirical foundation.[21]

It can be questioned whether sport can live up to the high expectations of policy makers. Can it play a role in mitigating the breakdown of social capital on the community level? But determining a direct causal relation between sport and pro-social development may be unfeasible or not even relevant. The success of one sports programme within a certain context will not necessarily lead to the same success within a different context. Consequently, it is relevant to investigate and determine which contextual conditions and organizational mechanisms can facilitate beneficial and sustainable outcomes on the individual, group and community level. This needs to be done by the systematic collection of practice-based evidence in which every case represents a possibility to learn. Sport only amounts to sport. It is not sport as such that can lead to such outcomes, but rather the context of sport.

The strategy of using sport for reaching out to socially deprived youth has been used in Flanders most often within a community sports development approach. In this perspective, sport is recognized as an opportunity to engage young people in a positive alternative and not just in terms of participation in activities, but across a range of issues including education, employment and training, community leadership, and healthy lifestyles. In recent years, this approach became known as 'sport plus' (or 'sport+') initiatives, because of the proclaimed added value beyond 'mere' participation.

But despite two decades of specific community sports initiatives in Flanders aimed at socially deprived youth, the present situation shows many deficiencies. For example, based on the views of 20 expert witnesses coming from a variety of sectors (i.e. sport, education, youth, welfare), it was concluded that most of today's sports stimulation initiatives in Flanders aimed at socially deprived groups do not operate in optimal conditions. According to the experts, most initiatives are characterized by inadequate social and pedagogical skills of coaching and teaching staff, limited structural cooperation with partner organizations, availability of sports facilities, and accessibility of activities. Notwithstanding the present deficiencies, these formats of community sports have become a well established and recognized concept for reaching out to socially excluded youth, and the methodology has been broadened towards other excluded groups in Flanders.

Neighbourhood sports: a local community approach

As the majority of community sports initiatives aimed at socially deprived youth in Flanders has been situated outside the 'regular' sports provision (i.e. local sports services and sports clubs), the limited availability of adequate sports facilities remains one of the major problems in reaching out to these youths. Among other things, this situation has led to the occurrence of an alternative sports organizational format in Flanders with an emphasis on high accessibility through the organization of events in public squares, streets and parks in socially deprived areas, which from the beginning of the nineties became known as 'neighbourhood sports'. The term 'neighbourhood sports' refers in essence to the use and the combination of specific methodologies that are different from the more traditional sports delivery formats. It is important to note that one overall neighbourhood sports format does not exist in the Flemish context. Findings of a study that attempted to determine the actual position of neighbourhood sports in Flanders (in which data were collected among representatives of 250 Flemish municipalities, as well as among 30 Flemish expert witnesses and 10 good practices) indicated that there is a wide diversity of organizational formats in neighbourhood sports.[22] This variety largely depends on the type of coordinating organization, as well as on the aims and specific target group. Neighbourhood sports are often regarded as an accessible means of sports stimulation and aims at those groups that are not, or only to a limited extent, participating in (organized) sports. While neighbourhood sports initiatives occasionally make use of regular sports facilities, they are often organized in a variety of facilities (from outdoor places such as public parks and squares to indoor facilities such as renovated warehouses, parking spaces, etc.).

The concept of neighbourhood sports originated as a football initiative. In 1989, the King Baudouin Foundation, in cooperation with the Royal Belgian Football Federation, launched a street football campaign.[23] Their aim was to improve the social integration of underprivileged youth through the organization of accessible football competitions on the streets in urban deprived areas. As the range of areas to organize the competitions became larger (i.e. public parks, squares, beaches, etc.), its name changed into 'neighbourhood football' in 1992. Two years later, the name changed into 'neighbourhood ball' as other ball sports were included (i.e. basketball and volleyball). Finally in 2001, it changed to its present name, neighbourhood sports, as more sports became part of the programmes. In most of these initiatives there has been an increased interest in working together at the local level with other structures coming from in and outside the sports sector. The choice of neighbourhood sports activities, as well as the organizational level and type of guidance approach, varies according to the target group and specific neighbourhood characteristics.

Today, the Flemish Government recognizes the value of neighbourhood sports. The decree on 'local sport policy', which was recently issued, states that municipal sports services are obliged to invest one-fifth of their total budget in alternatively organized sports initiatives (such as neighbourhood sports) in order to receive subsidies from the Flemish Government. This decree can be seen as a social correction of the local sports policy in which municipal services are encouraged to take up the role as directors of a local sports for all movement using an interactive governance style. Neighbourhood sports is in line with what has been described elsewhere as being the characteristics of community sports development: a flexible, adaptable, informal, interactive, people-centred approach, aimed at lowering the initial thresholds to participation in order to address the deficiencies of mainstream provision.[24] The innovative character of these neighbourhood sports initiatives for the Flemish situation can be found in the way they are embedded in regular structures (municipal sports and youth services) and the striving towards a formal cooperation network of different actors within the community context. The concept of neighbourhood sports can be compared with formats elsewhere, such as the Community Sport Networks in the UK and the neighbourhood-education-sport (Buurt-Onderwijs-Sport) approach in The Netherlands.[25] These networks are being established in an attempt to rationalize the fragmented structure of sports provision into a new 'delivery system of sport', tailored to the needs of the local context.

Two examples of neighbourhood sports initiatives in Flanders will be described in the next paragraphs, illustrating the multifaceted character of this sports organizational format: the case of neighbourhood sports project 'Ghent' and the neighbourhood sports project 'Mechelen'. What stands out in these two cases is the involvement of non-traditional actors in setting up a local delivery system of sports, embedded within a community context.

Neighbourhood sports project, Ghent

Ghent, Flanders second largest city with a population of 233,000 inhabitants, is the capital city of the Flemish province East Flanders. The coordination and implementation of neighbourhood sports in Ghent has for the most part been initiated outside the public and private sports sector, namely by the municipal youth service, youth welfare organizations and community development organizations. Ten neighbourhoods are defined as 'attention' areas (deprived communities) due to high percentages of ethnic minorities and high levels of unemployment. These neighbourhoods are mainly situated in the old workers' areas of the city, where there is a lack of sports clubs and sports facilities. One of those areas is Ghent-Nord, a densely populated and agglomerated neighbourhood where almost one-fifth of the population is unemployed and 40% comes from an ethnic cultural minority.

In searching for a solution for the lack of adequate sports accommodation, a community sports project was set up with local residents, community organizations and a multinational enterprise as its primary partners. The enterprise, a textile and chemicals manufacturing company involved in producing high-performance fabrics for aerospace, automotive and industrial applications, agreed to provide a part of its infrastructure to be used for the project. A plan was conceived in which the company's parking lot was converted into an indoor sports hall to be used during weekends. The makeover was financed by the company itself and an electricity distributing company sponsors the project by providing free electricity. The converted parking lot became known as the 'sports barn'. According to the organizers, one of the key success factors of the project is the cooperation of different stakeholders. Multiple sports activities are provided with a high degree of involvement of residents. Participants or residents are encouraged to actively take part in the project, thus increasing the ownership of the project and creating opportunities for voluntary work. These recruitments are based on distinct profiles. Membership and registration are not required to participate in the activities, although some basic rules are set forward with regard to safety, hygiene, time-frame of the activities and respect for infrastructure and equipment.

A major deficiency that has been pinpointed by the project coordinators is the limited involvement of the organized sports sector, which according to them, undermines the quality of the provided activities and hinders opportunities for a possible flow through of the participating youngsters towards local sports clubs.

Neighbourhood sports project, Mechelen

The city of Mechelen, located less than 25 kilometres north of the Belgian capital, Brussels, has a population of around 78,900 inhabitants, with 7.5% people of foreign origin, mostly Moroccan. In 1993, the municipal welfare service started its own sports project, which can be regarded as the actual start of the neighbourhood sports project Mechelen. Since its inception, the general aim of the neighbourhood sports project has been to provide a meaningful and accessible sports programme for unorganized six to 16 year-olds. Most of these youngsters live in socially deprived areas. Through its programme, the project attempts to communicate with youngsters within the context of the social practice of sport on a variety of topics (e.g. dealing with winning and losing, communicating with referees, opponents, team members, coaches and organizers). The project is also intended to be an alternative for the regular sports provision which holds a number of barriers for this youth group (e.g. financial, structural and cultural). Other goals relate to the provision of a possible flow through to regular sports clubs as well as offering social assistance at the individual level. Through the project, the organizers get to know the backgrounds of participants better. This enables them to detect problems and, if necessary, work with them individually in hands-on situations.

Although successful in reaching specific youngsters, during the first seven years of the project neighbourhood sports in Mechelen was regarded as a 'side phenomenon', receiving limited or no attention from local officials. While the project reached hundreds of children and youngsters every week and provided them with a regular sports provision, the sports sector as well as the local sports service did not show any interest in it. In the beginning of 2000, the Belgian Ministry of Internal Affairs started a number of preventive measures in preparation for the organization of the European Football Championship that was to be held later that year in Belgium and The Netherlands (Euro 2000). Next to measures aimed at escorting football fans, the authorities also wanted to start a number of local prevention initiatives in so-called 'transit cities', situated along important arterial roads that were going to be used by fans during the Championship matches and, as such, regarded as possible 'risk areas'. Because of its specific location, Mechelen was also selected as a transit city. These cities received considerable funding, which needed to be used to organize activities for youngsters in deprived areas during the time of the Championship to 'stay out of trouble'. After initial hesitation, the local government asked the help of the neighbourhood sports project. With these funds, the project decided to organize a large-scale neighbourhood football tournament during the time of Euro 2000. It is beyond any doubt that this event can be regarded as a very important incentive for the further development of the neighbourhood sports project of Mechelen. It has helped to enable a number of steps, which would probably not have been taken if the tournament was not organized. The tournament turned into a yearly event that has become the largest indoor football competition in Flanders, attracting more than 500 boys in three age categories (with a few mixed teams) each year. It includes a number of side activities (e.g. panna cage, human table football). The maximum has been set at 60 teams, due to capacity reasons. Half of the teams are recruited from other cities and several regular football clubs take part. In 2001, the neighbourhood sports project moved from the municipal welfare service to the local sports service, where it is still located at present. Neighbourhood football is now organized at different open-air locations and is one of the most successful activities to date. Other football alternatives have grown from it since. The various youth welfare organizations that started to work together are now officially recognized by the local government and, for the first time ever, they now even receive financial support by the municipality of Mechelen.

Although the evaluation of the effectiveness of this kind of initiatives remains complex, the project has convinced local officials of its value. Not only because it showed to them that accessible sports initiatives can attract youngsters that otherwise do not become involved in regular sports participation, but also because local police reports have mentioned a decrease in the number of problems with youngsters in specific deprived areas.

De-traditionalization of sport for all

Today an evolution can be observed in the way policy makers are viewing the organization, delivery and practice of sport for all. Since the start of the sport-for-all movement, the context of sports participation in Flanders has undergone some drastic changes. The sports sector cannot be looked upon any more as the exclusive partner in developing a local community sports provision. In comparison with non and alternatively organized sport, recent statistics show that club organized sport scores significantly lower.[26] A quarter of the adult population has an active membership involvement in a sports club, while almost half of the adult population practise sport on an individual basis. During the last two decades, individual sports participation has become the most popular form of practising sport, which among other things resulted in a declining volunteer base for sports clubs. On the other hand, sports participation numbers for youth reveal that for a large part young people still practise their sport in an organized context, although the popularity of non-organized sport shows a comparable popularity.[27]

It has been indicated that in order to be able to speak of a democratized sports participation, a further 'de-traditionalization' of sport is required.[28] This logically leads to a broader perspective on sports development that surpasses the traditional formats in which sport used to be organized and provided. New organizational formats in sport, often characterized by weaker ties between participants and sometimes referred to as 'light sports communities', have become increasingly popular.[29]

Commercial sport in Flanders

The commercialization and professionalization processes of sport are believed to be responsible for the success of non and alternatively organized sport.[30] Looking at the characteristics of sports participation in the beginning of the 21st century, an intensified commercialization process can be noticed that instigated and – for a large part – shaped the so-called 'second recreation wave', in which the market is encroaching on the territory of the state and the civil society in providing sports and recreation services. For example, the number of fitness centres in Flanders has increased by 54.9% over the last decade, while the number of sports clubs in subsidized federations has decreased by 8.2% in the same period. Also, participation data regarding the most popular sports in Flanders show that preferences among the population over 12 is gradually commercializing, as illustrated by the increased popularity of fitness, running (events) and skiing. Fitness, only to be surpassed by cycling and walking, has become more popular than swimming. In 2007, almost 16% of the active Flemish population was engaged in it.[31] It is interesting to note that fitness, a sector traditionally not subsidized by the state, has been to a large extent responsible for the increased participation of the population in Flanders and, more importantly, in bridging the gender gap in sports participation during the last decennia. This is a remarkable fact as the Flemish Government has never played a significant role in promoting and developing fitness based sports provision.

One actor that has surprisingly been left out of the picture in the sport-for-all movement in Flanders is the commercial sports sector. In Flanders this sector has become involved in so called mixed formats, such as public-private cooperation in the construction and management of municipal sports infrastructure or shared commercial-voluntary initiatives of sponsoring organized sports (e.g. private sponsors of sports clubs or initiatives such as Start 2 Run, Homeless World Cup Football). Market generated initiatives such as the 'Start to run – bike – swim – fitness – walk' campaigns can be put forward as low-threshold sports provisions that are reaching large sections of the population. A smart use of popular media channels, new technologies (e.g. ipods), and identifiable spokespersons (local celebrities) are important strategic elements within these initiatives. Partnerships within these 'start to . . . ' initiatives consist of a variety of sports-related organizations (that produce sports products and services) and sports-unrelated commercial organizations. Branch associated events such as the Nike Beach Aerobics Marathon, Tampax Beach Soccer, Ladies Runs, Ladies Bike, o.b. Beach Volleyball have also created possibilities in reaching groups of Flemish society. The above described initiatives can be regarded as practices within a sport-for-all context, and are exemplary for the involvement of the commercial sector in creating a low-threshold sports provision. Interestingly, through targeting specific sections of the population, the commercial sports sector seems to be able to attract some groups who are identified as 'hard to reach' customers in a traditional sports provision.[32] For example, a number of fitness centres in Flanders have set up 'Ladies Only' branches. Not so surprisingly, by using a specific public relation strategy and a format that acknowledges the requirements and characteristics of the target group, these Ladies Only branches are attracting Muslim women who are hardly being reached by the regular and alternative sports structures.

Next, some sports initiatives within the Flemish context will be highlighted that originated outside the traditional domains of the civil society and the state. There will be a focus on those commercial for-profit organizations that have been active at the local community level within the context of sport for all.

A wider role for commercial sport?

Until now, the Flemish Government has played a leading role in delivering funding for the organized non-profit sports sector and investing in heavy sports infrastructure in their sport-for-all promotional strategy. However, taking the limited involvement of the traditional sports system into consideration, as well as the current deficiencies of the public and other private non-profit providers of community sports initiatives aimed at socially deprived youth, it is interesting to investigate whether or not the commercial sports sector can play a role here. As there are several indications of an intensified commercialization process in Flemish sports provision over the past decade, it is worthwhile to investigate to what extent this sector can contribute in developing and delivering a sustainable community sports provision for socially deprived youth. While at first sight, this involvement might be very restricted because of the gap that exists between both worlds, a closer look, however, appears to produce another image. In fact, a number of mechanisms seem to exist which might provide some evidence that both worlds are not that far apart as it may seem. One of the mechanisms relates to the association of a commercialized sports provision with specific elements of contemporary youth culture. For example, in their attempt to reach out and attract youth, segments of the commercialized leisure industry have clearly linked up with the so-called 'urban street movement culture'. Among other things, this can be illustrated by the fact that leading soft drink companies (e.g. Coca-Cola, Pepsi) have become increasingly involved in supporting and organizing street sports events with street football, three-on-three basketball, BMX and skateboarding (e.g. 'Coca-Cola Street Striker'; 'Pepsi Street Skills'; 'Red Bull Street Style'; 'Sprite Urban Games'). Sports wear and equipment giants, such as Nike and Adidas, have also started to promote and organize freestyle sports events. Nike, for example, developed a series of 'Panna Knock Out' soccer events. In these events, players technically duel each other in arenas (circular cages). Elements of popular youth culture and role models are being integrated in the marketing concept of these Panna events in order to reach potential participants. By adapting street rules and expressions, organizers of these events are proclaiming themselves as the representatives of a new street-football generation. The created street-style atmosphere works like a magnet for youth in the communities where these events are organized. In several Flemish cities street-football events (e.g. Lotto street soccer 2008) have been set up by a cooperative alliance of commercial partners (i.e. media, sports wear, marketing), local and central governments, the National Lottery and the Royal Belgian Football Federation. An extra dimension within these city street-football tournaments is that a format is created in which the organizers are not only targeting youth, but also their direct social environment (peer group, siblings, parents). Another sports business player on the urban street-games market, whose influence is steadily increasing, is the computer-gaming industry. A sector that has, more than occasionally, associated itself with the street sports culture. In some events gaming producers are exhibiting their 'street' hardware where young people can try out their virtual street skills.

With their branding strategy in which the commercial sector associates itself with street culture ('street tribe') and organizes accessible competitions for inner-city urban youth, they have actually entered the domain of community (neighbourhood) sports providers who also use highly accessible and recognizable street-sports activities for these youths. These commercial providers are tapping into the networks of what has been described as symbolic societies by using the social and cultural influence channels of the target groups they wish to involve.[33] It appears to inspire many youngsters to become involved in street sports, which can be demonstrated through the vast amount of video clips available on YouTube in which young people show their street skills.

By organizing street-sports events, the commercial sector is offering similar community (neighbourhood) sports activities and might be taking up an active position within community sports provision. It is however important to look at the reason why these profit-based initiatives are getting involved in sports provision for inner city youth. What profit can be created by targeting young people who are seemingly not capable of giving a substantial financial return through their participation? Especially when taking into account that some of the street-associated manufactured sports goods (e.g. equipment, clothes) are in many cases more expensive than their original non-street versions. Interestingly, sometimes this association of street culture is also linked to passing on a number of explicit norms and values to youngsters, which relate to, among other things, denouncing a 'win at all cost' attitude and embracing virtues such as fair play, honour and creativity. Illustrative here is the 'Joga Bonito' campaign created by Nike. Joga Bonito (which means 'play beautifully' in Portuguese) is described as a football-oriented social network service. Through advertisements on the nikefootball.com website, 'Joga TV' promotes an alternative football approach, which emphasizes a pure experience of the sport's skills, stripped of the excesses of today's professional and highly commercialized football. As these virtues clearly resemble street-culture values, Nike tries to appeal to many youngsters. Former French international football 'star' player Eric Cantona appeared as one of the leading spokesmen for the campaign. One of the most famous campaign video clips shows Cantona feinting to break into a German TV studio and ending a live broadcast on football, stating the following: 'This is Eric Cantona, interrupting your transmissions. Broadcasting live from the heart of Germany. *Mes amis footballeurs*, for too long we let liars and cheaters make a fool of our game ... I am here to remind the world that this game is about skills, heart, honour, joy, team spirit. *Mes amis*, I need your help, your heart and your feet. Together, me and you, we can make it beautiful again. Beautiful! So step forward, my brothers in football and enjoy. Play beautiful.' It is noteworthy to mention that Cantona, in his days not only respected for his superb football skills, became also known for his numerous disciplinary problems with opponents, referees and even fans.

Clearly, the above-mentioned examples can be located in the branding strategy of companies, based on the notion that street culture is 'hot' and undoubtedly appeals to larger segments of today's youth. But perhaps more important is the question: in what way can communities where these initiatives are organized benefit from this association? Are these commercial initiatives just scratching the surface of community-based sports interventions or are they sustainable? Or to put it more bluntly, why is 'the circus' in town and what happens when it leaves town? After all, it is to be expected that commercialized initiatives primarily aim for economic profit, which, at first sight, is hard to obtain through focusing on socially deprived youth.

A second mechanism that can be detected, and seems to bring the commercial sector closer to community sports, is related to the corporate social responsibility strategy of specific companies. In its purest form, corporate social responsibility is described as a 'genuine attempt to return benefits of successful business back to the community that it is derived from'.[34] For example, over the years several major sports-goods companies have become involved in also benefiting the wider community and environment in which they operate (e.g. the Adidas Group, the Reebok Foundation). Among other things, their aim is to promote social and economic equality by funding non-profit organizations delivering programmes aimed at urban youth and under-served groups to empower them to fulfil their potential. As they also support or directly organize sports-development initiatives on a local level, there is a clear link to community sports. Illustrative here is the involvement of the Nike Foundation which has been active in Flanders in providing financial support to promising community-based sports initiatives. In most of these cases, 'the power of sport' has been advocated to beat the social exclusion, poverty, criminal behaviour, etc., of socially deprived groups in society, to rebuild their lives and offer new opportunities. In their contribution in this issue of *Sport in Society*, on sport business and social capital, Spaaij and Westerbeek also argue that the case studies on Nike and the Homeless World Cup suggest that the deployment of corporate social responsibility in and through sport offers substantial potential for community return. It will, however, be important to determine to what extent commercial initiatives can live up to these expectations and can offer an added value to existing non-profit community sports development initiatives. It can be assumed that much will depend on the kind of expectations that exist. For example, when looking at the case described earlier of neighbourhood sports of Ghent, it becomes clear that the involvement of the commercial sector on the local level (in this case the provision of extra sports facilities by a local company), can indeed result in added value. And other examples can also be described here, such as professional (commercialized) football clubs that offer opportunities to further develop community sports (e.g. through grass-roots community football facility and community projects). It is likely that most of these initiatives originated as a reaction against problematic behaviour of specific local youth groups and the resulting annoyance for the community (and its businesses). However, the choice of focusing on community development through sport can be viewed in a positive re-socialization perspective situated within a larger, corporate social responsibility strategy. Reference can be made here to the earlier described case of Neighbourhood Sport Mechelen, where the initial concern for controlling risk areas during a commercialized mega sports event (Euro 2000), has gradually turned into a structural provision of highly accessible sports initiatives in socially deprived urban areas.

The link between the commercial sports sector and community sports initiatives aimed at socially deprived youth has been described earlier in relation to two mechanisms. One of these mechanisms relates to a branding strategy in connecting the company's image to the urban street (movement) culture. Through this association, sports-goods manufacturers attempt to reach large segments of today's youngsters and their social environment by focusing on popular youth lifestyles which are characterized, among other things, by respect, honour and creativity. It has been put forward that in the coming years, lifestyle characteristics, and not so much social-economical factors, will need to be taken more into account in order to reach those groups that are not actively participating in organized sports.[35] In line with the symbolic societies theory, differences in sports-participation patterns would have to be explained not so much by the traditional social-economical background factors (positions), but rather by the differences created by influential socialization channels, such as the media, religion, education, etc., (sometimes referred to as neo-tribalism).[36] These are influential channels, with which increasingly more links can be detected in relation to the commercial sports sector. A potential seems to be present that could lead to a more dynamic sport-for-all policy and practice for, among others, socially deprived youth.

Community sport and commercial sport: partners or competitors?

In the last 15 years, public spending on sports in Flanders has decreased in real terms.[37] The power of the state to influence the sports market has been diminished due to economic recessions and the effects of a more (neo-)liberal monetary system (the 1970s' and also the current system) with the overall consequence that the state is pulling back in these sectors where it previously had a monopoly position. The funding resources of the state for sports associations and social projects have become stretched, and the role of the state in developing a sport-for-all provision is weakened simply by the position it is forced to take. This implies that the state may not be able to take up this task alone. There are some who would argue for the state to leave providers to compete for participants. This would allow the open market to provide for a range of public needs, without subsidizing public facilities and services, and take the burden away from the public sector.[38] However, others fear that commercialization of the sports-provision services will jeopardize societal objectives such as social integration and cohesion. It is indicated that the profit-oriented, competitive nature of the unregulated market creates inequality, exclusion and community breakdown in the first place.[39]

Through its subsidization policy, the state has always played an important role in the organization and development of sports in Flanders. As a result, the non-profit sports sector has a tradition of being very dependent on Government funding. More problematically, because of this prominent role the Flemish Government has played, the organized sports sector and associated organizations are not actively focusing on providing a genuine sport-for-all provision. It is also pointed out that there is a potential conflict between 'developing sports in communities' and 'developing communities through sports' and that perhaps these are different processes.[40]

Despite 40 years of sport-for-all policy in Flanders, distinct inequalities in sports participation among its population still exist. And, although a variety of community (neighbourhood) sports initiatives have been set up since the beginning of the 1990s in which other non-profit providers have been involved in the promotion of sports for specific deprived groups, a number of problems still remain. It can be questioned if it is desirable or sustainable that social cultural objectives are only associated with the public sports and recreation services and that economical objectives are as a rule exclusively linked to commercial services. This might be a too narrow perspective when looking at the broad societal field that sport is embedded in. As Taylor puts it: 'Equal opportunities is not just defined as the exclusive preserve of the social reformist agenda in the public and voluntary sectors, but can be a desirable aspect of the economics of the commercial private sector as well'.[41] Sport and sport business might as well play a role in reducing the constraints that exclude certain social groups.

As outlined in the present paper, the Flemish Government is creating opportunities for alternative providers to become involved in the development of community sports. It might even be a way to encourage the commercial sports sector to take up a wider role in a dynamic, local, sport-for-all delivery in which economic outcomes can be put in a broader perspective of social outcomes, manifested within corporate objectives and cooperation networks. As for the Flemish case, the traditionally organized sports sector seems to be unable (or unwilling?) to move beyond a policy of just creating equal opportunities for all.

A sport-for-all policy and practice need to encompass equal sports opportunities, equal sports conditions and equal sports outcomes for all. The commercial sports sector has inherently more flexibility to accommodate the needs of the potential sports participant, and seems to be able to navigate more agilely around barriers that are hindering certain groups of society from actively participating in sports provisions. It is unclear what the specific community return is and therefore more research is needed. Caveats need to be put forward about the involvement of the commercial sector within the context of developing sport within the community. A real threat exists that in the described cases of street-football events the urban street culture is being hijacked by the commercial sports sector. These events are mostly sponsored in the conventional way by companies keen to take advantage of an audience of children and their parents, without a genuine interest for community-generated benefits.[42] This necessitates scrutinizing the legitimacy of the involvement of the commercial sports sector when entering the field of community (neighbourhood) sports. Some have warned of the dangers of a fashionable 'community' label with virtually no recognition that a particular set of practices and values is implied.[43] Projects under the flagship of 'community' receive funding because they understand the salience of social goals in sports policy and the attractiveness of community sports in funding mechanisms.[44] This is a real threat, which is not only confined to the context of the commercial sector.

Developing regulatory mechanisms in which the free hand of the market can be managed to provide equal sports opportunities, conditions and outcomes for those groups who are not fully participating, will be the biggest challenge and responsibility of the state. This also implies that the state needs to create and facilitate a positive climate in which the commercial sports sector can develop itself within a community context (development of sport in the community). A balance needs to be found between the development of the community through sport and the development of sport in the community. Without regulatory mechanisms and an established methodology based on empirical research, one cannot expect sport to score in both of these fields. It is believed that the input of the state stays, nonetheless, necessary for creating a legal framework and for a desired adjustment of private sports spending.[45] Involvement of the public sector is imperative to provide a safety net for those most vulnerable and traditionally excluded.[46] One of the core tasks of the (local) government remains protecting the rights of all citizens that are residing in its territory. These rights also include the right for active sports participation.

Conclusion

In this paper we have described the context of the sport-for-all practice within the Flemish landscape. What stands out is the role that the Government has played in setting up structures to develop a sport-for-all format. Notwithstanding the substantial efforts the Flemish Government has taken in implementing a sport-for-all policy within a community context, specific groups of society are systematically being excluded from this. The failure of the organized sports sector to contribute in mitigating the systematically exclusionary mechanisms are the result of either the unwillingness or incapability of this sector. And as a result of the Government's prominent involvement, the organized sports sector has become – to some extend – inactive in taking up a wider role. This strongly challenges the views expressed within the European Sports Charter and the European's Commission White Paper on Sport on the perceived central function and responsibility of sports clubs and federations. In addition, sports clubs seem to have lost their touch with the world of today's youth, and are therefore losing their position and function.[47] The instrumental potential of sport, referred to as sport-plus, cannot seem to bear fruit within the context of this sector. It is argued that if sport is to be used as a means to deal with social issues, attention needs to be given to the social responsibilities of sport itself. It is up to sports organizations (i.e. clubs and federations) to clearly identify and communicate what they perceive their social responsibilities are. However it is believed that, to this day, the social responsibilities linked to sport remain underdeveloped.[48] More insight is needed on what these social responsibilities are, and in what conditions and for whom they are more likely to lead to sport-plus outcomes.

The debatable involvement of the organized sports sector within a broader community development context has paved the way for the appearance of alternative providers that are traditionally not linked to sports-delivery services. Within this paper, we have primarily focused on those programmes aimed at socially deprived youth, due to the supposed educational values sports participation brings with it and the attention that youth sport in general has received by Flemish policy makers since the nineties. In addition, alternative sports-delivery systems, coined 'neighbourhood sports' have been set up in the majority of Flemish cities, using a local stakeholder approach. But serious deficiencies remain that are hindering the development of optimal, local sport-for-all practices. An acute shortage of qualified coaches and the absence of systematic monitoring and evaluation practices stand out as the primary bottlenecks.

By recognizing and subsidizing an alternative sports-delivery system, the Flemish Government, however, seems to be opening more doors for the involvement of new players. The commercial sports sector has been delivering sports formats in which they are reaching large sections of the population. Particularly by targeting youth within an urban context, they have entered the work-field of youth and welfare organizations. Relating to socially deprived youth, two mechanisms have been identified for the active involvement of the commercial sports sector within the community sports landscape. The first one relates to a branding strategy in which a broader youth culture is being targeted (urban street culture). By tapping into influential socializing channels, they have succeeded in reaching youth in a sports community context, where other sports providers have not. The second mechanism relates to a corporate social responsibility ethos, in which for-profit organizations have tried to maximize their positive impact on their social and physical environment through the use of sport. Although the mechanisms can be identified, it is far more difficult to determine the community impact that is generated by these commercial initiatives and some caveats need to be put in perspective.

As illustrated by the cases of Ghent and Mechelen, the involvement of commercial partners has substantially contributed to the development of a community-sports format through a local partnership in which, from the point of view of the commercial sector, a 'stakeholder' rather than a 'shareholder' approach has been utilized. In other cases, such as the 'urban street movement', the community return for those excluded groups remains enigmatic, and more systematic analysis is needed to determine the scope of such sports formats instigated by for-profit organizations. By creating a well-defined partnership between commercial and community organizations, a more dynamic sport-for-all policy might be generated that can accrue into the structural provision of highly accessible sports initiatives in socially deprived areas. The role of the Government stays nonetheless a prerequisite.

Notes

[1] European Sports Charter, art. 1.i and art. 4.2.
[2] Van Tuyckom and Scheerder, 'Sport For All?'.

3 Vlaamse Regionale Indicatoren 2009.
4 Elchardus and Smits, *Anatomie en Oorzaken van het Wantrouwen.*
5 Vlaamse Regionale Indicatoren 2009.
6 Theeboom et al., *Handboek sportbeleidsplanning*; Vanlandewijck and Van de Vliet, 'Sportgedrag van Personen met een Handicap in Vlaanderen'.
7 Coalter, *A Wider Role for Sport.*
8 Van Lierde and Willems, 'Hoe goed zit je bij een sportclub?'.
9 Putnam, *Bowling Alone*; Verweel, Janssen and Roques, 'Kleurrijke Zuilen'; Breedveld and van der Meulen, 'Vertrouwen in de Sport'; Scheerder et al., 'Sport en Sociale Cohesie'; Van der Meulen, 'Alle Menschen werden Brüder'.
10 Delnoij, 'Ze zijn gewoon niet te binden'; Duyvendak and Hurenkamp, *Kiezen voor de Kudde.*
11 Rutten et al., *Jeugdsport en Morele Socialisatie.*
12 Elling, Theeboom and De Knop, 'Sociale Integratie in Sportbeleid in Nederland en Vlaanderen'.
13 Koolen, *De Meest Gestelde Vragen over Allochtonen en Sport*; Kruissink, 'Van padvinderij tot pretpark, van Vechtsport tot Volleybal'; van der Gugten, 'De Sport als Aangrijpingspunt voor Criminaliteitspreventie'; Van Dijk, 'De rol van sportbeoefening bij de preventie van criminaliteit'.
14 Van Geelen, 'Hedendaagse Ontwikkelingen Binnen het Sportbeleid in Nederland'.
15 Coalter, *A Wider Role for Sport.*
16 Bailey, 'Youth Sport and Social Inclusion'; Elling, *Ze zijn er niet voor gebouwd.*
17 Hylton and Totten, 'Community Sports Development', 13.
18 Theeboom and De Knop, 'Inventarisatie binnen het jeugdwelzijnswerk in Vlaanderen'.
19 De Knop and Walgrave, *Sport als Integratie, Kansen voor Maatschappelijk Kwetsbare Jongeren*; De Mol and Knops, 'Jeugd en Sport'.
20 Scheerder et al., 'Sport en Sociale Cohesie'.
21 Hoyng, De Knop and Theeboom, 'Functies en Betekenissen van Sport'.
22 Theeboom et al., *Sport en maatschappelijke achterstelling.*
23 Theeboom and de Maesschalck, *Sporten om de Hoek.*
24 Hylton and Totten, 'Community Sports Development', 113.
25 In the context of the UK the concept of 'neighbourhood sport' is being referred to as 'doorstep sports'. These sport initiatives have been brought under the StreetGames national network since 2007. Partners include Sport England, the Football Foundation, the Premier League, the Co-operative network. For more information see www.streetgames.org. Concerning the neighbourhood-education-sport (Buurt-Onderwijs-Sport) approach of the Netherlands, refer to www.nisb.nl.
26 Scheerder, *Tofsport in Vlaanderen.*
27 Smits, *Maatschappelijke Participatie van Jongeren.*
28 Scheerder, Vanreusel and Pauwels, *Breedtesport in Vlaanderen Gepeild.*
29 Delnoij, 'Ze zijn gewoon niet te binden'; Duyvendak and Hurenkamp, *Kiezen voor de Kudde.*
30 van Bottenburg, 'A Second Wave of Running'.
31 Scheerder, *Tofsport in Vlaanderen.*
32 De Knop et al., 'Implications of Islam'; Walseth and Fasting, 'Islam's View'.
33 Elchardus and Glorieux, *De Symbolische Samenleving.*
34 Smith and Westerbeek, 'Sport as a Vehicle'.
35 Scheerder, Vanreusel and Pauwels, *Breedtesport in Vlaanderen Gepeild*, 225–61.
36 Elchardus and Glorieux, *De Symbolische Samenleving*; Bennet, 'Subcultures or Neo-Tribes'.
37 De Knop and van der Poel, 'Het Sportbeleid in Nederland en Vlaanderen'.
38 Coalter, 'Leisure Studies'; LeGrand, 'Theory of the Government Failure'.
39 Ledwith, *Community Development.*
40 Coalter, 'Sports Clubs'.
41 Taylor, *Equal Opportunities*, 60.
42 Smith and Westerbeek, 'Sport as a Vehicle'.
43 Haywood, *Community Leisure and Recreation.*
44 Jackson, Totten and Robinson, 'Evaluating Projects'.
45 De Knop and van der Poel, 'Het Sportbeleid in Nederland en Vlaanderen'.
46 Clarke, Cochrane and McLaughlin, *Managing Social Policy.*
47 Theeboom et al., 'Sport en Jeugd', 370.
48 Smith and Westerbeek, 'Sport as a Vehicle'.

References

Bailey, R. 'Youth Sport and Social Inclusion'. In *Positive Youth Development through Sport*, edited by N. Holt, 85–96. London: Routledge, 2007.

Bennet, A. 'Subcultures or Neo-Tribes? Rethinking the Relationship between Youth, Style & Musical Taste'. *Sociology* 33, no. 3 (1999): 599–17.

Breedveld, K., and R. van der Meulen. 'Vertrouwen in de Sport. Een Empirische Analyse van de Relatie tussen Sportdeelname en Sociaal Kapitaal'. *Vrijetijdstudies* 20, no. 2 (2003): 37–49.

Clarke, J., A. Cochrane, and E. McLaughlin. *Managing Social Policy*. London: Sage Publications, 1994.

Coalter, F. *A Wider Social Role for Sport: Who's Keeping the Score?* London: Routledge, 2007.

Coalter, F. 'Leisure Studies, Leisure Policy and Social Citizenship: The Failure of Welfare or the Limits of Welfare?' *Leisure Studies* 17 (2007): 21–36.

Coalter, F. 'Sports Clubs, Social Capital and Social Regeneration: "Ill-defined Interventions with Hard to Follow Outcomes"?' *Sport in Society* 10, no. 4 (2007): 537–59.

Council of Europe, Committee of Ministers. *(Revised) European Sports Charter*, art. 1.i and 4.2, 2001.

De Knop, P., M. Theeboom, H. Wittock, and K. De Martelaer. 'Implications of Islam on Muslim Girls' Participation in Western Europe: Literature Review on Policy Recommendation for Sport Promotion'. *Sport, Education and Society* 1, no. 2 (1996): 40–8.

De Knop, P., and H. van der Poel. 'Het Sportbeleid in Nederland en Vlaanderen'. In *Sportsociologie: Het Spel en de Spelers*, edited by P. De Knop, B. Vanreusel, and J. Scheerder, 63–84. Maarssen: Elsevier Gezondheidszorg, 2006.

De Knop, P., and L. Walgrave. *Sport als Integratie, Kansen voor Maatschappelijk Kwetsbare Jongeren*. Brussel: Koning Boudewijnstichting, 1992.

De Mol, A., and G. Knops. 'Jeugd en Sport'. *Tijdschrift voor Lichamelijke Opvoeding* 3, no. 157 (1995): 8–10.

Delnoij, M. 'Ze zijn gewoon niet te binden: Hardlopers, Atletiekverenigingen en de Opkomst van Lichte Gemeenschappen'. Unpublished MSc thesis, Universiteit van Amsterdam, 2004.

Duyvendak, J.W., and M. Hurenkamp, eds. *Kiezen voor de Kudde: Lichte Gemeenschappen en de Nieuwe Meerderheid*. Amsterdam: Van Gennep, 2004.

Elchardus, M., and I. Glorieux, eds. *De Symbolische Samenleving. Een Exploratie van de Nieuwe Sociale en Culturele Ruimtes*. Tielt: Lannoo, 2002.

Elchardus, M., and W. Smits. *Anatomie en Oorzaken van het Wantrouwen*. Brussel: VUBpress, 2002.

Elling, A. *Ze zijn er niet voor gebouwd: In- en Uitsluiting in de Sport naar Sekse en Etniciteit*. Nieuwegein: Arko Sports Media, 2002.

Elling, A., M. Theeboom, and P. De Knop. 'Sociale Integratie in Sportbeleid in Nederland en Vlaanderen'. In *Waarden en Normen in de Sport: Analyse en beleidsperspectief*, edited by J. Steenbergen, A. Buisman, P. De Knop, and J. Lucassen, 261–79. Houten: Bohn Stafleu Van Loghum, 1998.

Haywood, L. (ed.) *Community Leisure and Recreation*. London: Heineman, 1994.

Hoyng, J., P. De Knop, and M. Theeboom. 'Functies en Betekenissen van Sport'. *Vrijetijdstudies* 16, no. 3 (1998): 33–55.

Hylton, K., and M. Totten. 'Community Sports Development'. In *Sports Development, Policy, Process and Practice*, edited by K. Hylton and P. Braham, 17–77. London: Routledge, 2008.

Jackson, D., M. Totten, and P. Robinson. 'Evaluating Projects in the Awards for All Programme'. *Yorkshire and Humber Regional Review* 13, no. 3 (2003): 27–8.

Koolen, R. *De Meest Gestelde Vragen over Allochtonen en Sport*. Arnhem: Nederlandse Sport Federatie, 1992.

Kruissink, M. 'Van padvinderij tot pretpark, van Vechtsport tot Volleybal'. *Justitiële Verkenningen* 14, no. 15 (1988): 66–85.

Ledwith, M. *Community Development: A Critical Approach*. Bristol: The Policy Press Publications, 2005.

LeGrand, J. 'The Theory of Government Failure'. *British Journal of Political Science* 21, (1991): 423–42.

Putnam, R. *Bowling Alone. The Collapse and Revival of American Community*. New York: Simon & Schuster, 2000.

Rutten, E., G. Stams, L. Vloet, and D. Dekovic. *Jeugdsport en Morele Socialisatie: Haalbaarheidsstudie naar een Interventie met Behulp van Forumtheater*. Amsterdam: SCO-Kohnstamm Instituut, 2003.

Scheerder, J. *Tofsport in Vlaanderen: Groei, Omvang en Segmentatie van de Vlaamse Recreatie-Sportmarkt*. Antwerpen: F&G Partners, 2007.

Scheerder, J., M. Theeboom, K. Van den Bergh, and P. De Knop. 'Sport en Sociale Cohesie: Een Overzicht van Onderzoeksmateriaal in Vlaanderen'. In *Sportbeleid in Vlaanderen*, vol. 2, *Studies*, edited by P. De Knop, J. Scheerder, and H. Ponnet, 77–85. Brussel: Publicatiefonds Vlaamse Trainersschool, 2006.

Scheerder, J., B. Vanreusel, and G. Pauwels. *Breedtesport in Vlaanderen gepeild: Trends en Profielen 1999–2006. Vlaanderen gepeild, 2007*. Brussel: Ministerie van de Vlaamse Gemeenschap, 2007.

Smith, A., and H. Westerbeek. 'Sport as a Vehicle for Deploying Corporate Social Responsibility'. *The Journal of Corporate Citizenship* 25, no. 1 (2007): 43–54.

Smits, W. *Maatschappelijke Participatie van Jongeren: Bewegen in Sociale, Vrijetijds- en Culturele Ruimte*. Brussel: Onderzoeksgroep TOR, 2006.

Studiedienst van de Vlaamse Regering. *Vlaamse Regionale Indicatoren 2009 (VRIND 2009)*. Brussels: Vlaamse Overheid, 2009.

Taylor, G. *Equal Opportunities*. London: Industrial Society, 1994.

Theeboom, M., F. Dekens, E. Dom, and J. Vertonghen. *Handboek Sportbeleidsplanning*. Brussel: Politeia, 2007.

Theeboom, M., and P. De Knop. 'Inventarisatie binnen het jeugdwelzijnswerk in Vlaanderen'. In *Sport als integratie. Kansen voor maatschappelijk kwetsbare jongeren*, edited by P. De Knop and L. Walgrave, 119–30. Brussel: Koning Boudewijnstichting, 1992.

Theeboom, M., P. De Knop, J. Scheerder, K. Martelaer, P. Wylleman, and A. Buisman. 'Sport en Jeugd'. In *Sportsociologie: Het Spel en de Spelers*, edited by P. De Knop, B. Vanreusel, and J. Scheerder, 359–72. Maarssen: Elsevier Gezondheidszorg, 2006.

Theeboom, M., J. Truyens, and R. Haudenhuyse. *Sport en maatschappelijke achterstelling: Een verkennend onderzoek naar de bestaande initiatieven in Vlaanderen en mogelijkheden naar de toekomst*. Brussel: Koning Boudewijnstichting, 2008.

Theeboom, M., and P. De Maesschalck. *Sporten om de Hoek: Een Brede Kijk op Buurtsport in Vlaanderen*. Sint-Niklaas: ISB, 2006.

van Bottenburg, M. 'A Second Wave of Running?' *Sport Marketing Europe* 1, no. 1 (2006): 26–30.

van der Gugten, M. 'De Sport als Aangrijpingspunt voor Criminaliteitspreventie'. *Justitiële Verkenningen* 14, no. 15 (1988): 86–112.

Van der Meulen, R. 'Alle Menschen werden Brüder: Lidmaatschap van Sportverenigingen, Vriendschappen, Kennissenkringen, en Interetnisch Vertrouwen'. *Mens & Maatschappij* 82, no. 2 (2007): 155–75.

Van Dijk, M. 'De rol van sportbeoefening bij de preventie van criminaliteit'. Paper presented at the conference Sport, Agressie en Vandalisme: Bestrijdend? Bevorderend?, Noordwijk aan zee, Landelijke Contactraad, 1987.

Van Geelen, W. 'Hedendaagse Ontwikkelingen Binnen het Sportbeleid in Nederland'. *Sportgids*, June, no. 10 (1988).

Van Lierde, A., and T. Willems. 'Hoe goed zit je bij een sportclub?' In *Sportbeleid in Vlaanderen*, vol. 2, *Studies*, edited by P. De Knop, J. Scheerder, and H. Ponnet, 127–135. Brussel: Publicatiefonds Vlaamse Trainersschool, 2006.

Van Tuyckom, C., and J. Scheerder. 'Sport for all? Social Stratification of Recreational Sport Activities in the EU-27'. *Kinesiologia Slovenica*, 14, no. 2 (2008), 54–63.

Vanlandewijck, Y., and P. Van de Vliet. 'Sportgedrag van Personen met een Handicap in Vlaanderen'. In *Sportbeleid in Vlaanderen*, vol. 2, *Studies*, edited by P. De Knop, J. Scheerder, and H. Ponnet. Brussel: Publicatiefonds Vlaamse Trainersschool, 2006.

Verweel, P., J. Janssen, and C. Roques. 'Kleurrijke zuilen: Over de Ontwikkeling van Sociaal Kapitaal door Allochtonen in Eigen en Gemengde Sportverenigingen'. *Vrijetijdstudies* 23, no. 4 (2005): 7–22.

Walseth, K., and K. Fasting. 'Islam's View on Physical Activity and Sport: Egyptian Women Interpreting Islam'. *International Review for the Sociology of Sport* 38, no. 1 (2003): 45–60.

Commercial sport and local communities: a market niche for social sport business?

Hans Westerbeek

Institute of Sport, Exercise and Active Living, Victoria University, Melbourne, Australia and Free University of Brussels, Brussels, Belgium

This article reflects on the contributions made to this special issue by the different authors. It further defines the concept of social business and proposes to apply the concept to sport, in order to generate a more sustainable, and more (social) value adding sport business environment.

In this special issue of *Sport in Society,* entitled 'Global Sport Business: Community Impacts of Commercial Sport', a range of pressing matters that comse with the arrival of sport as a global product of commercial exploitation were considered. Allow me as the editor of this special issue, to highlight some of the concluding comments of the contributing authors, and using these, suggest an additional conceptual approach to conducting sport business with and in communities. It is clear that sport has become an activity that has substantial commercial value to be mined by business entrepreneurs. The most recent wave of globalization incorporates technological advancement that has led to achieving global reach concerning communicating with potential customers. Sport entered a marketplace that offers tremendous financial rewards for those who manage to control the international governing bodies of sport and the events that these organizations are the custodians of. Not only did contributors to this special issue raise some of the most important driving factors that lead to sport's global attractiveness, but they also tackled important positive and negative impacts of commodified sport on communities of sport's (potential) fans, participants, beneficiaries and benefactors. Fittingly this special issue features case examples from a diverse range of localities, such as, India, Kenya, Belgium, Japan, the UK and Australia.

Two articles focus on the incredible influence that the media – and television in particular – has had on the globalization of sport. Television continues to redefine how humans collectively remember, how identities are formed – at the individual and the communal level – and how people share histories and form connections. Broadly speaking the articles consider the power of sport as a mediating factor in (trans)forming communal identity and as a direct derivative, strengthening or redefining human behaviour(s) based on national or regionally informed culture. Raymond Boyle considers the relationship between sport and the media in the UK media landscape and how new hybrid communities of mediated sport fans are appearing. Members of those communities demand not only attention from the owners of sport but also enforce significant involvement in the production of mediated sport. Boyle counsels that if the transformation of the sport/media nexus is solely driven by free market principles, European media regulators will:

struggle to strike a balance between the commercial and cultural role of broadcasting and media in society and ask, what should be the continued role of public service broadcasting? Where do notions of the public good fit into media and political discourse? How do we combat 'market failure' in media content provision? In the same context, sports should also reflect on their relationship with the range of diverse stakeholders who sustain the industries, both financially and also culturally.

Boyle's likening of the media sports relationship as part of a long revolution makes him conclude that tensions are developing between older notions of sporting communities and the newly forming hybrid communities of mediated sport fans.

> The challenge is for the governing bodies of sport to respect and seriously engage with, rather than pay lip-service to, notions of stakeholder democracy within this emerging, complex new landscape. The sports media relationship has always been one of change, shot through with strong patterns of continuity. It is the cultural component of this process of connection, through shared collective memory, identity, tradition and history that makes sport such a compelling, competitive and potentially powerful cultural form, informed by the local, but connected to the global. The long-term health of sporting culture will depend on the ability of sports to meaningfully engage with all the differing communities that move within its orbit.

Raymond Boyle, and Shakya Mitra arrive at the conclusion that if media ventures, driven by a capitalist profit incentive, can influence the (re)formation of sport community (cultures), it is of the utmost importance we continue to actively assess what sport 'is' and what we as communities of sport's stakeholders want 'it' to be in society.

Mitra describes the fascinating case of the Indian Premier League (IPL) Twenty20 cricket competition. In what at best can be described as a developing sport business nation - India - it is quite mindboggling to observe how a new sporting competition can become commercially successful in less than three years, where more established sporting leagues such as the English Premier League (football) and the US-based National Football League (NFL) have taken more than a century to achieve a similar outcome. Admittedly cricket is probably the only sport popular enough in the Indian subcontinent to achieve such a rapid rise to sport business fame but it is intriguing nevertheless to see both customers (fans) and sponsors/owners embrace a new sport product with such gusto and fervour.

Overall it is shown by Mitra that 'the best of many worlds' in terms of the structure and management of a professional sport league can be brought together in a new competition to leap ahead of professional sporting competitions in more advanced sport business economies. By 'simply' adopting a franchise structure, quite innovatively auctioning off the available team licenses to eagerly bidding city/corporate syndicates, and then introducing proven equalisation and competitive balance tools such as a salary cap and revenue sharing (of broadcast income), the managers of the IPL have created something out of nowhere. Where Indian cricket fan communities were limited to satisfying their thirst for thrilling cricket action via television or by watching matches between irregularly visiting national teams and the Indian side, the IPL has transformed the sport spectator landscape in three short years. In many ways the IPL is a best practice example of how quickly latent demand for sport entertainment can be transformed into a product that attracts a whole new community of sport fans.

Koji Kobayashi, John M. Amis, Richard Unwin and Richard Southall debate the effects that globalizing forces have had on the culture of corporate management in two Japanese sporting goods manufacturers. Although national culture and identity continue to strongly influence managerial practice, the authors conclude that traditional Japanese values were forced to hybridize with western-style values and cultural practices in order to remain competitive in the international sporting goods industry. Kobayashi et al. argue that,

This study also offers intriguing implications for Japanese and western management. First, differences appear to be diminishing as managers in Japanese and western firms seek to develop ever more effective global management practices by learning from each other. However, despite such intense forces of globalization, the differences still and prominently lie in managerial elements which strongly reflect national cultures and values. In this study, Asics and Mizuno have managed to retain key Japanese values and indeed actively spread 'Asicsism' and 'Mizunoism' while emerging as global corporations.

It should be noted in this context that *for profit* sporting goods companies such as Nike have had a significant influence on establishing and influencing youth culture as a result of their aggressive sport celebrity marketing driven branding and sales campaigns. Nike's influence has been such that it has lead to the formation of Nike iconography that is revered by youngsters in both the west and the rest of the world. It can be hypothesized that Nike's marketing focus directly results from Nike's corporate culture that has naturally rooted in a free market business environment in the USA, whereas the two Japanese companies discussed by Kobayashi et al. express their national origins in a culture that is traditionally top-down and manufacturing driven. Realizing that I am proposing a conceptual leap here, it might be that successful sporting goods *manufacturers* less so than companies that focus on *marketing* can strongly influence the formation (of the needs) of communities of sport or lifestyle consumers. Where Nike aggressively tells the customer they need the swoosh to belong to an in-crowd, Asics and Mizuno have for a long time assumed that absolute product quality is what the customer wants. Ultimately, the power of Nike's ability to influence market demands has forced the two Japanese companies into adopting a style of management that not comes naturally from the perspective of national culture and values.

In an effort to locate sport business in contemporary debate about the potential of sport to contribute to generating social capital, Ramon Spaaij and Hans Westerbeek propose a typology of markets for social capital in the sport business environment. The contribution of this article is the realization that although (global) corporations may well have the ambition to deploy their social responsibilities across all markets that they operate in, the reality remains that successful creation and maintenance of social capital is a localized, hands-on, face-to-face activity. It is also noted that although the potential for generating social capital through sport may be high, most of the corporate social responsibility activities are self-regulated and non-enforceable which puts the responsibility on sport business(es) when push comes to shove. To ensure that social contributions are made,

> Arguably, it does not really matter whether the production of social capital is largely dependent on first generating an economic profit or surplus, as long as corporate governors realize that economic gains will ultimately be higher if the stock of social capital is increased as well. A strong focus on the financial success of organizations is reasonable given their need to survive in a competitive business environment, but improved knowledge of the relationship between social gains and economic success may well lead to increasing investment in the achievement of social outcomes. This is likely to be beneficial for both profit seekers and those organizations that aim to reinvest surplus in the advancement of non-profit objectives.

In a way this argument is further founded by Fred Coalter in his article on the potential value and measurability of sport-for-development programmes, and what we can and cannot expect of such programmes. Part of his argument revolves around the form of organization of such programmes and how 'organization' impacts the relationship between forms of sport and types of social capital. Again the conclusion is that local success (or impact on local communities of stakeholders) of sport-for-development initiatives highly depends on the continuity of support organizations, and how these organizations themselves can guarantee longevity. More often than not these organizations are reliant on short-term corporate funding, and as such they are not independently (self-sustaining) operations. As noted by Coalter

> The case study of MYSA illustrates a number of issues about the danger of decontextualized, overly romanticized, communitarian generalizations about the 'power' of sport-for-development. It seems that it is not simple sports participation which can hope to achieve most desired outcomes, but *sports plus*; it is not 'sport' which achieves many of these outcomes, but *sporting organizations;* it is not sport which produces and sustains social capital, enters into partnerships and mobilizes sporting and non-sporting resources, but certain types of social organization. Further, evidence would suggest that some of these organizations are consciously and systematically organized to maximize the possibility of achieving such outcomes. . . . A further key issue relates to the nature of the processes involved in the formation and sustaining of different types of social capital. There is broad agreement that prescriptive policy-led attempts to construct social capital may fail, as social capital is based on activities, relationships and norms freely engaged in by individuals. Such an analysis raises significant issues for organizations that are wholly aid-dependent and are encouraged to offer an economy of solutions to a wide range of social, political and economic problems.

Stated differently, social capital as a direct expression of a perceived need in the community emerges bottom up and is hard to be policy 'manufactured'. This argument extends to how – in this case – sport is organized and on whom it depends for ongoing recourses. It is much better to depend on end consumers than being at the mercy of (corporate or government) benefactors who choose (or choose not!) to invest in social capital generating sport programmes.

Finally, the most 'localized' contribution comes from Marc Theeboom, Reinhard Haudenhuyse and Paul De Knop, who reflect on community sport programmes that have purposely been set up to stimulate participation among socially deprived groups. Their argument revolves around the fact that traditional providers of such programmes have consistently shown that they are not capable of responding adequately and timely to the constantly changing demands of the marketplace. This has led to an increasing number of commercial sport providers entering the domain of community sport provision, sometimes as pure commercial providers, sometimes taking over as the (government) subsidized provider of services from traditional non-profit organizations. The authors conclude that well defined and negotiated partnerships between commercial and community organizations may well lead to a more diverse and dynamic sport-for-all policy landscape. They continue to consider central and local government as important and continuing providers of resources and of directors of policy.

They contend that,

> Developing regulatory mechanisms in which the free hand of the market can be managed to provide equal sports opportunities, conditions and outcomes for those groups who are not fully participating, will be the biggest challenge and responsibility of the state. This also implies that the state needs to create and facilitate a positive climate in which the commercial sports sector can develop itself within a community context (development of sport in the community). A balance needs to be found between the development of the community through sport and the development of sport in the community. Without regulatory mechanisms and an established methodology based on empirical research, one cannot expect sport to score in both of these fields. It is believed that the input of the state stays nonetheless necessary for creating a legal framework and for a desired adjustment of private sports spending.

In the opening article I stated that a special issue offers the opportunity to thematically focus, and to raise issues outside the mainstream of research in the discipline area. One undertakes the publication of a special issue journal by broadly describing a proposed theme, and thinking of a catchy title for the journal, and then hopes that appropriate and exciting submissions are received. For this special issue I can say that quite a few submissions were not what I was expecting, but they were exciting and inspiring nevertheless. The submissions made me recast and expand my personal view of what is sport business and what impact it can (and should) have on a variety of communities. Viewpoints projected by Muhammad Yunus briefly alluded to in the opening article provide a look into a possible future for sport business as well. He argues that capitalism is only a half-developed structure, a mono-dimensional world in which people only focus on competing in a free market and where success is solely measured by profit. Sport business has certainly shifted a long way towards a money grab by a wealthy few in a free market. But sport has traditionally not been such a line of business and, for that reason, may well have an early mover advantage to transform some of its practices to social business activities. According to Yunus,[1] social business complements capitalism in that its success is measured in achieving social outcomes. Social business is not charity, not corporate social responsibility, not 'not for profit', and not government either. His fundamental argument is that any business or organization not based on social business principles will ultimately need to operate in a 'for profit' modus – even when it is a not-for-profit, NGO, or governmental organization – in order to survive, and as such will be judged on its ability to break even or achieve a profit. In the words of a former US president, you are either with us or against us – in this context – favouring free market capitalism or rejecting it. However, rather than having to choose one over the other, for-profit business and social business can be each other's perfect complements. The founding objectives for social business are fundamentally different from for-profit businesses. A social business is set up to achieve social outcomes, but operates on normal business principles. Money invested in social business is not returned to investors in multiples, but returned in full after the social business has had sufficient time to achieve a break-even business operation. Most cases presented in this special issue are either examples of for-profit (sport value capitalizing) business, or sport value derived business (where sport is used to positively impact communities). In both cases sport remains highly dependent on (inconsistent) contributions from parties external to the sport business, such as sponsors, donors or government. Both forms of organization will not deliver maximum output regarding social outcomes – the first not because it seeks a profit as a primary outcome and the second not because it depends on third-party contributions in the process of generating sufficient resources. In many ways the club-based sporting system that originated in Europe is an example of how sport could be delivered through applying social business principles. However, as noted by Theeboom, Haudenhuyse and De Knop, the organized sport system seems unable to branch out towards delivering on social objectives that are outside their traditional scope of founding values. It will be up to the creativity and ingenuity of social entrepreneurs to come up with social sport business plans that successfully tackle social issues – issues in society that currently remain the purview of government, charity or not-for-profit organizations.

Ultimately social sport businesses will find that not for all socially worthy objectives, to be achieved through or with the assistance of sport, there is a market. In those cases long-term (ongoing) government or corporate investment remains critical and innovative social business partnerships need to be conjured up. Nevertheless, at this point in time of sport business evolution it is opportune to add the paradigm of social business to the range of options that are available to sport exerting its positive influence in society.

Note

[1] M. Yunus, *Creating a World Without Poverty: Social Business and the Future of Capitalism*, New York: Public Affairs, 2007.

Index

Routledge
Taylor & Francis Group

Sport in History

Published on behalf of the British Society of Sports History

EDITOR-IN-CHIEF:
Professor Matthew Taylor, *De Montfort University, UK*

EDITORS:
Dr Paul Dimeo, *University of Stirling, UK*
Dr Martin Johnes, *Swansea University, UK*

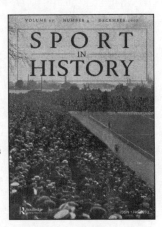

Sport in History is a history journal that publishes original, archivally-based research on the history of sport, leisure and recreation. The journal encourages the study of sport to illuminate broader historical issues and debates. Includes an extensive reviews section, an annual compendium of sports-related accessions to British archives and a 'Sport in Public History' section dealing with issues of sports-related heritage and memory in society.

To view free articles please visit **www.tandf.co.uk/journals/rsih** and click on News & Offers.

To sign up for tables of contents, new publications and citation alerting services visit **www.informaworld.com/alerting**

@**updates**
Taylor & Francis Group

Register your email address at **www.tandf.co.uk/journals/eupdates.asp** to receive information on books, journals and other news within your areas of interest.

Powered by
informaworld

For further information, please contact Customer Services at either of the following:
T&F Informa UK Ltd, Sheepen Place, Colchester, Essex, CO3 3LP, UK
Tel: +44 (0) 20 7017 5544 Fax: 44 (0) 20 7017 5198
Email: subscriptions@tandf.co.uk

Taylor & Francis Inc, 325 Chestnut Street, Philadelphia, PA 19106, USA
Tel: +1 800 354 1420 (toll-free calls from within the US)
or +1 215 625 8900 (calls from overseas) Fax: +1 215 625 2940
Email: customerservice@taylorandfrancis.com

View an online sample issue at:
www.tandf.co.uk/journals/rsih

Leisure/Loisir

Official publication of the Canadian Association for Leisure Studies
Revue de l'Association canadienne d'études en loisir

Volume 34, 2010, 4 issues per year

New to Routledge in 2010

EDITOR:
Bryan Smale, *University of Waterloo, Canada*

Leisure/Loisir strives to publish a diverse collection of scholarly papers in all areas of leisure, recreation, arts, parks, sport, and travel and tourism. Reflecting the multi- and interdisciplinary nature of these areas of study, the journal invites papers that use a wide range of perspectives and research methods. Submissions may include, but are not limited to: empirical research papers (qualitative, quantitative, or mixed methods), conceptual papers, comprehensive review papers, policy and economic impact analyses, and pedagogical aspects for leisure educators.

Leisure/Loisir is the official publication of the *Canadian Association for Leisure Studies/Association canadienne d'études en loisir (CALS)*. While **Leisure/Loisir** is based in Canada and offers a primary outlet for individuals affiliated with Canadian institutions, the journal encourages international submissions. As a Canadian journal, both English and French manuscript submissions are encouraged.

For more information or to read free articles from **Leisure/Loisir** visit the journal homepage at
www.tandf.co.uk/journals/rloi

To sign up for tables of contents, new publications and citation alerting services visit **www.informaworld.com/alerting**

Register your email address at **www.tandf.co.uk/journals/eupdates.asp** to receive information on books, journals and other news within your areas of interest.

For further information, please contact Customer Services at either of the following:
T&F Informa UK Ltd, Sheepen Place, Colchester, Essex, CO3 3LP, UK
Tel: +44 (0) 20 7017 5544 Fax: 44 (0) 20 7017 5198
Email: subscriptions@tandf.co.uk

Taylor & Francis Inc, 325 Chestnut Street, Philadelphia, PA 19106, USA
Tel: +1 800 354 1420 (toll-free calls from within the US)
or +1 215 625 8900 (calls from overseas) Fax: +1 215 625 2940
Email: customerservice@taylorandfrancis.com

View an online sample issue at:
www.tandf.co.uk/journals/rloi